ACCENTS ON SHAKESPEARE

General editor: TERENCE HAWKES

Shakespeare Without Women

Shakespeare Without Women is a controversial study of female impersonation and the connections between dramatic and political
representation in Shakespeare's plays. In this original and challenging book, Callaghan argues that all Shakespeare's actors were, of
historical necessity, (white) males which meant that the portayal of
women and racial others posed unique problems for his theatre.
What is important, *Shakespeare Without Women* claims, is not to be-
moan the absence of women, Africans, or the Irish, but to determine
what such absences meant in their historical context and why they
matter today. Callaghan focuses on the implications of absence and
exclusion in several of Shakespeare's works, including:

- the exclusion of the female body from *Twelfth Night*;
- the impersonation of the female voice in early performances of
  the plays;
- racial impersonations in *Othello*;
- echoes of the removal of the Gaelic Irish in *The Tempest*;
- the absence of women on stage and in public life as shown in *A
  Midsummer Night's Dream*.

Dympna Callaghan is currently William P. Tolley Professor in
the Humanities at Syracuse University, New York. She is the author
of *Woman and Gender in Renaissance Tragedy* (1989), co-author of *The
Weyward Sisters. Shakespeare and feminist politics* (1994) and co-editor
of *Feminist Readings of early modern culture*

ACCENTS ON SHAKESPEARE
General Editor: TERENCE HAWKES

It is more than twenty years since the New Accents series helped to establish "theory" as a fundamental and continuing feature of the study of literature at undergraduate level. Since then, the need for short, powerful "cutting edge" accounts of and comments on new developments has increased sharply. In the case of Shakespeare, books with this sort of focus have not been readily available. Accents on Shakespeare aims to supply them.

Accents on Shakespeare volumes will either "apply" theory, or broaden and adapt it in order to connect with concrete teaching concerns. In the process, they will also reflect and engage with the major developments in Shakespeare studies of the last ten years.

The series will lead as well as follow. In pursuit of this goal it will be a two-tiered series. In addition to affordable, "adoptable" titles aimed at modular undergraduate courses, it will include a number of research-based books. Spirited and committed, these second-tier volumes advocate radical change rather than stolidly reinforcing the status quo.

IN THE SAME SERIES

Shakespeare and Appropriation
Edited by Christy Desmet and Robert Sawyer

Shakespeare Without Women
Dympna Callaghan

Shakespeare Without Women

Representing gender and race on the Renaissance stage

DYMPNA CALLAGHAN

London and New York

First published 2000
by Routledge
11 New Fetter Lane,
London EC4P 4EE

Simultaneously published in
the USA and Canada
by Routledge
29 West 35th Street,
New York, NY 10001

Routledge is an imprint of the
Taylor & Francis Group

Typeset in Baskerville by
Ponting–Green Publishing Services,
Chesham, Buckinghamshire
Printed and bound in Great Britain by
TJ International Ltd, Padstow, Cornwall

British Library Cataloguing in
Publication Data

A catalogue record for this book is available
from the British Library

Library of Congress Cataloging in
Publication Data

Shakespeare without women / Dympna
Callaghan
    p.   cm. – (Accents on Shakespeare)
    Includes bibliographical references and
index
    1. Shakespeare, William, 1564–1616 –
Characters – Women. 2. Shakespeare,
William, 1564–1616 – Characters –
Africans. 3. Shakespeare, William,
1564–1616 – Stage history – to 1625.
5. Theater – England – casting – History
– 16th century. 6. Theater – England –
casting – History – 17th century.
7. Feminism and theater – England –
History. 8. Female impersonators –
England – History. 9. Theater and society
– England – History. 10. Africans in
literature. 11. Blacks in literature.
12. Women in literature.
I. Title II. Series.
PR2991.C337 1999
822.3′3–dc21   99–15659
                                            CIP

ISBN 0–415–20231–0 (hbk)
ISBN 0–415–20232–9 (pbk)

For Laurie Maguire

Contents

Plates

General editor's preface

In our century, the field of literary studies has rarely been a settled, tranquil place. Indeed, for over two decades, the clash of opposed theories, prejudices, and points of view has made it more of a battlefield. Echoing across its most beleaguered terrain, the student's weary complaint "Why can't I just pick up Shakespeare plays and read them?" seems to demand a sympathetic response.

Nevertheless, we know that modern spectacles will always impose their own particular characteristics on the vision of those who unthinkingly don them. This must mean, at the very least, that an apparently simple confrontation with, or pious contemplation of, the text of a 400-year-old play can scarcely supply the grounding for an adequate response to its complex demands. For this reason, a transfer of emphasis from "text" toward "context" has increasingly been the concern of critics and scholars since World War II: a tendency that has perhaps reached its climax in more recent movements such as new historicism or cultural materialism.

A consideration of the conditions, social, political, or economic within which the play came to exist, from which it derives, and to which it speaks will certainly make legitimate demands on the attention of any well-prepared student nowadays. Of course, the serious pursuit of those interests will also inevitably start to undermine ancient and inherited prejudices, such as the supposed distinction between "foreground" and "background" in literary studies. And even the slightest awareness of the pressures of gender or of race, or the most cursory glance at the role played by that strange creature "Shakespeare" in our cultural politics, will reinforce a similar turn toward questions that sometimes appear scandalously "non-literary." It seems clear that very different and unsettling notions of the ways in which literature might be addressed can hardly be avoided. The worrying truth is that nobody can just pick up Shakespeare's plays and read them. Perhaps – even more worrying – they never could.

The aim of *Accents on Shakespeare* is to encourage students and teachers to explore the implications of this situation by means of an engagement with the major developments in Shakespeare studies of the last ten years. It will offer a continuing and challenging re-flection on those ideas through a series of multi- and single-author books which will also supply the basis for adapting or augmenting them in the light of changing concerns.

Accents on Shakespeare also intends to lead as well as follow. In pur-suit of this goal, the series will operate on more than one level. In addition to titles aimed at modular undergraduate courses, it will include a number of books embodying polemical, strongly argued cases aimed at expanding the horizons of a specific aspect of the subject and at challenging the preconceptions on which it is based. These volumes will not be learned "monographs" in any tradi-tional sense. They will, it is hoped, offer a platform for the work of the liveliest younger scholars and teachers at their most outspoken and provocative. Committed and contentious, they will be report-ing from the forefront of current work and will have something new to say. The fact that each book in the series promises a Shakespeare inflected in terms of a specific urgency should ensure that, in the present as in the recent past, the accent will be on change.

Terence Hawkes

Acknowledgments

Earlier versions of chapters one, two, and three of this book were previously published in *Textual Practice*, *Alternative Shakespeare 2* ed., Terence Hawkes, and the *Journal for Medieval and Early Modern Studies*.

I am grateful for the many gifts of scholarship and friendship I have received in the course of writing this book. First and foremost, I am grateful to my wonderful students and colleagues at Syracuse University and secondly, to the many new friends I have made at the Newberry and Folger Libraries, at Queen's University, Belfast, and at Clare Hall, Cambridge.

It is hard to single out individuals because so many people have offered helpful comments and references, but among them are Mary Beth Rose, Charles Whitney, Al Braunmuller, Ann Jenalie Cook, Alan Sinfield, Bruce Smith, Kate Shaw, John Elliott, R.S. White, Leeds Barroll, Mark Thornton Burnett, Ginger Vaughan, Susan Zimmerman, Theodora Jankowski, Philip Ford, Chris R. Kyle, Susan Snyder, Margaret Maurer, Ramona Wray, Juliet Dusinberre, Pat Parker, Georgianna Zeigler, Lena Cowen Orlin, Brian Vickers, Alan Nelson and Barbara Mowat. My colleague, Pat Moody has been a constant source of support. Andrew Murphy, Hiram Morgan, and Eugene Flanagan were kind enough to lend their expertise on matters Irish, while Werner Gundersheimer, in addition to invaluable intellectual leadership at the Folger, offered his services as James I in

Jonson's *Irish Masque*. Jim Binns offered kind assistance with Latin texts, and to Paul Noordhof I am indebted for comments on the philosophical dimensions of my argument. Rosaria Champagne, Steve Cohan, Crystal Bartolovich, Peter Mortenson, and Gail Paster were kind enough to read portions of the manuscript and offered tremendously helpful comments. Michael Dobson offered crucial good humor and superb advice at critical stages of the writing.

I am especially grateful to the people I have known through the entire course of the project. Jyotsna Singh and I have the phone bills to prove the duration of our friendship. Bernadette Powell, Helen Francis, and Elizabeth Ridout have been unfailingly supportive. One of my great privileges is to have had Felicity Nussbaum as a colleague while she was at Syracuse. She remains a beloved friend and a vital and magnanimous source of intellectual advice and feminist inspiration. Although Phyllis Rackin will not agree with everything in this book, my arguments have been shaped in very significant measure by my dialog with her and I owe an enormous amount to her generous engagement. My much loved friend, Frances Dolan, to whom these thanks are long overdue, has been there from first to last. It has been my great good fortune to be on leave with her both in Chicago and DC where I had the benefit both of her erudition and marvellous intellectual and personal generosity. I cannot begin to describe how important Jean Howard's intellectual influence has been. She has also offered sage advice, solace, criticism and encouragement on everything I have ever written. For this, and much more, Jean remains my ideal of the feminist intellectual.

I am fortunate to have so many brilliant (in every sense) friends, and I am particularly grateful for my Cambridge comrades. Juliet Fleming valiantly read my work in quantity, and did so with unfailing kindness and generosity. I have learnt an enormous amount from her impeccable eloquence but even more from her cherished friendship. Pippa Berry's erudition and insight at every level never cease to amaze me. Her intellectual generosity and friendship are among my most precious gifts.

Jeff Parker and Kathy Romack, in addition to being inspiring students, have my thanks for helping me get the manuscript out of the computer, while Mary Tonkinson helped me get the manuscript out the door. Sharon Moss and Kokkie Buur made me understand the purpose of doing so, and, in the process, have enriched my life tremendously.

Terry Hawkes has been immensely supportive and helpful as series editor. I would also like to give my thanks to Talia Rogers and her team.

Most of all, I am grateful for the world's most wonderful parents, Nora and Eamonn Callaghan, and for my shining, gifted sister, Margaret Newcombe.

The book is dedicated to Laurie Maguire, whose friendship I value beyond measure. She has given me unparalleled encouragement throughout and has been a wonder of intellectual inspiration, not only on the beaches of Halki, but also on the perilous voyage out.

In the wake of such blessings, all that remains to say was probably best said in the Renaissance: "I pray thee, Courteous Reader, with patience to amend the faults which may fall out to be more than either we had thought or could by our diligence (which was not wanting) prevent."

Some good body, tell me how I do,
Whose presence absence, absence presence is.
(Sir Philip Sidney, *Astrophil and Stella*)

Introduction
Cleopatra had a way with her

"*Enter Blackamoors with music*" reads the stage direction in Act V, scene ii, of *Love's Labour's Lost*. This cue holds forth a prospect that stage directions like "A street in Athens," "A Tavern in Eastcheap," etc., cannot, namely that of a perfect coincidence between dramatic representation and reality; the possibility of presence, in this case, exotic and tantalizing. Unlike "*Exit, pursued by a bear*" in *The Winter's Tale* (III. iii. 58), which may well have involved a real trained bear rather than an actor in a bear-suit[1] (though not, of course, a bear actually in deathly pursuit), "*Enter Blackamoors*" undoubtedly signals the entrance not of actual Africans but of English minstrels in blackface.

Of course, the printed direction "*Enter Blackamoors with music*," dating from 1597 at the latest, was not available to Shakespeare's audience any more than the expectation that, even if impersonated *ad vivum* by virtue of mimetic and cosmetic proficiency, these musicians might be real Africans. Although English monarchs employed black musicians from the reign of Henry VIII – Henry had a "blacke trumpet" while Elizabeth I is depicted with a group of black minstrels and dancers in a painting dated *c.*1577 and attributed to Gheeraerts the Elder, and James I later had a troupe of black minstrels – there is no record of black performers being borrowed from royal or aristocratic households to play roles onstage (Fryer 1984: 4,9; Walvin 1973: 9). There is, however, a wealth of evidence about how early modern performers achieved racial impersonation by means of theatrical integument. The stage direction, then, signals not that the players borrowed royal musicians but that they are dramatizing the richness and exoticism of court culture (Vaughan and Vaughan 1997).

However problematic or fleeting the possibility of presence it implies, this stage direction shares an epistemological affinity with Stanley Cavell's account of the apocryphal incident of the Southern yokel, "who rushes to the stage to save Desdemona from the black man" (Cavell 1969: 327). The "joke" is not so much that the yokel thinks that Desdemona – a white actress performing in the antebellum South – is really being killed, but rather, that he believes that the white actor playing Othello is really black. Though he nowhere remarks upon it, Cavell's yokel is not simply a naive spectator who contrasts with "the state of mind in which we find the events in a theatre neither credible nor incredible" but a racist spectator whose fear of miscegenation inhibits his capacity to distinguish between dramatic representation and reality. That is, the problem of representation in this incident coincides with specific problems attendant upon the dramatic depiction of gender and race.

What is significant about the blackamoors in the stage direction from *Love's Labour's Lost* and Cavell's yokel is that they bespeak fantasies of presence about people who, for reasons far in excess of problems of geography and practicality, could not possibly have been onstage. *Love's Labour's* blackamoors and Cavell's yokel thereby exemplify the subject of this book, namely the specifically political dimension of the dense philosophical problems posed by dramatic representation. For this book is about what, or rather who, is *not there* on Shakespeare's stage – particularly women (who certainly were not exotic entities on the streets of London), Africans, and the indigenous Irish, a denigrated constituency who, unlike the Anglo-Irish, were probably as scarce and unusual in Shakespeare's London as their exoticized Moorish counterparts. I am especially concerned with whether such absence matters and, further, curious about what complex admixture of elements – including sympathetic representation, misrepresentation, non-representation, and, crucially, the structural effects of mimesis itself – constitutes the absence of these groups.

Despite the absence of women and Africans from early modern public theatre, the only visual record we have of a Shakespearean

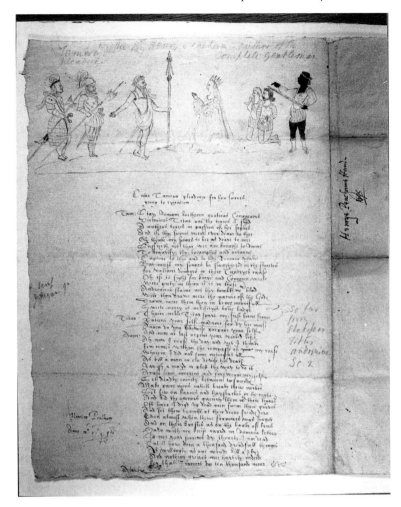

Plate 1 Drawing of *Titus Andronicus* (Henry Peacham). Reproduced by permission of the Marquess of Bath, Longleat House, Warminster, Wiltshire, Great Britain.

performance, Henry Peacham's drawing of *Titus Andronicus* (Plate 1), vividly depicts racial and gendered difference and seems to point to the inclusivity of Shakespeare's stage. A Roman spear marks centerstage, while stage right a kneeling Tamora pleads for her sons' lives. Tamora's role is literally out of proportion here because, even kneeling, Peacham's drawing renders her altogether bigger than the Roman she supplicates. Aaron is the only standing figure on this side of the drawing. Black and gesticulating, he offers a stark and conspicuous contrast to the nondescript Romans lined up stage left. The picture emphasizes Africans as visibly different from Europeans, an intriguing phenomenon in Western art history.[2] As Don Hedrick has observed: "the ideology of the visual image ... pertains to race in ways that differ from the discursive meaning of race or ethnicity" (Hedrick 1995).

In the context of the iconography of racial representation, Peacham's picture, and especially Aaron's hypervisibility within it, makes for a fascinating juxtaposition with an observation made by the late Betty Shabazz, Malcolm X's widow: "Malcolm said if you are looking at a picture of the world and you don't see yourself in it, your task should be obvious: to get in the picture."[3] That Aaron, whose villainy makes him a distorted image of African identity, *is* in the picture is itself problematic and constitutes evidence of the troubled contiguity between cultural representation and representation understood in the broader political sense. Certainly, as Shabazz's comment indicates, we in the twentieth century have come to equate visibility with power. Although, as Peggy Phelan has pointed out, if mere visibility really constituted power, "then almost-naked young white women should be running Western culture" (Phelan 1993: 10).

Many of Shakespeare's contemporaries did not share our faith in representation. Theatricalists and antitheatricalists alike feared the encroachments mimetic representation made upon the real. Thomas Heywood argued defensively:

> To see our youth attired in the habit of women. [W]ho knows not what their intents be? Who cannot distinguish them by their names, assuredly knowing that they are but to represent such a lady, at such a tyme appointed? Do not the universities, the fountains, and well springs of all good arts, learning and documents, admit the like in their colleges? [A]nd they (I assure myself) are not ignorant of their use. In the time of my residence at Cambridge, I have seen tragedyes, comedyes, historyes pastorals and shows publickly acted, in which the graduates of good place and reputation have bene specially parted.
>
> (Heywood quoted in Chambers 1923: vol. I, 252)

Alas, in Oxford these fine distinctions between transvestite males and women, between representation and reality, were not so clear and became the cause of heated controversy between the Puritan John Rainoldes and the combined forces of William Gager and Alberico Gentili (Binns 1974: 95–120; 1990: 135, 326). The social struggle about representation is played out on an apparently lighter note when a grocer and his wife commandeer the play in Beaumont and Fletcher's *The Knight of the Burning Pestle*. This play satirizes the aspirations of audiences who want to see themselves, their tastes and concerns, directly reflected in plots inappropriate to their social standing. In other words, the desire for theatrical representation is seen as a spurious and irredeemably bourgeois goal.

Far from equating cultural representation with political power, the Puritans (who were, in Marxist terms, the vanguard of the new economic and social order) deplored as lewd and idolatrous what went on at the playhouse, and did so despite the fact that representational practises of all kinds became necessary as part not only of an economy based on increasingly abstract systems of exchange but also on a social system which replaced "the visible or patent form of sovereign power with an invisible and resolutely *latent* form of economic domination" (Halpern 1991: 5). That is, the coercion that inheres in social relations whereby the aristocracy secures and maintains power gives way to an invisible function of the economic system itself. Thus visibility, which at a later historical moment comes to signify representation in its political sense (namely, representing the interests of a particular constituency rather than mere depiction), becomes prominent precisely at the moment when crucial aspects of power and economic exchange become invisible. Further, in 1642 with the advent of the Commonwealth period, those who had been the nonentities of English history gained representation for the first time, and the site of that representation, singularly, was not in the theatres (see Dutton 1991: 248).

The perils of cultural representation seem to have been much more apparent in pre-Hollywood eras. The status of actors, such as Nathan Field, who was barred from receiving communion in his parish church, makes it clear that the practise of theatrical representation was parlous. Likewise, in bastardy legislation men become conveniently invisible and women visible. In the statute of 1610, women's visibility was constituted by the fact that they had become an economic liability on the parish: "Every lewd woman which shall have any bastard which may be chargeable to the parish, the justices of the peace shall committ [*sic*] such woman to the house of correction, to be punished and set to work, during the term of one whole year" (quoted in Breitenberg 1996: 19). In stark contrast to the dangers of visibility in early modern England and to Cleopatra's fears about squeaking boys, certain groups in the twentieth century – especially, as we see from Shabazz's comment, people of color but also gays and lesbians, and other marginalized communities – have tended to regard even misrepresentation as the necessary cost of visibility: "Representation at any price." [4]

Historically, however, in relation to Shakespeare, marginalized groups have *not* felt under-represented and invisible. Indeed, generations of readers and playgoers, many of them "cultural others," have experienced the powerful and pleasurable perception that in Shakespeare they are indeed represented. Witness Maya Angelou's famous declaration: "I *know* that William Shakespeare was a black woman" (Erickson 1991: 111, 117). This may be because, as Stephen Greenblatt observes, "[S]o absolute is Shakespeare's achievement that he has himself come to seem like great creating nature: the common bond of humankind, the principle of hope, the symbol of the imagination's power to transcend time-bound beliefs and assumptions, peculiar historical circumstances, and specific artistic conventions" (Greenblatt 1997: 1). Roberto Fernandez Retamar, for instance, who was active in the Cuban revolution, writes in a tradition of reading in *The Tempest* the script for resistance to colonialism: "I know no other metaphor more expressive of our cultural situation, of our reality ... what is our history, what is our culture, if not the history and culture of Caliban?" (Retamar 1989: 14). Pioneering theatre director Joseph Papp recalls: "I grew up in a home where Yiddish was spoken, and English was only a second language, I was acutely sensitive to the musical sounds of different languages and had an ear for lilt and cadence and rhythm in the spoken word. ... Although Shakespeare lived and wrote hundreds of years ago, his name rolls off my tongue as if he were my brother" (Papp 1988: ix, xiv). In the complex structure of his distinctly humanist identification, it is notable that Papp does not identify with a particular character; Shylock, for instance. Indeed, identifications regularly entail rather elusive correlations of self and Shakespearean character or situation. At a conference I attended in Providence, Rhode Island, in response to a paper on Shakespeare's histories, a woman in the audience stood up and explained the powerful impact the plays had had on her as an adolescent reader struggling with her sexual identity. "I came out," she declared, "with *Henry V.*"

Like the AfricanAmerican rock singer, Joan, in Gayl Jones's novel, *The Healing*, we have to keep reminding ourselves: "You know, even Shakespeare's sweet bitches are still a man's idea of a sweet bitch" (Jones 1998: 103).

I have chosen to concentrate on Shakespeare rather than Jonson, Middleton, Marlowe, or whomever else, precisely because the idea of exclusion jars with the full and vivid characters who populate his plays and who seem to represent all of us in our myriad and multiple degrees of otherness. The starting point of my project has been a certain philosophical skepticism about the mechanisms of dramatic representation as well as a specifically political skepticism about the benefits of representation, understood as cultural visibility, for marginalized groups. On Shakespeare's stage, as a result of both all-male mimesis and the production of racialized others in racially homogenous acting companies, the problem of representation in general – that it necessarily represents what is not actually there – becomes exacerbated in historically specific relation to femininity and racial difference.

Whatever alleged "exceptions" might have existed in early modern culture to the implicit but nonetheless *systematic* prohibition against female mimesis, there were no women on Shakespeare's stage.[5] My title, *Shakespeare Without Women* centers on the absence of women in particular and uses the problem of female impersonation in Shakespeare to focus on wider problems in feminism about what it means to secure cultural and political representation in patriarchy for women and other oppressed groups. One has only to think of Cleopatra, who serves simultaneously as a symbol of woman, of female sovereignty, of racial difference, and of subjected nationhood, in order to recognize that race is not an ancillary representational category. In the specific historical context of the Renaissance, the institutionalized practise of female impersonation, which, because more than half the population was female, is by far the most pervasive form of impersonation (more so, for example, than the impersonation of aristocrats or racial others), epitomizes the process of substitution inherent in dramatic representation at the same time as it signals the exclusions on which the dramatic signification of difference is founded. Hence the representation of absent women encapsulates and exemplifies (though, of course, it cannot fully encompass) my concerns about the production of difference on the Renaissance stage.

Indeed, no analysis that excludes race and class can properly claim to be feminist. For feminism is not just the idea that women should be equal to men but a radical interrogation of all the categories – not just those of gender – which constitute the epistemological structures and power relations of our history. In particular, the insistence that gender, race and class are categories always simultaneously in play in relation to all human and, for that matter, academic subjects constitutes the most crucial conceptual advance made by recent black feminist work.[6] Women are always marked by their social status as aristocrats, fishwives, citizens' wives, or prostitutes, while their beauty is always troped by racial markers, such as the English white and red, or the "foul Ethiope." Issues of presence, representation, absence, and exclusion thus cannot be understood in isolation from questions of racial representation and issues of class. For these reasons, in the pervasive system of exclusions naturalized beyond the threshold of visibility, the intricate play of presence and absence it is my purpose to address, does not apply to women alone. Therefore I deliberately de-emphasize cross-dressing as that which positively encodes absence and exclusion as transvestite presence because it tends to occlude the connections between female impersonation and racial impersonation. Throughout, I choose to focus on absence rather than presence because racial alterity in Shakespeare's theatre has the same status as the female body, namely, absent from the processes of representation.

Yet to focus on absence from representation, to argue that, in any sense, Shakespeare "left out" those who bore the marks of gender and race in the culture, may seem to point the politically correct finger at what can only be regarded as a deficiency. In fact, absence and deficiency can be equated only from the perspective of historical nostalgia that omits precisely the complex historical and aesthetic formations whose detailed elaborations I am concerned to trace. Worse still, my claim that early modern women were absent from Shakespeare's stage may be understood to deny them agency and make women passive victims. I have written very consciously against the critical trend whereby some endeavours to ascribe female agency almost deny women's oppression altogether. Exclusion from the stage, in my view, indeed bespeaks an aspect of women's secondary social status and is not remedied by those rare instances of female performance, but such recognition of women's oppression does not *de facto* render women abject victims of patriarchal culture, or deny them agency.

Certainly, one of my objectives is to challenge the fetishistic insistence on presence in Shakespeare, evident in the notion that there must be women on Shakespeare's stage, at least in every sense that counts, because there are representations of women on Shakespeare's stage. Such reasoning, in fact, recapitulates the dynamics of spectatorship itself. On the many occasions I have encountered this line of argument in the course of writing this book, I have felt frustration akin to that of Laurence Sterne's Parson Yorick in *A Sentimental Journey* (1768), who cannot convince his bishop that he is not the King of Denmark's jester: "'Good God!' said I, 'You might as well confound Alexander the Great with Alexander the Coppersmith, my lord.' – 'Twas all one,' he replied" (Sterne 1986 [1768]: 110).

As Yorick reminds the bishop that he is not the skull from *Hamlet*, we have to remind ourselves that no matter how much we feel Shakespeare represents all of us he had never heard tell of us, did not write for us, and seems, indeed, to have had little or no concern for literary posterity. For all that, or rather *because* of that, to indict Shakespeare for failing to engage in twentieth-century casting practises, or to blame him for the sex and race prejudices of his era – let alone those of our own – would be futile and anachronistic. I neither know nor, frankly, do I much care to speculate about whether it would have been "better" if Shakespeare had used a real African rather than Richard Burbage to play Othello or Aaron, or real women to play women's roles. If there *must* be an answer, it is that it would have been "different." Such hypothetical (not to mention ahistorical) issues do not trouble me here, because I am arguing that *presence cannot be equated with representation any more than representation can be equated with inclusion*. With this in mind, I want to use Shakespeare as the site from which to address the stakes of representation, especially for those who, in spite, or perhaps because, of their hypervisibility, have been historically its objects and not its subjects.

On the philosophical register, Shakespeare's plays both demonstrate and complicate the paradox whereby theatrical representation depends for its functioning – even in its moments of self-reflexivity – on the absence of the thing it represents (see Walton 1990: 117, 26–8). This intractable problem remains even in instances of perfect coincidence between any given element of a particular representation and that which it represents. (Even if, for example, the blackamoors in *Love's Labour's Lost* had been real, they would not really be playing at the court of Navarre.) That absence and substitution are the motors of representation is perhaps nowhere more apparent than in that watershed in the history of Western dramatic representation, Shakespeare's *Hamlet*. Hamlet positions his mother as the origin and cause of a complex chain of absence and substitution with which he is incestuously obsessed. Claudius is his absent father's substitute not only on the throne but also in his mother's bed. These circumstances fuel Hamlet's misogyny and articulate a crucial alignment between representation and femininity in which the woman's own body, the female orifice – what Hamlet terms the woman's "nothing" (as opposed to the phallic "thing") – contains the site of her absence: "That's a fair thought to lie between a maid's legs" (III. ii. 119).

Reiterating a commonplace about the omission of the hobby-horse, apparently as a result of Puritan objections, from the May games, Hamlet laments: "For O, for O, the hobby-horse is forgot" (III. ii. 133). The hobby-horse signifies wanton femininity, the genital woman, woman as the site of her own absence as in Leontes's tirade in *The Winter's Tale*: "my wife, a hobby-horse. ..." By coincidence, E. H. Gombrich also explicates the problems of representation in relation to the hobby-horse. In a memorable passage from *Meditations on a Hobby Horse*, he asks:

> How should we address it [the hobby-horse]? Should we describe it as an "image of a horse"? ... Luckily there is another word in the Dictionary which might prove more accommodating: "representation. To ... stand for, be specimen of, fill place of, be substitute for." A portrayal of a horse? Surely not. A substitute for a horse? Yes. That is it. Perhaps there is more to this formula than meets the eye.
>
> (Gombrich 1985: 1)

In the historically specific circumstances of the May games, however, the hobby-horse was rather more than a substitute for a horse. Tied around the waist of a male dancer moving with suggestive gyrations, the hobby-horse served as a prosthetic phallus, as it does in many productions of *Two Noble Kinsmen*. Further, in part because of its suppressed status, the hobby-horse became, as the Arden editor notes, the type of what is not there. The hobby-horse as the symbol of substitution marks out the difference between what Wallace Stevens called "the nothing that is not there and the nothing that is" (Vulpi 1996: 47–8). That is, the definable, delimited, containable nothing can be represented ("the nothing that is") and is opposed to the unthinkable, infinite nothing ("the nothing that is not there") which cannot. It is only the "thing" (Elizabethan slang for the penis) that can figure forth those absences which are troped as feminine (see Shershow 1995: 86). The hobby-horse, then, reveals representation, at least in the context of seventeenth-century popular culture and religious discourse, as inherently phallic and dependent upon a construction of the feminine absence.

While within this scheme female characters on the stage can be positive, negative, or even proto-feminist, the gap between representation (always a relatively autonomous entity) and social "reality" sometimes yawns oppressively wide. If I seem to revert here to a simplistic formula for the relation between representation and that to which it refers, consider, for instance, Donne's alleged remark to Ben Jonson that his *Anniversaries* described "the idea of a Woman and not as she was" (see Tayler 1991). Yet the relation between representation and reality is notoriously elusive. Theatre tends to confound the distinction between representation and its referents because it is based on illusion, on the failure of the empirical to secure the real (see Taylor 1996: 97–142). The dominant paradigm structures this relation as being between the representation and "the thing itself" and has been more recently contested by the notion that there is no ontological grounding in bedrock "reality" but only an ever-receding complex of cultural representations whose meaning is relational rather than absolute. Thus it is not always possible to distinguish immediately between the representations of femininity/negritude, etc., and real gendered and raced social identities. Indeed, stage impersonations should not be understood as attempts to grasp a coherent, authentic identity that always resides outside its representations and which somehow always outreaches them. There are, rather, complex dislocations and coincidences between women and representations of femininity, between Africans and representations of negritude, and so on, making these representations complicit with the lived conditions to which they refer. Racist representations, for example, helped to produce and reproduce racism with which real racial others – from Pocahontas to the Moroccan ambassador – then had to negotiate (see Tilton 1994: 8).

Virginia Woolf gestures to this perplexing fissure between real women and cultural representations of them when she ponders the hypervisibility of women in classical and Renaissance theatre: "[T]he paradox of this world where in real life a respectable woman could hardly show her face alone in the street, and yet on the stage woman equals or surpasses man, has never been satisfactorily explained"

(Woolf 1929: 65). Woolf addresses the chasm between precisely *positive* images of women and the restricted nature of women's lives: "Imaginatively she is of the highest importance; practically she is completely insignificant. She pervades poetry from cover to cover; she is all but absent from history" (43). This is very different from the emphasis of seventies feminism, which, recognizing that negative stereotypes are a significant component of sex oppression because they mold and discipline women and their desires, sought to improve images of women by making them more realistic and diverse. That is, the images-of-women approach erroneously accorded representation the status of a primary determinant. Woolf's emphasis is also quite distinct from later feminist criticism, which shifted its attention from the image to the axis of vision itself (the male gaze, questions of specularity, and so on). In contrast, Woolf's paradox, which remains to be addressed by feminism, concerns the limits of women's participation in culture versus their hypervisibility in the dramatic literature (though it must be noted that women are not equally visible in all genres), as well as the more specific contradiction that simultaneously produced women's relative absence from the scene of literary production and powerful representations of femininity on the stage.

The density of Woolf's paradox is particularly apparent when we examine the connection between raced and gendered alterity in what Ania Loomba calls "the double-play that produced non-European women on stage" (Loomba 1996: 190). This production, of course, occurred without the inclusion of the women represented, and did so most memorably in what I am tempted to call the palpable femininity of Shakespeare's Cleopatra. As Woolf remarks, "Certainly, if we consider it, Cleopatra must have had a way with her" (Woolf 1929: 64). In Cleopatra, Shakespeare is thought to have captured the very essence and allure of womanhood, the epitome of powerfully erotic, oriental femininity. More important, Cleopatra is a figure singularly capable of representing herself. She speaks more than any other female character in Shakespeare and infamously controls the speech of those around her (Loomba 1996: 175). When Antony begs to speak while dying on the monument, Cleopatra refuses and interjects "Let me speak" (IV. xv. 45) (Dusinberre 1996: 49).

For all Cleopatra's assertiveness, however, and for all the fact that scene division and stage directions imply performance, there is no record of the play ever having been performed during Shakespeare's lifetime. Thus it is just possible that what for generations of readers and playgoers has seemed like the incontrovertible womanhood of Cleopatra, a role that must have presented an immense challenge to even the most gifted male impersonator, may never have been embodied on Shakespeare's stage.[7] Judith Cook observes, "One has known boys who would do very well as Cressida. But what about … Cleopatra? One can only suppose that the emotional and intuitive potentialities of youths were more fully realized by the Elizabethans [*sic*]" (Cook 1977: 8). Unwittingly, perhaps, Cook hits upon the way in which one can read Cressida's arrival in the Greek camp, for example, as an intensely homoerotic scene, a counter to the more straightforward relation between Achilles and Patroclus. That is, Cressida is so much a pawn of relations among men, that there is a level at which she refers not to women but to the masculinities she negotiates. Certain characters, especially the cross-dressed heroines of the profoundly homoerotic comedies, of which Rosalind in *As You Like It* is the preeminent example, may not have been representations of women at all. Similarly, while Cleopatra, the cross-dressing queen, may be, indeed, all woman, a deliberate attempt to refer to a femininity quite outside the technical and aesthetic apparatus of the stage itself, it is equally possible that she is a glittering travesty of female sovereignty in the vein of Heywood's *If You Know Not Me, You Know Nobody* (see Jankowski 1992: 189–206). Whatever the reasons, performance history of the hypervisible and powerful Cleopatra demonstrates that she has too often been found to be unrepresentable, and the play has been performed only a handful of times up until this century.

Whether she is thoroughly feminine or thoroughly homoerotic, that Cleopatra is so compelling a *female* character role written for a male actor (whether or not it was ever performed by one) indicates the impossibility of pure sexual or gender categories. The crude category of woman, defined only by biology and outside the text and insulated from the ways in which cultural representations produce and reinforce assigned subject positions, is a classification of no more substantial existence than the most outlandish fiction. Representation thus contributes to, rather than being distinct from, the invention of the cultural subject. The paradox of representation is that it both produces and occludes subjectivities and while it may service the production and reproduction of subjectivities, it cannot wholly determine them. Representation exerts a pull on subjectivity, which can be variously, or even simultaneously, coercive and disciplinary, seductive and enthralling. That the categories of "woman",

"African", etc., are always bound up with representation renders them profoundly cultural and complex rather than biological and essential – though no less real.

Have we now arrived at a position where Sterne's bishop is right after all? In what sense can women and racialized subjects be understood to be, especially in the absence of essentialist categories of identity, evacuated from the scene of representation? Astonishingly, Stephen Orgel claims "Everyone in this culture [early modern England] was in some respects a woman" (Orgel 1996: 124). Being a woman, however, entails more than a relatively disadvantaged position in a rigidly stratified hierarchy. Certainly actors, very much at the bottom of the totem pole, as Marianne Novy has argued, were in a position not structurally dissimilar to that of women (Novy 1984: 92). For all that, actors were not women. That is, gender categories were neither reversible nor sufficiently flexible to allow women on the stage.

Thus raced and gendered bodies at large in the material world beyond the stage do not have immutable inherent characteristics but constitute the social and historical marks of oppression and privilege rather than their cause. Such identities are not grounded in nature or biology but by particular forms of labor – access to (even enslavement within) certain forms of production and exclusion from others. Evidence of this is perhaps to be found in the 1599 record of a university production at Oxford when female impersonators sat in the audience. The fact that they finally ascended the stage was regarded as proof of their real, male identity: "[N]either were known to bee men ... until they suspected it, seeing them entreated by the wooers to rise and danse upon the stage" (quoted in Shapiro 1996: 36). Access to dramatic representation is here defined, *de facto*, as male.

As Jean Howard has pointed out, the fundamental contradiction of early modern English drama is that women were excluded from the theatre as performers and playwrights and included as paying customers (Howard 1994: 1–46). In this, women's relation to representation is significantly different from that, for example, of Africans or the Irish. Unlike Africans, who constitute a tiny albeit significant and highly visible proportion of Shakespeare's characters but a tiny segment of the London population, and little or none of its audience, women constitute more than half the population and possibly half the audience. Anglo-Irish agents of colonialism such as Lord Thurles (who while in the company of the countess of Essex provokes an affray at the playhouse when the feather in his hat restricts the view of theatregoers behind him) are quite distinct from the indigenous Irish, who are not to be found in the theatre audience (Gurr 1987: 28). Whatever images of Moors, Turks, and wild men appeared on the English stage, they were rarely in the audience to take exception to the proceedings. English women were another matter. They were the objects and the consumers of the very representations they could not produce, and by extension, the bearers, not the makers, of meaning. The fact that women enjoyed the theatre or that they exercised the power of the gaze does not mitigate the fact that their exclusion from the stage was itself oppressive. No doubt the viability of theatre depends on female consumption, but we cannot then assume, especially given how little we know about women in Shakespeare's audience – and we know almost nothing from the perspective of women themselves – that such consumption constitutes approval. Here again, Cleopatra is a case in point. As Juliet Dusinberre observes, she is the one character in Shakespeare who, despite all critical assertions about the pleasure women took in the spectacle of all-male performance, commits suicide in order to avoid seeing herself performed by a boy (Dusinberre 1996: 53). One wonders with Dusinberre: "Would she [Cleopatra] have felt equally threatened by the concept of a woman performer?" (ibid.).[8]

For all the novelty and inventiveness of the playhouse, the new institution of emergent capitalism, unique in Europe (even the Spanish *corrales*, though both permanent and public, were not purpose-built) incorporated an implicit and long-standing prohibition against female players as European theatre did not (McKendrick 1989: 183–5). That they did so is in one way entirely predictable. As Majorie Garber has noted in her comprehensive analysis of the pervasive cultural fascination with cross-dressing: "[I]t might be contended that transvestite theater is the norm, not the aberration" (Garber 1992: 39). What is distinctive about the early modern prohibition on female performers, however, is that it occurred not in the theatre of a feudal or classical tradition (as was the case in Japan, China, and Greece) but was a feudal practise appropriated in the new context of the English public theatre. The stage became a specific and more absolute site of exclusion than in the cyclical, ritual dramatic cycles of the medieval era, records of which document payments to women who may have been engaged in actual performance.

Yet matters were not rectified by what, on the theoretical register, we might describe as the instantiation of presence, that is, by the

introduction of actresses. Women's arrival on stage was not an un-
mitigated "improvement" because representation, as Horkheimer
and Adorno remark in *The Dialectic of Enlightenment*, is always one
step forward and two steps back: "the capacity of representation is
the vehicle of progress and regression at one and the same time"
(Horkheimer and Adorno 1972: 35). On the one hand, as Elizabeth Howe has pointed out, actresses were often subject to sexual
harassment and: "The presence of women's bodies on the stage
encouraged lurid, eroticized presentations of female suffering, and
was designed to tantalize, rather than to attack violent masculine
behavior" (Howe 1992a: 176).[9] On the other hand, a handful of
women had gained access to a conspicuously public space even if
they usually did so at the price of their reputations. A few women
also became involved in theatrical management, and so represented
a small but significant gain. By now, however, the theatre imitated
Continental dramaturgy not only in the matter of female performers but in being an exclusive venue attended by fewer spectators
from the lower orders and further in having a virtually sex-
segregated audience (Roberts 1989: 81).

Female presence, which evolved from the innovations of two foreign queens, did make a cultural contribution, and its capacity to
upset the applecart was visible early on in William Prynne's condemnation of women actors as "notorious whores" in the wake of
Henrietta Maria's 1633 performance in Walter Montague's court
production of *The Shepheard's Paradise* (published in 1629; and 1659).
As Sophie Tomlinson observes, the female body and voice onstage
"challenged the order of things which placed women on the side of
absence and silence. The threat of the actress lay in the potential for
presenting femininity as a mobile, expressive force: the spectacle of
the woman actor summoning up the specter of the female subject"
(Tomlinson 1995: 9).

Despite the limitations of female performance, there is a feminist urge to celebrate the arrival of women on the stage as an
unqualified improvement regardless of the fact that acting had
always been considered a pretty degraded profession even for men.
Jacqueline Pearson writes: "The introduction of actresses must
have affected the drama of the period profoundly. Love and marriage and adultery could be enacted with a frankness and realism
impossible in a theatre where all performers were male" (Pearson
1988: 26).

One feminist writer who did not believe that women's arrival on the stage was a great leap forward is Alice Clark, author of the foundational and now intensely debated text on women's changing economic status with the advent of capitalism, *Working Life of Women in the Seventeenth Century* (1982 [1919]). Clark argues that women were squeezed out of the workforce as the seventeenth century progressed and became the necessary pool of cheap labor that later fueled the textile and woolen industry and thus the industrial revolution:

> The period under review, namely the seventeenth century, forms an important crisis in the historic development of English-women. The gulf which separates the women of the Restoration period from those of the Elizabethan era can be perceived by the most casual reader of contemporary drama. To the objection that the heroines of Shakespeare on the one hand and of Congreve and Wycherley on the other are creations of the imagination, it must be replied that the dramatic poet can only present life as he knows it.
>
> (Clark 1982 [1919]: 2–3)

Clark demonstrates a rather literal-minded reflectionist model of the relation between dramatic literature and society. Ignoring the transvestite nature of Shakespeare's stage, she reads the drama as a direct representation of women and as evidence of profound change in the character of women in the course of the seventeenth century (ibid.: 3). For Clark, drama is a barometer for the condition of women in the seventeenth century, and however naive this notion of the relation between drama and society, there were indeed many ways in which representations of womankind deteriorated rather than improved with the introduction of the actress. Further, she points out, demand for women as actresses occurred at a time when they had been almost totally excluded from other professions. Whatever disagreement there may be about her conclusions, Clark's economic analysis leads us to confront the problem of constructing a narrative – which is as much a theoretical as a historical problem – of women's exclusion and participation in culture. Though it is always dangerous to generalize, Clark also raises the possibility that women were better represented (and by this I mean more fully represented as well as less sexually commodified) on Shakespeare's stage by the bodies of male actors of rather dubious moral and social standing than they were by Restoration actresses – who were of even more dubious moral and social standing.

Debates about the arrival of the actress, however, exemplify a problem that applies to racialized "others" as much as to women – the limits of presence in the structure of mimesis. When actors of genuinely African heritage finally began to play Shakespeare, black performers could not, try as they might, fully redeem a character such as the evil Aaron. Similarly, because of the increasing racism of audiences and directors alike in the face of an actual black actor, Othello became less sympathetic than he had ever been when played by Richard Burbage. Less of a hero and more of a savage, his tragedy was simply that of reverting to his uncivilized "nature." In a more recent example of the limits of corporeal presence, a director who chose to dramatize the figure of the Indian boy in *A Midsummer Night's Dream* (a figure who is alluded to but does not have a role in Shakespeare's play) did not manage to represent the role of race in the play, but, as Margo Hendricks has shown, only to reenact and solidify the play's orientalist fantasies (Hendricks 1996: 37–60). Thus the realization of the fantasy of "presence" in the body of the performer serves more to uncover the limits of representation rather than to undo them. That we expect otherwise testifies to the hold of the fantasy itself, to our enormous investment in cultural representation, as well as its conflation with political representation.

What is crucial here are neither the merits (or lack thereof) of Restoration theatre nor the first uses of black performers but the fact that change in representation alone does not bring about political change. Such change requires a radical alteration in production at every level – theatrical, economic, political, and cultural. Even Horkheimer and Adorno's slightly revised evolutionary narrative of representation, from forward movement to forward-and-back, fails to account for such complexity. When all colors, shapes, levels of physical ability, sexualities, and so on, are to be seen on TV, we still cannot be sure that we will be fully represented; we will still have to decide exactly what representation means as a political and cultural goal, who gets represented, who gets access to representation, who feels represented, and what counts as representation.

Under pressure of these questions, I can neither dismiss the fictional nature of Shakespearean femininity nor make a nostalgic case for the importance of bodily presence and lament, "If only there had been women in Shakespeare!" I make, instead, a historical case for absence – for what was rather than what should or might have been. I am concerned to analyze the constitutive absences and the imprints of erasure in Shakespeare's plays. This presents, of course, something of a methodological problem since what is under erasure is not literally present in the text itself. As scholars who address the breach between playtext and performance have long known, looking at what is not there is hardly a matter of inventing and fantasizing new content for the plays (see Berger 1989). Rather, looking at what is not there entails regarding very steadily the chiaroscuro and contours of dramatic presence, making visible the agility with which literary representation both gives shape and takes form on the horizon of history.

In this project, then, I aim more to discern the butterfly in motion than to pin it in the case. I hope to do justice to the plays as vivid, complex, aesthetic formations as well as wonderfully dynamic social acts. Finally, by insisting on absence, I also hope to unravel some of the philosophical and political dimensions of representation in culture.

Throughout the book, I focus in particular on three categories of persons who were not actually present on Shakespeare's stage: women, Africans, and the primary subjects of racist discourse in early modern England, the Irish. Despite their contiguity, these three categories, pose, as I have already hinted, quite distinct problems in relation to representation. For instance, cosmetically blanched to signify women's beauty, female impersonators on the stage served to figure whiteness as a racial category as much as they signified gender difference. Again, while there was an implicit prohibition against female mimesis, women were not exhibited as such in pageants and sideshows, whereas Africans and American Indians were prominent objects of such display. Women were, however, occasionally displayed as freaks or circus acts: the "hairy wench"; the "hog-faced woman"; "Dancinge on the Ropes performed by a woman & also A Baboone" (Thompson 1996: 104–5). Further, women's bodies, especially the genitals, were sometimes displayed by men in individual acts of sexual assault, and women were exhibited in the punitive practise of whipping and stripping those convicted of prostitution:

> [S]pecial commissions are set up, and when they meet with a case, they punish the man with imprisonment and a fine. The woman is taken to Bridewell … where the executioner scourges her naked before the populace. And although close watch is kept on them, great swarms of these women haunt the town in the taverns and playhouses.
>
> (quoted in Gurr 1987: 214)

Here, women, in stark contrast to their male clients and pimps, are subject to the full range of specular practises from surveillance to punitive display. Another point of contrast among the three groups is that Africans and women are both hypervisible objects of impersonation, whereas the Irish, whose glibs and mantles mark them as irredeemably other and whose relation to representation in English culture is extraordinarily complex, hardly figure at all in Shakespeare and are, as Michael Neill has shown, like the American Indians, disproportionately under-represented in the dramatic literature in general (Neill 1994a: 1, 1–132). This absence (Captain MacMorris is Anglo-Irish rather than Gaelic Irish) is historically coincident with, though not causally related to, endeavors to raze those native populations from the territories they occupied – in the starvation of Munster, for example, and in the proposal to remove the natives of Ulster in early plans for the plantation of that province. Indeed, if the Irish are conspicuous in Shakespeare, it is *only* by their absence.

Restrictions specifically on women's access to cultural institutions were not limited to theatre. Although, of course, there were women writers in early modern England, there were specific practical impediments to women's literacy especially to writing and Latinity, and these were quite distinct from both the obstacles, and the rationalization behind them, that faced lower-class men. The degree of women's participation in and resistance to male-controlled sites of representation was hardly commensurable with the implacable structures of material power and authority exercised by men (see Shershow 1995: 12). Yet class also made a difference for women. Indeed, the difference between the masque and the public stage, I would argue, is primarily one of class rather than one of gender. In the masque aristocratic women did indeed represent themselves, though whether or not they engaged in mimesis is arguable (see Barroll 1997: 112–26). Especially in the craze for blackface masques, aristocratic women also took it upon themselves not so much to represent others but to control the production of blackness as a category.

English women are also distinguished from Africans and from the Irish, whose possession of their own rich and distinct forms of cultural expression was acknowledged as the traditions specific to women were not. Loomba's remarks on the East are equally applicable to the Irish: "The cultural difference between it [the Orient] and Europe could not be expressed as one between unlettered and lettered cultures. The East was not, at least not then, Europe's silent 'other.' Colonial discourses may have subsequently muffled the voice of the colonized people around the world, but the processes of silencing differed" (Loomba 1996: 176). In that there are restrictions on English women's cultural representation within their *own* culture, the form taken by women's exclusion from the production of representation in early modern English culture is markedly distinct from the situation of Africans and the Irish within cultural representation.

However, not all the persons physically absent yet conspicuously represented on Shakespeare's stage are marginalized groups. There are, for instance, no real kings on the stage any more than there are real women or real racial others (see Pye 1990; and Billington 1991). The difference is that sovereigns did not lack access to representation. Women, in contrast, did lack such access by virtue of exclusion from the stage, while racial others were not present in sufficient numbers in English society in order to secure it. Sovereigns, on the other hand, staged spectacles of power outside the theatre, and the court masque and the royal progress were theatrical forms exclusively their own. The crown exercised control over the public theatre by means of the Revels office as well as specific injunctions against depicting a living Christian prince onstage.[10] The fact that Middleton's *A Game At Chess* (1626) slipped through the Revels office at a time when it served the crown's anti-Catholic interests to lampoon the Spanish sovereign – and, incidentally, to do so by implicitly racializing religious difference via the rhetoric of black and white – signals that this prohibition was selectively enforced.[11] Absence of the sovereign from the public stage thus constituted supercultural regulation of the entire social apparatus of representation rather than exclusion from it.[12]

I have been struggling, then, with questions of visibility, power, and the meaning of representation and have used the Shakespearean corpus as a way of understanding the positions of women, Africans, and the Irish both within and outside theatrical culture. Above all, I have come to recognize the necessity of reading simultaneously exclusion from and representation in (as opposed to participation in) early modern culture. Race and gender in this scheme are not just related themes but categories that become visible only in relation to each another. Thus, while my analysis is always feminist, it does not always take women as its sole object. Indeed, only one of the chapters that follow (Chapter 1, "And All is Semblative a

Woman's Part") takes women as its sole focus, while the last chapter, "What Is An Audience?" addresses both women and groundlings in Shakespeare's audience and is informed by the problem of the class status of Shakespeare's actors. Class, however, never appears in this book as a separate category; it is, in my view, qualitatively different from race and gender in that all subjects in early modern English culture, even aristocratic ones, are always class-marked, whereas white English men constitute the unmarked racial and gender categories of early modern England. Nonetheless, it remains important that the vehicles of Shakespearean representation, the actors, were not, as we have noted, privileged members of the society, but social anomalies sometimes regarded (as in the legislation of 1572) as unproductive persons on the level of vagabonds and beggars. Thus it is not the case that the lower classes lacked representation on Shakespeare's stage; it is rather the case that such representation was viewed as almost entirely derogatory. The chapters on castration, black masculinity, and the Irish (both men and women) do not take women as their primary focus either, but they demystify patriarchal logic around the issues of female impersonation, the construction of white femininity, and patriarchal history, respectively.

The first chapter examines *Twelfth Night* and the problem of material exclusion of the female body, which is, nonetheless, literally graphically represented in this play in the form of a scandalous pun on female genitalia in the letter to Malvolio. While I believe this is an important point within the context of theatre history, I hope also to offer an intervention in recent feminist preoccupation with the body. In contrast to the tide of feminist commentary that focuses on the female body as an element of the mind-body binary that structures Western thought, I argue that the body, understood as absolute presence, leaves us within the confines of the same problematic and with an impoverished understanding of the material as brute facticity rather than as a component of the dialectic of historical materialism.

Chapter 2, "The Castrator's Song," looks at the impersonation of the female voice as the most vulnerable aspect of the woman's part for the boy-actor (see Charney 1979: 37–43; Rastall 1996: 316). I have to admit to writing this chapter at a point when I was feeling much misunderstood, when responses to my project assumed that saying Shakespeare was without women, or indeed anything short of complete plenitude on any count, was to somehow be a feminist against Shakespeare, and even against-men. I decided, tongue-in-cheek, to take my critics at their word, and assiduously applied myself to the surgical treatises on castration. (Let it not be said that feminists lack a sense of humor.) Since it was widely recognized that castration altered the vocal chords, I was interested here to explore another anomaly of the English stage, namely the absence of the castrati so popular elsewhere in Europe.[13] Shakespeare's theatre was more markedly aural that any that succeeded it, and, as Margaret Lamb has argued, "The Elizabethan stage voice may well have relied more on range of pitch and less on stress than modern Englishmen do; with ... more musical and varied tone" (Lamb 1980: 29). Yet the voice remains the most under-historicized part of the transvestite stage, studies of which are almost entirely focused on the visual elements of impersonation. In a sense, a profoundly Lacanian one, this critical omission is not surprising, since in castration, the psychoanalytic paradigm for presence and absence, the phallus and "lack" is totally absorbed with seeing. For Freud there is a moment when the little boy sees with horror, recognizing "in a flash," what the little girl has not got, and interprets her lack as evidence that she has been castrated. Teresa de Lauretis remarks: "this femininity is purely a representation, a positionality within the phallic model of desire and signification; it is not a quality or a property of women. Which all amounts to saying that woman, *as* subject of desire or of signification, is unrepresentable; or, better, that in the phallic order of patriarchal culture and in its theory, woman is unrepresentable except as representation" (de Lauretis 1987: 20). That is, the cultural imperative to view a woman as a castrated man is completely reliant on visual apprehension. The predominance of the visual in the psychoanalytic register, which gives priority to the phallus as a conspicuous object, relegates female genitalia to the order of the invisible, to the horror of nothing-to-see. The feminist solution cannot be just visibility – the female genitals are not, after all, invisible and have certainly been the object of scrutiny in practises ranging from gynecology to pornography – but a rearrangement and reconceptualization of the scopic field, a radical depriviledging of phallomorphism. I have tried to accomplish this by offering a brief history of the then new operation of surgical castration in the period in order to access the articulation and subsumption of woman's difference under the rubric of possessing or not possessing the phallus.

The following two chapters address specifically the question of race. Chapter 3 deals with racial impersonation in *Othello* as part of the period's representational spectrum from exhibition to mimesis. I argue that women in the play serve to mark whiteness against Othello's negritude, and that the play of race and gender needs to be read, first of all, in terms of theatrical integument. For all the long critical history of Othello and of whether or not he is a veritable Negro or just off-white, there has been very little attention paid to the bald fact that both black Othello and Desdemona were played by white males. Attention to the materiality of early modern performance makes these issues both visible and important, but the way in which history has rendered this circumstance invisible, just as it has rendered the vocal apparatus undetectable, fascinates me. I argue that one of the reasons it is so difficult to discern the play of difference on the Renaissance stage is the advent of the commodity and the system of representation required by it, in the development of which theatre played no small part. Commodities are reified because the labor that produces them becomes invisible, and with the burgeoning slave trade, the exotic, the African became itself a commodity alienated from its own humanity.

Chapter 4 is about the annihilation of a people and their culture, the Gaelic Irish; and, try as I might to infuse it with humor, it remained a bleak story redeemed only by the fact that I believe that in *The Tempest* Shakespeare, consciously or otherwise, leaves a space for the appreciation of cultural difference. In an act of reverse positivism, I have looked very hard at this palpable space, at the aporia of representation until, finally, there came into focus the absent Irish, proximate yet invisible; at their culture; and, at one point in the essay, even the absent woman I am pleased to call the Irish Sycorax, Granuiale. In an oblique way this chapter speaks to my own identity and to why I, too, feel enmeshed in the messy, often wrong-headed, yet empowering identifications with Shakespeare.

I conclude with the place in which I had expected to find incontrovertible material evidence of women's participation in theatre – in the audience. But find it I could not. There are certainly women in the audience, but I discovered that their presence is heavily mediated by male accounts of theatre attendance and by a pervasive fantasy about female spectatorship. That is, male mimesis requires a female spectator, and so projections about female sexual and specular receptivity become necessary to the functioning of theatre.[14] I focus in particular here on *A Midsummer Night's Dream* because it is so concerned with the philosophical aspects of representation and also because it presents those problems as a function of gender-and-class differentiated labor within the structure of theatre itself. This chapter puts pressure on the critical certainty about women's presence in the audience, that is, on our own fantasy of women's inclusion in culture, and juxtaposes the exclusion of women with the concept of a theatrical exclusivity based on class.

Taking Shakespeare's transvestite stage as its primary trope, this book is simultaneously an examination of and an exercise in faith in representation.

1

"And all is semblative a woman's part"
Body politics and *Twelfth Night*

I

Once a marginalized object in traditional literary scholarship, the body has emerged as a crucial category of critical inquiry. In Renaissance studies it has become the focus of attention as the site of emergent notions of the modern subject and attendant concepts of privacy and intimacy hitherto viewed as natural and transhistorical. Transformations wrought by the Reformation and by the shift from feudalism to capitalism rendered the body subject to what Norbert Elias has called "the civilizing process" (Elias 1978–82 [1939]; Gent and Llewellyn 1990: 1–10). More specifically, Renaissance theatre itself had a corporeal, sexual identity. It was a place where, to use Dekker's redolent term, "stinkards" gathered, where patrons engaged in those sexual practises so often vilified by anti-theatricalists: arousal, prostitution, perhaps even copulation itself (Gurr 1987: 38). The Renaissance body, then, especially in the arena of theatre, has been recognized as political, that is, as a site for the operation of power and the exercise of meaning, and one "fully social in its being and in its ideological valency" (Barker 1984: 13).

That the Renaissance seems peculiarly concerned with the somatic might seem justification enough for a study of the body in Shakespeare. We might concur with Carroll Smith-Rosenberg, who argues: "During periods of social transformation, when social forms crack open ... ideological conflict fractures discourse ... sexuality and the physical body emerge as particularly evocative political symbols" (Smith-Rosenberg 1989: 103). But the resurgence of the body in Renaissance studies (and elsewhere) is not a perennial, cyclical phenomenon. Rather, the intensity of focus on the body is related to very specific, historically situated developments in poststructuralist theory.

In *The Ideology of the Aesthetic* Terry Eagleton draws attention to the politics of current concern with the body:

> [F]ew literary texts are likely to make it nowadays into the new historicist canon unless they contain at least one mutilated body. A recovery of the importance of the body has been one of the most precious achievements of recent radical thought. ... At the same time, it is difficult to read the later Roland Barthes, or even the later Michel Foucault, without feeling that a certain style of meditation on the body, on pleasures and surfaces, zones and techniques, has acted among other things as a convenient displacement of a less immediately corporeal politics, and acted also as an *ersatz* kind of ethics. There is a privileged, privatized hedonism about such discourse, emerging as it does at just the historical point where certain less exotic forms of politics found themselves suffering a setback.
>
> (Eagleton 1990: 7)

The body is simultaneously situated here as *de facto*, "exotic," a "precious achievement," and a "displacement" of serious politics. The emancipatory potential projected onto the body (by feminist and Queer theorists as much as the doyens of poststructuralism) versus the political limitations of current fetishizations of the body seems to put the "undecidable" and the "dialectical" perilously close. Nevertheless, Eagleton draws our attention to the fact that the body becomes in much critical discourse the site of "micropolitics" (in centrist or "ludic" readings of the postmodern as opposed to resistance postmodernism),[1] which is believed to have replaced the grand conceptual, liberatory narratives of political economy (see Zavarzadeh 1991). Ludic postmodernism produces a naive notion that social transformation can be articulated at the corporeal level. Foucault falls into this utopian vision of the body at the end of *The History of Sexuality*. The body, as a site of opacity almost exempt from meaning, becomes the privileged locus of resistance: "The rallying point for the counterattack against the deployment of sexuality ought not to be sex-desire, but bodies and pleasures" (Foucault 1981: 157).[2] While "bodies and pleasures" mark Foucault's distance from Derridean and Lacanian desire, in the end the ideological effect is the same, namely one of privileged, privatized hedonism. Similarly Bakhtin, whose rhetoric is more that of mouth and anus than zone and surface, nonetheless deploys a populist, utopian view of the disruptiveness of the grotesque body (see Stallybrass and White 1986).

Paradoxically, too, micropolitical analyses are frequently presented as "materialist." For example, both Foucault's techniques of the subject and Bakhtin's grotesque realism have been viewed as such, in what Eagleton dubs "the modish, purely gestural uses of that most euphoric of radical buzz-words" (Eagleton 1986: 80). In some instances popular and politically specific uses of the term *materialism* are employed as if they were synonymous. Lucy Gent and Nigel Llewellyn, for example, in their fairly traditional, thematic approach to *Renaissance Bodies*, argue for the pure material reality of the body as opposed to "abstraction and distance"; that is, the discursivity of the "figure": " 'Body,' by contrast, suggests the solidly central un-represented fact of existence, a materiality that is of itself inarticulate. It is the mute substance of which 'figure' is a more nervous and expressive shadow" (Gent and Llewellyn 1990: 2). Yet this appearance of substance occurs only because this is how, within the transactions of discourse, the body is rendered intelligible in our culture. When Gent and Llewellyn refer to the body's sheer physicality, the mute facticity of its materiality, they reduce the material to the elemental. This definition of the material as the density of things one can touch is classically humanist. Mas'ud Zavarzadeh explains:

> In the discourses of ludic postmodernism, "politics" is an exemplary instance of totalitarian "conceptuality." The micropolitics of the body, on the other hand, is politics without concepts: the local politics of material experience. However, *material* in these theories ... means the immediate elements of the medium of the political, that is to say, the discourses that articulate subjectivities and thus produce the micro-political. It is, in other words, a materialist politics only in the sense that, for example, focusing on the "photochemical reality" of film makes the film maker a "materialist" film maker. An idealist materialism isolates single issues and their mode of enunciation from the global structures of the political economy.
>
> (Zavarzadeh 1991: 48)

Such critical discourses, then, invoke the body as substantive, ontologically grounded *raw* material devoid of any agenda for social transformation. Alternatively (and sometimes simultaneously) in its textualist rendition, the material is defined *as* discourse, as the material part of the sign to which the body contributes, as Barthes has proposed, through the phatic dimension of speech.[3] Thus a characteristic deconstructionist maneuver places the opacity of both the signifier and the body as the "material" dimensions of the production of meaning. This depoliticized materialism conveniently coincides with both post-marxism and those reactionary elements of the (ludic) postmodern to which it is also causally related. In this way contemporary discourse on the body, as Eagleton argues, has become alienated from the "more traditional political topics of the state, class conflict and modes of production," that is, from historical materialism as it has been previously and more rigorously understood (Eagleton 1990: 7). The body, then, even when it is understood not as simple transhistorical fact but as "a relation in a system of liaisons which are material, discursive, psychic, sexual, but without stop or centre" (Barker 1984: 12), may signal, nonetheless, the displacement of the political defined as the global, totalizing agendas relegated to obsolescence in much postmodern theory. Thus, while ludic postmodern discourses of the body offer accounts of the body substantially different from humanist understandings, their ideological effects are in the end disarmingly similar.

Materialism, as I have argued, cannot be reduced to raw physicality or to the so-called materiality of signs; both constitute "idealist materialism." In terms of discourse on the body, this contention denies neither the "real" ontological existence of the body nor the materiality of discourse (see Barrett 1988: xxviii; Wolff 1990: 133). However, the material should not be confined to the binarism brutematerial/discursive, but rather considered as the way the social and cultural always *exceed* the discursive. For this is precisely what is at stake in the question of the material. An example may clarify the point: that certain classes of women were particularly marked out as rape victims in the Renaissance (servants, for example) and that women continue to be viewed as sexual terrain to be possessed, violated, and commodified constitute physical, social, and cultural aspects of rape as opposed to purely physical or "textual" ones (see Bashar 1983: 24–46). (Women are thus no more vulnerable to rape as an inherent fact of biology than men are to castration.) Rape has, then, both a physicality and a politics that in a patriarchal culture expresses relations *between men* in which women are property, and as such it cannot be separated from issues of class and ownership. That is, the discursive construction of the gendered body is implicated in the materiality of the nondiscursive, and the latter is not simply raw materiality but also the social and cultural.

I have chosen an example pertinent to feminist struggle because the politics of the body are exacerbated and more urgent there: as the object of patriarchal subjugation, women are uniquely identified with their anatomy, which has been simultaneously and problematically marked as the ground of feminist resistance. The problem is whether the body intrinsically constitutes an appropriate and effective site of resistance to the increasingly dense, subtle, and comprehensive conceptual trap of late-capitalist patriarchy. The danger is that "its pre-existing meanings, as sex object, as object of the male gaze, can always prevail and reappropriate the body" (Wolff 1990: 121). It is not clear that we reclaim women's bodies – especially denigrated female genitals, which are culturally marked as the source of women's oppression – without regressing into biological essentialism (the very rationale for women's subordination), the phenomenology of lived experience, or the political evasions of poststructuralism.[4] Nor can we reclaim past representations of female corporeality in any simple, celebratory way.

In what follows I want to use a more politically effective understanding of materialism than the one current in cultural criticism of the body in order to focus on the absent-presence of female genitals in *Twelfth Night*. My analysis of the play's representations of the female body operates in terms of global rather than local structures and resists the characteristic poststructuralist notion that undecidability is liberating. Further, I want to resist the pervasive tendency in Shakespeare criticism, in both its humanist and poststructuralist manifestations, to conflate "matter" and materialism, a trivialization that blocks the emancipatory potential of this radical concept.[5] For the female body, while not literally present on the Renaissance stage, was constantly and often scabrously constructed in masculine discourses in ways that reinforced larger patriarchal institutions and practises.[6]

II

In Shakespearean comedy the female body is most obviously a problem at the (secondary) level of the text's fiction, where female characters such as Viola and Rosalind disguise themselves as eunuchs and lackeys. But the female body is also problematized at the primary level of Renaissance theatre practise, in which boys played "the woman's part." Lisa Jardine argues, " 'Playing the woman's part' – male effeminacy – is an act for a male audience's appreciation"; she asserts that that "these figures are sexually enticing *qua* transvestied boys, and that the plays encourage the audience to view them as such" (Jardine 1983: 31, 29).[7] As the complexity of this state of affairs has been emphasized, however, there has been something of a displacement of the initial feminist recognition that transvestism is an aspect of misogyny based on the material practise of excluding women from the Renaissance stage – the "boy actress" phenomenon.[8] Thus, while Stephen Orgel in a now-famous contribution to *South Atlantic Quarterly*'s special issue on homosexuality contends, like Jardine, that homosexuality was the dominant form of eroticism in Renaissance culture, he also argues (and this is indeed a crucial recognition) that the homoeroticism of the Renaissance stage was not inevitably misogynist (Orgel 1989: 17).[9] Transvestism could not have had particularly insidious implications for women, he argues, because plays depended for their success on the large numbers of female playgoers. Nevertheless, the *exclusion* of women from the stage and their simultaneous *inclusion* as customers – the fundamental characteristic (contradiction) of the institution of theatre in early modern England – does not exculpate theatre from charges of misogyny. This should not lead us to conclude, of course, that women's appearance on the stage at the Restoration should be read simply as "progress." In those countries where female players were allowed on stage, women were no less oppressed than in England.[10] Rather, the point here is to recognize the flexibility, the historically and geographically variable nature of patriarchy, while insisting on the exclusion of women from the Renaissance stage as the determinate material condition of the theatre's production and representation of femininity.

Catherine Belsey's essay, "Disrupting Sexual Difference: Meaning and Gender in the Comedies," written in the 1980s performed the important task of bringing a feminist-deconstructionist reading to the comedies. This approach takes the destabilization of meaning to be in and of itself "political," and urges separation of the positive play of transvestism from the systematic and structural oppression of women. From this perspective the endless play of meaning inherent in transvestism becomes inherently subversive –

undecidable – and therefore, "for us to decide" (Belsey 1985: 190). But since all meanings in language are inherently unstable, the limits of this approach are that transvestite destabilizations do not necessarily offer any especially liberating possibilities for feminism.[11] Comic transvestism, particularly in *Twelfth Night*, may indeed take "the most remarkable risks with the identity of its central figure" and permit us "to glimpse alternative possibilities" (Belsey 1985: 166–7). But it is very likely that these new possibilities would equally provide the basis for control and self-surveillance (Wolff 1990: 127).

In contrast to this strain of criticism, I want to argue that in the carnivalesque world of *Twelfth Night* the female body's capacity for resistance and disruption is severely curtailed by the fact that the transvestite actor is "as likely to be portraying women with contempt as with respect" and the fact that the male body, "the very instrument of the art of the theatre" (Gibbons 1980: 64), repeatedly and ritually enacts the displacement, exclusion, and discipline of its female counterpart.

III

In the Renaissance the mimicking of social superiors by wearing their clothes was as much a violation of natural order as the assumption of a sexual identity other than that dictated by one's anatomical destiny. Antitheatricalists tirelessly inveighed against the latter. A fairly typical example of such an attack is to be found in Philip Stubbes's infamous book, whose very title, *The Anatomy of Abuses*, invokes the corporeality of deviance:

> Our apparell was given as a sign distinctive, to discern betwixt sexe and sexe, and therefore one to wear the apparell of an other sex, is to participate with the same and to adulterate the veritie of his owne kinde.
>
> (Stubbes 1583: 38)

Cross-dressing is an obvious target for antitheatricalists given the biblical injunction against it: "the Lord forbideth men and wemen to chaunge raiment," and the 1620 pamphlet controversy about androgynous dress, *Hic Mulier* and *Haec Vir* (Jardine 1983: 14, 155–6). Nevertheless, *two* types of transvestism prevailed: that which violated the boundaries of gender demarcation and that which violated class hierarchy. On this matter, Jonas Barish summarizes the representative view of Puritan antitheatricalist William Perkins: "Distinctions of dress, however external and theatrical they may seem to us, for Perkins virtually belong to our essence, and may no more be tampered with than that essence itself" (Barish 1981: 92).[12] Thus, for the likes of Perkins and Stubbes, essence resides in apparel rather than in what lies beneath it. To divest oneself of the appropriate social signifiers is to alter one's essence, to adulterate God-given nature. From this point of view the soul resides in the clothes, not just for Parolles but for all humanity.

That there is a structural identity between gender and class transvestism is demonstrable in the fact that the profound hostility to transvestite actors was related to the revival of medieval sumptuary laws, which prohibited the confusions of "degrees" and "callings" ordained by God (see Orgel 1989: 15). This is so much the case that Malvolio's obedience to the injunction contained in a forged letter that he wear yellow stockings and cross-garters all but overwhelms the Viola/Sebastian plot from which it singularly diverts the audience's attention. Malvolio's cross-gartering, his "transvestism," is, then, structurally and symbolically related to gender inversion, and it is no further removed from anatomical inscription than is Viola's disguise. Malvolio adopts attire that might be suitable if worn by a young gentleman suitor to Olivia but is incongruous and ridiculous when worn by a servant who sees himself as fit to be her husband.[13] As the Elizabethan "Homily Against Excess of Apparell" contends, such behavior constitutes a violation of both decorum and decree:

> many a one doubtless should be compelled to wear a russet coat which now ruffleth in silks and velvets, spending mo[r]e by the year in superfluous apparell than their fathers received for the whole revenue of their lands.[14]

Having indulged in these improprieties, Malvolio really is, in a sense, mad, because it is, as Raymond Ruyer remarks, such eccentricities and deviations from the naturalized orthodoxy of decorum which are "the small change of madness" (quoted in Stallybrass 1986: 123; see also Tennenhouse 1989: 67).

Notably, the only record we have of a Renaissance performance of the play does not so much as mention Viola's transvestism.[15] John Manningham's contemporary response places Malvolio at the play's core:

> At our feast we had a play called Twelfth Night or What You Will, much like the Commedy of Errors or Menechmi in Plautus,

but most like and near to that in Italian called Inganni. A good
practise in it to make the Steward believe his Lady Widdowe was
in love with him by counterfeyting a letter from his Lady in
generall terms, telling him what shee liked best in him and pre-
scribing his gesture in smiling his apparaile etc, and then when
he came to practise making him beleeve they tooke him to be
mad.

(quoted from King 1971: 97)

Similarly, Charles I, embracing the title's invitation to tag the play,
"What You Will," inscribed *Malvolio* opposite the title of the play in
his copy of the Second Folio. A 1623 performance of the play also
refers to it by that title.[16] Although we cannot account for all the
textual changes that may have occurred from the time of the first
recorded performance to the version we have received (Olivia is
not a widow for instance, and we have no way of knowing whether
this represents Manningham's error or a reference simply to the
costume of a widow or a change in the text), there is good reason to
concur with Margaret Maurer, who contends, "Frankly, he
[Malvolio] has upstaged the twin device" (Maurer, unpublished:
2). However, Malvolio does not merely upstage the comedy of the
main plot: he notoriously disrupts the festive spirit of *Twelfth Night*.
The unrecuperable "I'll be reveng'd on the whole pack of you" (V.
i. 377) troubles all the charm and delight that critics and audiences
have found in the play. It is also possible that Malvolio's desire for
revenge is directed at women, and at Olivia quite specifically for
her "Alas, poor fool, how they have baffled thee!" (V. i. 368). It
would seem, then, that class transvestism is more threatening than
that of gender, which can be resolved rather more readily.[17] In this
respect Malvolio's cross-gartering is more subversive than any instance of cross-dressing because it is Malvolio who menaces the
romantic coupling with which the play concludes.

Because traditional criticism has often been at pains to gloss over
or dissolve the discordant tone produced by Malvolio's promise of
revenge, it has never been linked to the other major source of dis-
harmony, namely, the " 'discord' between the romance and the broader
comedy of the play" (Craik and Lothian, eds 1981: liv; Levine 1986;
Westlund 1984). The dimensions of significant corporeality enacted
in both gender and class transvestism and the feminized carnal excesses
constitutive of the play's bawdy are crucially interarticulated. Recognizing this interconnectedness, the way the female body is complexly

imbricated in other social categories, especially class, renders the female body in *Twelfth Night* not as a merely localized phenomenon but as a pervasive cultural one. Here I want to contest specifically the notion that "The primary, physiological distinction could not, of course, be represented on the stage" (McLuskie 1989: 100; see also Pequigney 1995: 178–85). In other words, in my reading what is at issue is not *whether it could be* represented but *how it is* represented. That is, the monstrous female genitalia in the play's representational register are not merely a localized "theme" but rather depend on and produce the exclusion and denigration of women and the ridicule and punishment of men who attempt to change their status in the social hierarchy. This is nothing less than the maintenance and reproduction of patriarchy.

Let me elaborate first on the text's bawdy, the raw physical humor that often disconcerts critics who favor the ethereal lyricism held to be the definitive characteristic of romantic comedy. Eric Partridge in a revised edition of his famous book, *Shakespeare's Bawdy*, is obliged to retract an earlier declaration that *Twelfth Night* is "the cleanest comedy except for *A Midsummer Night's Dream*" (Partridge 1968). Further, since *Twelfth Night* is by critical consensus the culmination of Shakespeare's work in the genre, when he "completely masters and exhausts the possibilities of this form of drama" (Rose 1988: 41), and since comedy is inherently corporeal, that range of possibilities necessarily includes the bawdy body. Stephen Greenblatt observes: "Shakespearean comedy constantly appeals to the body and in particular to sexuality as the heart of its theatrical magic; 'great creating nature' – the principle by which the world is and must be peopled" (Greenblatt 1988: 86; see also Craik and Lothian, eds 1981: lii). Such a view while it once again ignores the exclusion of real female corporeality, none the less grates against Granville-Barker's contention that Shakespeare's was a celibate stage devoid of physical representations of sexuality, where transvestism functioned as an aesthetic device to foreground theatrical artifice (Granville-Barker 1952: 15). For all the critical reluctance to address it, the "broad humor" of the play is perfectly appropriate to its celebration of Twelfth Night, the Feast of Misrule, when licensed inversion is the order of the day; as Feste remarks: "To see this age! A sentence is but a chev'ril glove to a good wit – how quickly the wrong side may be turned outward!" (III. i. 11–12). Here the fleshy grotesque body reigns supreme. Stallybrass and White describe the symbolic components of this structural inversion as follows:

Grotesque realism images the human body as multiple, bulging, over-or under-side, protuberant and incomplete … with its orifices (mouth, flared nostrils, anus) yawning wide and its lower regions (belly, legs, feet, buttocks and genitals) given priority over its upper regions (head, "spirit," reason).

(Stallybrass and White 1986: 9)

The play's laughter is thus produced by comic violations of social and somatic decorum integral to the culture of "cakes and ale," "masques and revels" (I. iii. 111–12), which has its most ardent devotees in Sir Toby Belch and Sir Andrew Aguecheek. Sir Toby, who epitomizes the corpulent excess of the carnival grotesque, vows to remain a drunkard as long as there is passage in his throat and drink in Illyria (I. iii. 39–40). Should he renege on this oath, Sir Toby avers, "call me a cut" (I. iii. 186). In the spirit of carnivalesque inversion, such derogatory references to the female genitals constitute much of the play's humor – not to mention its misogyny – thwarting the attempt of hegemonic, twentieth-century criticism to find in the play the good clean fun of benign (verging on the beneficent) comic romance.

Malvolio's class transvestism, as I have argued, is the central inversion of the play and is closely related to the play's representation of femininity, as well as its bawdy humor. In accordance with its carnival theme, *Twelfth Night* places female genitals at the heart of Malvolio's gulling, the play's most famous scene:

Malvolio: [*Taking up the letter*] By my life, this is my lady's hand: these be her very C's, her U's, and her T's, and thus makes she her great P's. It is in contempt of question her hand.
Sir Andrew: Her C's, her U's, and her T's: Why that?
Malvolio: [Reads] *To the unknown beloved, this, and my good wishes.* Her very phrases! By your leave, wax. Soft! and the impressure her Lucrece, with which she uses to seal: 'tis my lady! To whom should this be?

(II. v. 87–96)

Sir Andrew's exclamation is in part a rhetorical question emphasizing the scandalous pun, which Malvolio spells out in slow, excruciating detail: "CU[N]T." On another level the query justifies this crude jest because, of course, no C, U, or T exists in the superscription of the letter (Craik and Lothian, eds 1981: 67). At that literal, textual level we never really do know why there is a "CU[N]T" in

Twelfth Night. Symbolically, however, Malvolio, in taking seriously the possibility of trading a steward's servility for sexual service with his mistress – "She that would alter services with thee" (II. v. 157–8) – has, as Maria promised, been gulled into a "nayword" (II. iii. 135–6). That is, he has become, "liver and all," feminized, ridiculed, castrated; his corporeal being in its entirety has been reduced to the most denigrated body part – a "cut" (see Astington 1994: 23–49). Malvolio is already primed for this by his earlier fantasies of social advancement, which begin to forge the connection between debased femininity and social aspirations: "To be Count Malvolio" (II. v. 35). Count and cunt were probably homonymic in Elizabethan English as we see from Katherine's interpretation of the English word for "la robe" in *Henry V*, III. iv., as the "*mauvais, corruptible, gros, et impudique*" "*le count.*" Malvolio's is a stern lesson on the dangers of wish fulfillment. His degeneration into femininity is a reversal of the transformation from female to male believed biologically feasible in the Renaissance on the grounds that nature strove for perfection. In short, Malvolio's gender reversal constitutes an unnatural act. Thus his social ambitions implicate him, albeit inadvertently, in a species of deviance far more dangerous than Viola's deliberate transgression.[18]

The resonance of female genitalia is, however, more comprehensive than that. It signifies Maria's ambivalent sexual identity as Amazon Queen, Penthesilea (prefiguring in the denouement's genitally undecipherable "fancy's Queen"), and as the text's author, and Olivia's private parts. The audience is thus presented with the dynamic between Olivia's political authority and the (mis)representation of her body. To some extent the letter reveals all representation of the aristocratic body, which Leonard Tennenhouse has shown is necessarily female in the Elizabethan era (Tennenhouse 1989: 79), as untrustworthy mimesis. Olivia's authority is undercut by her status as semi-Petrarchan object of diverse passions – Orsino's idealizing and Malvolio's idiocy – and compounded by the letter's further dislocation of her power.

That Malvolio's "CUT"[19] does indeed have implications for Olivia's power is established by the banter with Cesario about how, without ceding her virginity, Olivia might leave to the world some copy of her beauty. In the wordplay on (corporeal) reproduction and (discursive) representation, Olivia works to retain at least linguistic sovereignty over her body. In one sense she plans to extend this control even to the grave, but, in another, female sovereignty of the body is merely dominion over a corpse: "I will give out divers schedules of my beauty. It shall be inventoried, and every particle and utensil labelled to my will. As, item, two lips indifferent red; item, two grey eyes, with lids to them; item, one neck, one chin, and so forth" (I. v. 247–51). Olivia's inventoried body is its representation after her decease in her *will*. The word will signifies both sexual desire and, literally, the legal document containing instructions about the disposal of her property. Command over one's body consists of command over its representations, its reproductions – something that would have resonated with Elizabethans, whose queen carefully supervised the reproduction and dissemination of her authority by controlling the use of her image as stringently as she controlled marriage plans prepared on her behalf.

Of course, Olivia cannot know that in the very next act, without her consent, her private parts will be on display for everyone's amusement. It is significant, too, that Olivia is the object of this form of ridicule since she is clearly the female figure with most authority in the play and the one with the most inclination to use it independently of men. Not only is the sexual function of the pudendum ridiculed but also its urinary one in the jest on Olivia's micturition – "her great P's." The allusion further deforms veiled, cloistered, aristocratic femininity into the grotesque and, paradoxically, more suitable object of Malvolio's sexual and social ambitions. "Her great P's" also bring us closer to the source of Olivia's excitement, "folds adjacent to the meatus urinarius on the female," which when tumescent can result in tribadism, as Ambrose Paré's *On Monsters and Marvels* fearfully points out: "they grow erect like the male rod, so much so that they can disport themselves with them, with other women" (Paré 1982 [1573]: 188; see also Laqueur 1990: 116, 188). Olivia's private parts, preposterously resembling the phallic proportions of a full-grown man, make her ridiculous (as female character, as boy actor, and as wooer of Cesario). The clitoris, the site of female desire, is in a sense a phallic imposter, as Jane Sharp's midwifery guide asserts: "It will stand and fall as the yard [penis] doth and makes women lustful and delight in copulation" (quoted in Laqueur 1989: 105). As the "phallic" woman in her advances toward Viola, Olivia has a cultural parallel in homophobic accounts of women whose clitoral hypertrophy makes them similarly aggressive suitors of other women.[20] Nicholas Tulp's treatise on anatomy gives an account of a German woman's predilection for exposing her clitoris, which extended some way from the vulva, in order to engage in "licentious sport with other women" (quoted in Laqueur 1989: 115). The boy actress Olivia thus becomes the "hypersimulation" of a woman[21] because despite the allusions, there is, of course, no female body as such in the "C.U.T." passage (just as there is none in the play).

It is worth exploring the cultural resonance of women's genitals, particularly in the arena of theatre. Andrew Gurr offers one of Henry Peacham's anecdotes from *The Compleat Gentleman* which has a certain positive, erotic connotation, rather than one aimed at violence or ridicule. Nonetheless, it suggests that the most important thing about both a woman's "cut" and a woman's purse (metaphorically related in contemporary psychoanalytic theory) is that both belong to her husband and can therefore be stolen by other men:

A tradesman's wife of the Exchange, one day when her husband was following some business in the city, desired he would give her leave to go see a play; which she had not done in seven years. He bade her take his apprentice along with her, and go; but especially to have care of her purse; which she warranted him she would. Sitting in a box, among some gallants and gallant wenches, and returning when the play was done, returned to her husband and told him she had lost her purse. "Wife, (quoth he,) did I not give you warning of it? How much money was there in it?" Quoth she, "Truly, four pieces, six shillings and a silver tooth-picker." Quoth her husband, "Where did you put it?" "Under my petticoat, between that and my smock." "What, (quoth he,) did you feel no body's hand there?" "Yes, (quoth she,) I felt one's hand there, but I did not think he had come for that."

(Gurr 1987: 6–8)

Even if, as Leah Scragg suggests, the "C. U. T." of *Twelfth Night* is an admonition to the audience to beware pickpockets; to feel themselves up and pat themselves (or their neighbors) down, its implications may not be so innocent as an issue of warning about potential financial loss. (This is particularly the case when we recollect that the appellation Moll Cutpurse in *The Roaring Girl* connotes her identity as both thief and "codpiece daughter" [II. ii. 89].)[22] Given the prevalence of pleasure in critical discourse at present, perhaps we should also consider the possibility that this admonition may signal a meaning of the word *cut* that is not entirely pejorative; it may have erotic connotations. Indeed, while the public exposure of female genitals by women was rare, it was considered an explicit invitation to sexual activity. That Malvolio comically presents himself as familiar with Olivia's private parts can also be read as a claim to have engaged in mutual masturbation, which seems to have been a very common form of premarital sex, as in the case of one virgin whose intimacies entailed lying on the bed while her partner "combed her private member" (Quaife 1979: 169).[23] While we may read the potential eroticism of the suggestion of mutual masturbation in *Twelfth Night* as comic and positive, it is counterbalanced by the contravention of social hierarchy, which, as it relates to Malvolio and Olivia's "relationship," is resoundingly negative. The argument for the scene as a benign jest on women's sexual pleasure – which could be rationalized in terms of Laqueur's claim that female pleasure, specifically orgasm, was thought to be necessary for conception – is severely compromised by the fact that this theory was also used as a way of dismissing rape charges (Laqueur 1990: 2–3, 161, 182). Magistrates were advised that women who were impregnated during rape must have been pleasured and therefore must have consented (Quaife 1979: 172). This points up not only the difficulty of reading the gulling scene in terms of female pleasure but also the fact that the episode depends for its humor on the conspicuous absence of Olivia's "consent."

The "C.U.T." scene is connected with the social enactment of women's oppression. Numerous women lodged legal complaints about men trying to touch and manipulate their genitals: "Whiles he was thus soliciting her, his hand was always grappling about her plackett, striving to have felt her privy part" (quoted in Quaife 1979: 168). Many of these incidents have been usefully assembled from court records in G. R. Quaife's *Wanton Wenches and Wayward Wives.* One man apparently told his friends of how he had groped a woman's genitals and told the woman herself, "Faith Mary, thou hast a soft cunt." Another case, perhaps even more pertinent to that of Olivia, is that of one Margaret Woods, who was held by the privates so long that she urinated in the man's hands (Quaife 1979: 168). Further, the public exposure of women's genitals could have unambiguously violent meanings and effects. One man from Batcombe "did violently take up the clothes of Elizabeth Numan and showed her nakedness to many," and a husbandman from Halse

> made an offer to divers then present that for a penny a piece they
> should see his wife's privities and there withal did take her and

throw her upon a board and did take up her clothes and showed her nakedness in most beastly and uncivil manner.

(quoted in Quaife 1979: 168)

Predictably, however, *men* are recorded as having found such violence both comic *and erotic*. One inn servant jumped in terror from a window after being thus abused, but it is quite clear from the account of a fellow female servant that her drunken assailants felt otherwise:

> throwing her down Jay, Willis and Sherwood holding her legs and arms down by force did one after another lift her clothes up to her girdle and then thrust their hands shamefully between her legs and feel her privities and look upon them. After which done Jay (who named himself the knight of the castle) sat upon a bench, taking and holding Edith between his legs, placing a stool before her face, and holding her arms fast. And then and there drawing their wicked rapiers and laying them upon the table made proclamations in these or the like words viz: "Oyes, whosoever dareth to break down the walls of grimcunt castle let him approach ... Henry Sherwood come forth and appear at grimcunt castle." Whereupon Sherwood came forth with a glass of beer in his hand and taking up Edith's coats above her knees felt her privities and then threw the glass of beer at the same.
>
> (Quaife 1979: 170)

The histrionics of this incident share certain features of the "C.U.T." scene in *Twelfth Night*. There is a fantasy of exalted social status (knighthood), male bonding (recall that Maria exits directly before the gulling and re-enters directly after it), and abuse directed quite specifically at the pudenda. Also, like Olivia's household, this gathering was amused by the graphic exposure of the woman's genitals and relished it as a focus of their theatrics.

The "graphic" display in *Twelfth Night* is, of course, precisely that, a written representation, linguistic rather than somatic, allowing the company to be hugely entertained. The elusiveness of "graphic" display renders female genitalia present in pornographic detail and absent as the "real" beyond representation.[24] What is palpably present, however, is "anatomized" femininity. Olivia's "hand" is both a limb and writing; in this case a blatant misrepresentation – a forgery. There is also the figure of Lucrece, who would seem to interject this scene with a more sober rendition of the feminine as object of male violence.

The usurped seal depicts Lucrece, probably portrayed in the "noble" act of stabbing herself, the self-penetrating reenactment of her violation that constitutes the only recourse of the ravished woman who seeks to preserve her moral integrity.[25] Lucrece is an appropriate figure for a seal, made to be ruptured by the letter's recipient in an act loosely analogous to sexual violation. To "open" a letter – to read it, to interpret it, is in some sense to breach its integrity. We are thus left with images of comically debased and tragically valorized femininity, each of which are specifically associated with writing as a mode of representation. In fact, the "licence of ink" with which Sir Toby urges Sir Andrew to taunt Cesario (III. ii. 42–3) is precisely the liberty taken by Maria's missive. For writing offers freedom from anatomical and class designations. Its maneuverable discursivity is emblematic of the power of (mis)representation which constitutes theatrical license itself and does so most vividly in the various forms of transvestism I have detailed here.

In order to consolidate (and complicate) the connection between the business of representing corporeality and the overall implications for a reading of *Twelfth Night*, I want to turn briefly to Stephen Orgel's comments on the play. He writes:

> Viola announces in the final moments of *Twelfth Night* that she cannot become a woman and the wife of Orsino until her woman's clothes have been recovered – a dress borrowed from Olivia or a new one purchased for the occasion apparently are not options – and that this will require the release of the sea captain who alone can find them, which in turn will necessitate the mollification of the enraged Malvolio, who has had the sea captain incarcerated: this all *materializes out of nowhere* in the last three minutes of the play. And Malvolio at the play's end offers no assistance but runs from the stage shouting "I'll be revenged on the whole pack of you." For Viola to become a woman requires, in short, a new play with Malvolio at its center.
>
> (Orgel 1989: 27, my emphasis)

Orgel is right that the play's production of femininity is dependent upon Malvolio, but it is so in more ways than he imagines. For, as I have argued, we do not need a new play because we already have Malvolio at the center of a plot where femininity is little less than an impossible condition, and female authority a ridiculous one. For if the play, as Leonard Tennenhouse asserts, involves the explicit transfer of patriarchal power into the body of a woman, who then returns it, now in "a more humane and less violent form" via marriage, the play must persuade us of the urgency of the final transaction (Tennenhouse 1986: 68).

Twelfth Night, then, treats the corporeal representation of sexuality, which is equated with femininity. Sue-Ellen Case summarizes the cultural rationale for this maneuver as follows:

> The female gender had become the custodian of male sexual behavior, which it instigated and elicited. The female body had become the site for sexuality. If women performed in the public arena, the sexuality inscribed upon their bodies would elicit immoral sexual responses from the men, bringing disorder to the social body.
>
> (Case 1988: 209–22)

Thus the very thing that justified women's exclusion from the stage is graphically foregrounded in this play. But the play does not therefore subversively evade the strictures against female bodies on stage; rather it adds weight to them by presenting the female body in its most biologically essential form – the cunt.[26] For the critic, *Twelfth Night* illustrates the problem of recovering the female body for feminism. We cannot make a female body "materialize" from nowhere; we can only register the complexity of its exclusion.

IV

Jane Gallop recalls that in *Les Bijoux Indiscrets* the protagonist is given a magic ring in order to confer the power of speech, and thence sexual revelation, upon female nether parts. Diderot's narrative, recounted by Gallop in 1988, almost exactly parallels her own rendition of the rank, raucous pudendum in *The Daughter's Seduction*, where, taking her cue from Freud's remarks on the odor of menstrual blood, she constructs an opposition between vaginal aroma and the veiled, impassive specularity of the phallus: "the cunt clamours for attention, makes a big stink" (Gallop 1982: 32; 1988). In the later analysis of *Les Bijoux Indiscrets* she elaborates on the protagonist's desire for a female pudendum that will speak with the "feminist" fantasy of one possessing powers of intellection – a shift from the stinking to the talking/thinking cunt. Gallop's is a fascinating effort to disrupt the mind/body dualism structuring Western thought. But as I noted at the start, the articulation of corporeal female desire is always open to appropriation by patriarchy.

Twelfth Night, as we have seen, invokes the raucous articulation of desire in the process of its ritualized deregulation. In its world, if you are fortunate enough to evade the castrating effect of the letters "C.U.T." (as Malvolio cannot), you may become or possess "What You Will." Will, as is apparent in the sonnets, is bawdy for both penis and pudenda. Its bawdy humor derives from the articulation of inappropriate desire, especially female desire. Female desire is not clearly affirmed in this inverted world, just as in actual social sites of symbolic inversion, such as carnivals, women were as likely to be sexually abused as given sexual license. Thus, there is as much violence against women in the tradition of carnivalesque transgression as in the authoritarian suppression to which it was formulated as a response (see Stallybrass 1989: 45–76; and Stallybrass and White 1986).

Nonetheless, the corporeality of sexual desire, which tends to be identified with the feminine, is articulated in this play as food, olfaction, noise, plague, and pestilence. To give but a brief example from the "C.U.T." scene, Malvolio's desires make him a "brock," a badger, a stinking beast. Eating and hunting as emblems of the erratic course of sexual desire open the play, as Orsino is alternately pleasured and tormented by all his sensory capacities:

> If music be the food of love, play on,
> Give me excess of it, that, surfeiting,
> The appetite may sicken, and so die.
> That strain again, it had a dying fall:
> O, it came o'er my ear like the sweet sound
> That breathes upon a bank of violets,
> Stealing and giving odour. Enough, no more;
> 'Tis not so sweet now as it was before. …
> …
> *Curio*: Will you go hunt, my lord?
>
> (I. i. 1–16)

Olivia is identified with a scent, both that of the hunted hart (into which Orsino rhetorically metamorphoses when pursued by his own uncontrollable desires) and that which "purg'd the air of pestilence" (I. i. 20). She is the food that whets his appetitive sexual desire and sates it all too quickly, "Enough, no more." Orsino maintains his dignity by responding with lethargy to the onslaught upon his senses.[27] This corresponds with the notion that sexual attraction was immanent in the body of the desired object. It is an illusion that characterizes desire itself, "a wish to locate the arousal, the erotics, in some object rather than in an intersubjective dynamic" (Gallop 1988: 139). And of course Olivia does not actually desire Orsino any more than she does Malvolio. Still, she manages to usurp her own dignity and "a smooth, discreet, and stable bearing" (IV. iii. 19) of her authority by marrying an effeminate boy of dubious social standing.

In the letter that dupes Malvolio, the "dish of poison" that is set for him by Maria, we come closest to Gallop's fantasy of the thinking, (almost) vocal cunt:

[*He opens the letter.*]

Fabian: This wins him, liver and all.
Malvolio: [*Reads*] *Jove knows I love;*
　　　　　But who?
　　　　　Lips, do not move,
　　　　　No man must know.
　　　　　"No man must know!" What follows? The numbers
　　　　　altered! "No man must know!" – If this should
　　　　　be thee, Malvolio!
Sir Toby: Marry, hang thee, brock!
Malvolio: [*Reads*] *I may command where I adore;*
　　　　　But silence, like a Lucrece knife,
　　　　　With bloodless stroke my heart doth gore;
　　　　　M. O. A. I. doth sway my life.

(II. v. 96–109)

In one sense the letter has itself become a cunt clamoring its desire but forced either to feign passivity or actually be quiescent, "Lips, do not move." The bawdy implications of the earlier "C.U.T." are not abandoned either; as both "lips" and "know" have carnal connotations, as Paré observes:

> Moreover, at the beginning of the neck of the womb is the entrance and crack of the woman's "nature," which the Latins call *Pecten*; and the edges, which are covered with hair, are called in Greek Pterigomata [*sic*] as if we were to say wings, or lips of the woman's crown, and between these are two excrescences of muscular flesh, one on each side, which cover the issue of the urine conduit; and they close up after the woman has pissed.
> (Paré 1982 [1573]: 188)

The woman's part also requires considerable powers of exegesis:

"No man must know. … The numbers altered!" Voracious female sexuality, it would appear, despite the injunction to silence, speaks for itself and yet demands the careful attention of interpretation, referring us also to the extra-diegetic reality of the boy actress's sexual equipment. Similarly, Viola's dubious sexual identity appears to give itself away, to sound off:

> For they shall yet belie thy happy years,
> That say thou art a man; Diana's lip
> Is not more smooth and rubious: thy small pipe
> Is as the maiden's organ, shrill and sound,
> And all is semblative a woman's part.
>
> (I. iv. 30–4)

The maiden's organ is both voice and genital femininity. Thus for Viola: "A little thing would make me tell them how much I lack of a man" (III. iv. 307–8). Here, however, contrary to the feminist fantasy of the inherently disruptive qualities of the female genitals in the phallocentric order, Viola must speak on behalf of her sexual parts because, ambivalent as they are, they incite her to discourse. Kathleen McLuskie writes of the endless complications of signifying woman on the Renaissance stage, "The frustrated critic may wish, like the puppet in *Bartholomew Fair*, simply to lift the skirts and expose the reality behind the signification, but the result, as in Jonson's play, would simply be a disconcerted silence" (McLuskie 1989: 111). In *Twelfth Night*, however, we have anything but that; we have an elaborate, fanciful instance of patriarchal ventriloquism.

I have attempted here to give a theoretical and critical context for my partial reading of the female body in *Twelfth Night*. In it, I have insisted on the materiality of woman's exclusion from the stage even while examining the representation of her private parts. To do so is to some extent to halt the play of possibilities envisaged by much contemporary cultural analysis of transvestism in order to take a political position that works to open up new space for the purposes of resistance postmodernism rather than leaving us suspended in the poststructuralist space of the undecidable (see Case 1989: 282–99; Butler 1990: 136; Garber 1992). I have also tried to confront the exclusion of women from the Renaissance stage without denying the complexity of the representation of the female body. This claim requires some small elaboration; for we have reached a moment when "complexity" is now routinely invoked as a reactionary formulation of "undecidability" in order to claim that things were not so bad for women in the Renaissance after all (see Callaghan 1989: 9–27). What is complex is the way in which apparently benign representations of women operate as regulatory fictions for the suppression, exclusion, and containment of those who, in their corporeality, lived the Renaissance condition of femininity. In this I hope that my analysis constitutes an intervention for current feminist politics by using the body in a Shakespeare text as a way of articulating the problems of its reclamation at this historical juncture for a materialist-feminist agenda.[28]

V

It has become a commonplace of criticism, one that recurs in interesting ways in analyses of Renaissance transvestism, that the anarchic, transformative possibilities of Renaissance Drama, especially those relating to the status of women, were foreclosed by the Puritan-motivated closing of the theatres (see Case 1988). There is no evidence, however, that identifies the closing of the theatres as a major component of either the progressive deterioration of women's status during the seventeenth century or the subsequent post-Enlightenment regime that now recruits our subjectivities.[29] For it was not, of course, the Puritans who were the agents of the then-emergent politics and sensibility that we now live, although it is possible that the closing of the theatres offers some explanation for why the revolution failed. Rather, the Puritans were the radical forces of change whose revolution was foreshortened by Royalist victory.

This confusion coincides with a persistent tendency to conflate women cross-dressers abroad in the streets of London and the institutional practise of theatrical transvestism necessitated by the exclusion of women from the stage. The issue of women in men's clothing is one to which the romantic comedies only obliquely refer (see Rose 1988: 91). While the phenomena of stage and social transvestism are connected, they are not identical. Thus even the case of *The Roaring Girl* does not involve a woman cross-dressing on stage – it entails that only as part of the plot's fiction, not a systemic aspect of the operation of theatre. Further, no antitheatricalist would have been mollified by the suggestion that if female actresses played women, the evil of stage transvestism might happily be avoided. This option is simply not available within the conceptual horizon of early modern England. For it is the presence of women in any and all of its manifestations that posits a situation either horrifying or unthinkable. Further, in social life women dressed as men, but in theatre men dressed as women, and the latter is to *some degree* an arena for licensed inversion.[30] No matter how heinous antitheatricalists found theatrical transvestism, they never found it necessary to inveigh against men gadding about London dressed as women. That men did not dress as women in social (as opposed to theatrical) practise is a phenomenon ignored by those who argue for theatre as preeminently a site of gender instability.[31] Nor did the political radicals of early modern England share the enthusiasm of contemporary critics about theatrical transvestism. Jean-Christophe Agnew remarks:

> What is clear from the protracted debate over stage transvestism … is the Puritans' utter disbelief in the traditional corrective virtues of travesty. How could they countenance a remedy that was so difficult to distinguish from the disease?[32]
>
> (Agnew 1986: 131)

From the perspective of my own analysis, the Puritans had a point.[33]

2

The castrator's song
Female impersonation on the early modern stage

Frobosco: I'll strike it in the nick, in the very nick, chuck.

Felice: Thou promisest more than I hope any spectator gives you faith of performance. (*To Antonio*) But why look you so dusky, ha?

Antonio: I was never worse fitted since the nativity of my actorship; I shall be hiss'd at on my life now.

Felice: Why, what must you play?

Antonio: Faith, I know not what, an hermaphrodite, two parts in one; my true person being son to the Duke of Genoa, though for the love of Mellida, Piero's daughter, I take this feigned presence of an Amazon, calling myself Florizel and I know not what. I a voice to play a lady! I shall ne'er do it.

Alberto: O, an Amazon should have such a voice, virago-like. Not play two parts in one? away, away; 'tis common fashion. Nay if you cannot bear two subtle fronts under one hood, idiot go by, go by, off this world's stage. O, time's impurity!

Antonio: Ay, but when use hath taught me action to hit the right point of a lady's part, I shall grow ignorant, when I must turn young prince again, how but to truss my hose.

Felice: Tush, never put them off; for women wear the breeches still.

(John Marston *Antonio and Mellida* (*c.* 1599), II. 63–85)[1]

John Marston's interest in genitals – writ large in this passage from *Antonio and Mellida* – is inscribed in his name. "Marston" is a pun on damaged testicles, or the act of doing such damage – "mar-stone" (*stone* meaning testicle in early modern parlance). In 1598, the playwright published a satire, *The Scourge of Villainy*, under the pseudonym W. Kinsayder. "Kinsayder" reflects both the pun in Marston's name and his description of his own authorial voice as a "barking satirist," since it means, variously, "dog-gelder" and "dog-gelder's song." This fascinating though seemingly trivial biographical information reveals, on closer examination, the traces of a contentious exchange with Joseph Hall, who had written of Marston that "[t]he dog was best cured by cutting & kinsing [*sic*; castrating]."[2] In this altercation, castration figures as the site of defensive humor, anxiety, and threat. Castration, however, was not only a prominent cultural trope but also a practise – one which, as the English well knew, was elsewhere in Europe associated with the popularity of castrati on the stage.[3] It is the relationship between castration and representation, especially the representation of femininity in its vocal aspect, that is the subject of this chapter.

Marston's induction scene to *Antonio and Mellida*, performed by the boys of St. Paul's, begins with Frobosco, who is to play the role of a parasite, bragging about his skills as an actor who will "strike it in the nick." The theme shifts from the process of acting in general, to a humorous account of the particular problems of female impersonation on the early modern stage in England, and to the problems of staging a spectacle of femininity which is not only visually plausible but also aurally effective. To play both prince and lady involves sartorial and sexual choices that are punningly expressed as phallic manipulations: when the young actor has "hit the lady's part" (vagina), that is, become adept in the matter of coitus, he won't know what to do with, or where to put, his penis (how to "truss his hose" – arrange his genitals in his drawers). The emphasis throughout is on the necessity of playing "two parts in one," of learning one's role and then shifting it abruptly. The further bawdy suggestion is that the actor must become acquainted with both active and passive sexual positions. The joke is exacerbated, of course, by the fact that the boys (depending on their ages) may possess neither the requisite genital equipment to play the man in heterosexual relations nor the genital and vocal equipment to play the man on the stage.[4] That they *do* have, however, the necessary orifice (the anus) to play the woman's part turns our attention to the sexual possibilities available to pubescent or prepubescent boys. This is the sexual initiation (buggery) insinuated in the opening joke about casting: "I was never worse fitted since the nativity of my actorship." Indeed, Marston's passage alludes not so much to women but to a range of indeterminate sexual categories: the virago, the Amazon, and the hermaphrodite. Thus the induction presents the self-conscious construction and performance of hybrid and permeable sexual classifications rather than the sedimented and discrete divisions of male and female.[5]

The disparity between the boys and sexual maturity makes the cultural prohibition against female mimesis even more curious than it would seem in the case of adult male performers.[6] That female impersonation on the early modern stage is understood as a practical necessity, that is, as an unquestioned assumption, a naturalized convention, is the source of much humor and comic stage business. It was culturally unthinkable that the serious difficulties entailed in the phallic substitution of femininity inherent in female impersonation, to which Marston's induction comically alludes, might easily be avoided by a practise common and extremely popular elsewhere in Europe, namely the use of female actors. In fact, I will argue, it is not the perfect similitude of woman that was the goal of early modern dramatic representations of femininity but the production of an aesthetic of representation that depicts sexual difference defined as the presence or lack of male genitalia.[7] This dynamic of difference is signalled in the passage from *Antonio and Mellida* by the verb *to truss* and specifically connotes a manipulation of the penis as an object. Its range of meanings include the manner in which the penis hangs in clothing ("trussing hose") and the complete retraction of testicles and penis (perhaps achieved by binding the genitals to the body) practiced by the Patagons, who allegedly "trusse their Genitall members so, as it is hiden within their body" (Bulwer 1653: 353).

A representational schema that understands sexual difference completely within the parameters of masculinity does not require women: it occurs entirely within a material economy of males. Visible and audible sexual difference, that is, femininity, on the early modern stage comprised a subspecies of masculinity. Femininity was *defined in and as a relation to* masculinity, and bore only a troublesome and secondary commensurability with women. However, this cleavage between femininity and women in the process of male mimesis need not involve the denigration of women as such. For

while the premise of all-male performance is misogynist – in that it is based on the exclusion of women, who are placed entirely outside its circuits of representation – in its execution the performance of femininity might even champion women. Indeed, some plays (such as *The Taming of the Shrew*[8]) are overtly misogynist in their content, while others (*The Changeling*, for example) vigorously assail patriarchal privilege. Nor did the fact that Renaissance audiences were aware that they were watching boys playing women annul the cultural articulation and demarcation of sexualities and gender. It must be emphasized moreover, that the all-male theatre did not eradicate difference but simply produced it within a visibly homogenous economy of gender.

The production of sexual difference within the all-male mimesis of the English stage is, however, shadowed by a culturally and anatomically closer option for achieving a dramatic fabrication of femininity than the use of female performers, and it is one that would be vocally as well as visually compelling, namely the castrato. Castrati (for whom there was historical precedent in the castrated actors playing female roles in ancient Roman theatre) often appeared alongside female performers in Europe rather than within an all-male system of dramatic representation because they were regarded as being vocally superior to both sexes. The castrato hangs over the English stage as an (in)credible threat. Symbolic yet plausible, the castration embodied by the castrato actualized the articulation of difference on which male mimesis was based.

Crucially, genital mutilation produced an ideal vocal aesthetic untrammeled by the cumbersome (though fetishized) physical apparatus of visible gender identity – the trussing of hose and pulling down of breeches. For while clothes lend gender a certain malleability and visibility (they can be put on, taken off, hidden, or revealed), there is far less flexibility in the vocal dimension of performance. Unlike beards, codpieces, and so on, voice is not available as a stage property. Embodied rather than prosthetic, the voice accords presence (Koestenbaum 1993: 155). This is why it is on the vocal rather than the visual register that the spectacle of femininity on the English stage reaches its breaking point. The crisis produced by the broken voice does not, however, necessarily concern the failure of simulation but of a simulation superior to woman herself; the artistic endeavor to grasp and articulate an aesthetic ideal.[9] The likes of a "squeaking Cleopatra" draws attention, then, not so much to the rift between femininity and its enactment (which is the substance of

Cleopatra's speech, as opposed to its performance) but to a crisis in the enactment of masculinity itself.

Stephen Orgel's question "Why Did the English Stage Take Boys For Women?" freed early modern theatre studies from the narrow confines of empirical theatre history (Orgel 1989: 7–29). I want to expand the terms of Orgel's query to ask what are the differences, in both the historical and the psychosymbolic register, among a boy, a castrato, and a man? (Women, as I have argued, have no place in this discussion because they were the consumers not the producers of theatre.) In posing this question, I will historicize a profoundly psychoanalytic and symbolic concept, castration, both as a threat and as a practise. I begin by examining instances of surgical castration, not with the tactical aim of providing dense historical context but with a conceptual goal – namely, to demonstrate that it was at this most fundamental, physiological level that contemporaries contemplated the connection between the vocal and the testicular which was the principal constituent of Antonio's dilemma about representing femininity on the stage ("I a voice to play a lady!").

While I do not intend to offer a conventional history of castration or a review of castration as a theme in drama, I do want to put in place a certain chronology, beginning with the Renaissance and ending with an analysis of the Lacanian concepts that motivate my inquiry. I will follow this trajectory, in schematic fashion, from surgical removals of the male genitals in the early modern period through the conceptual and physiological connections between castration and the vocal ideal and, finally, to the infamous Lacanian Phallus/ penis problematic. Far from being an anachronistic and belated application of psychoanalytic concepts to early modern culture, such a procedure, I maintain, is a way of historicizing the relation between the literal and the symbolic. This relation provides the conceptual underpinning both of women's absence from the stage and of our continuing predicament in culture.

The operation

Barber-surgeons shops in early modern England, where fairly minor surgical procedures were usually undertaken alongside haircutting and beardtrimming, were places of entertainment, offering to the exclusively male clientele music, drinks, gaming, and tobacco (Beier and Finlay 1986: 95). Not only were these shops themselves places of diversion, but there was, in addition, a preponderance of all forms of surgical practise around places of vice and resort, such as theatres and brothels (87). This was the result of rampant venereal disease in the metropolis and accounts for a conceptual as well as a geographical proximity between the theatre and the surgical procedure of castration.

Syphilis reached epidemic proportions during the seventeenth century, and there developed also a "new" disease, *morbus Gallicus*, or the French pox.[10] In advanced cases of venereal disease, castration was often the only remedy. Surgical removal of the penis (as opposed to the testicles) was not an uncommon last recourse, as instanced by this account from later in the period: "I knew a little old Man, whose Yard was cut off, for the *Lues Venerea* by the ordinary Chyrugion" (Scultetus 1674: 337–8).

The late sixteenth and early seventeenth centuries accordingly witnessed a rapid advance in medical technology. In "A note of particular ingredients for a Surgeons Chest," John Woodall, in *The Surgeon's Mate or Military and Domestic Surgery* first published in 1617, lists an array of sharp objects, including rather cumbersome saws for hewing off limbs, an assortment of knives, and that most delicate instrument of excoriation, the "dismembering nippers" (Woodall 1639 [1617]: n.p.). The surgical performance of Renaissance refashioning quite literally entailed cutting (an art refined since the medieval era)[11] with precision tools capable of increasingly careful incisions. Thomas Brugis's *Vade mecum: or a Companion for a Chirurgion Fitted for Sea, or land; Peace or War* (1640), published in seven editions by 1681, provides a comprehensive inventory of his instruments. For instance the incision knife:

> The use of this Instrument is to cut the Skin or Flesh upon needful occasions. … Let this Instrument be alwayes kept clean and bright, by being rubbed dry, after it hath been used, and sharp as any Razor. Let the Artist ever hide it from the Patient's sight with a Cloth, and also all other sharp Instruments for divers Reasons.
> (Brugis 1681: 3)

The surgeon as "Artist" conveys a sense of pride and relish in the whetted tools of his trade. The necessity of their concealment betrays the understandably acute anxiety of patients about to be cut without the benefit of anaesthetic.

That excision was a principal operation of surgical practise is perhaps evidenced by Woodall's remark, "If the Surgeons Mate cannot trimme men, then by due consequence there is to be a barber to the ships company" (Woodall 1639 [1617]: n.p.). The cleaving, sawing, dissecting, severing, and slicing of animate human anatomy was performed not by those given the theoretical training in medical arts, the physicians, but by a new class of barber-surgeons, some of whom, like Ambroise Paré, the most famous surgeon in Europe, gained tremendous reputations for their treatments. Even Paré had humble beginnings in the quasi-butchery of barber-surgery before going on to become court surgeon to four French monarchs. Surgeons such as Paré often garnered their experience on the battlefield, where their services were more in demand than ever as a consequence of the Western use of gunpowder. War, like syphilis, brought these members of the medical profession into direct contact predominantly with the male body (Young 1890: 125–6).[12]

Among its several objects of inquiry and excision, surgery took a fresh look at the organs of male vulnerability. Thomas Gale's translation of Vigo, for example, describes the penis (yarde) as follows:

> The yarde is a member verie full of sinnowie lacertes, with manie ligaments, veines, and arteries. It is hollowe, and that hollowness is full of ventositie or winde, engendered in the pulling veines, by which ventositie the elevation of the same commeth. This elevation proceedeth chiefelie of the arteries which come from the heart, for the heart giveth voluntarie motion to the sayd arteries. The ligamentes of the yarde proceede from the bonens of the thighes. And the sinowes grow from the nether part of the Nuke, and by reason of those sinnowes the saide yarde is of great feeling.[13]
>
> (Gale 1586:16)

Among the new articulations about male genitals, a discourse emerges that is curiously tantamount to a testicular aesthetic. Helkiah Crooke's *A Description of the Body of Man* (1631 [1615]), an anatomical rather than a surgical text, describes the testicles as "like to a leather sachell" (Crooke 1631 [1615]: 210). The testes "hang out under the belly at the rootes of the yarde, partly to abate lustful desires. … And because it was neither profitable nor handsome that they should hang bare; for the receiving and clothing of them, the *scrotum* or Cod was made as a purse or bagge" (204). The divine plan for anatomy seems to have given way to certain aesthetic considerations in the fashioning of "handsome" testicles. Aesthetic concerns also motivate a moral objection to circumcision: "Circumcision, a strange and smart invention of man, is a very ancient device practised to the diminution of the naturall comelines of this part" (Bulwer 1653: 366).

While surgery becomes a discourse about the fashioning of masculinity, there is an attendant trepidation about it as the scientific instrument of castration, which becomes explicit not in a surgical textbook but in John Bulwer's *Anthropometamorphosis: Man Transformed* (1653). Bulwer's treatise, a compilation of earlier sources, fulminates against human vanity, especially as manifested in bodily adornment and self-mutilation, and betrays its author's salacious pleasure in the catalog of behaviors he ostensibly condemns. Inveighing against the evils of castration, Bulwer concedes: "*And verily a dispensation may be granted in case of these inexorable, and otherwise incurable diseases.*" But Bulwer hastily adds:

> But upon any other pretence whatsoever, to adulterate the coin and image of Nature by so grosse an allay as makes them not current for men, or willingly to degenerate into the nature of women, suffering themselves to be transformed from the Masculine to the feminine appearance (a false copy) is to offer as great an Injury to nature as the malice of mans refractory wit can be guilty of: And it is so manifestly against the Law of Nature to tamper with the witnesses of mans virility that our Laws have made it Felony to geld any man against his will.
>
> (Bulwer 1653: 362)

Bulwer's tone implies that "the witnesses of mans virility" are in some immediate danger. Once the testicles are cut away, the patient does not become a woman but rather grows to embody a patently fake simulation of femininity: "a false copy." The implication is that there are (astonishingly) men who pose something of a social threat by willingly submitting themselves to castration and, significantly, by opting out of reproduction. This would surely require a commitment to the rearrangement of conventional sexual identities and gender relations far in excess of any merely careless degeneration into effeminacy consequent upon a failure in vigilance about one's manhood. A marginal note to the text describes precisely the vulnerability to which physiological masculinity may succumb:

> Two waies there are of this unnatural dilapidation of the body, one is performed by contusion, the other by excision, the last being more approved of; for they who have suffered the contusion of their Testicles, may now and then affect to play the man.
>
> (Bulwer 1653: 359)

In the case of contusion (that is, where the testicles have been crushed by means of a heavy blow, without breaking the skin), the faint residue of virility produces natural resistance to unmanliness and suggests the amorous possibilities that remained for some eunuchs in the simulation of a definitively masculine behavior. Bulwer's castration anxiety, however, may be traced not only to barbarous Continental practises but also to the necessity to which his first sentence alludes, to the legitimate castration of surgical procedures.

For the symbolic threat of castration took on more literal dimensions as surgical operations with high risk of morbidity and mortality became routine.[14] More people came under the surgeon's knife in the early modern period than ever before, and in particular, drastic measures were frequently administered to non-venereal "griefs of the yard" (Beier and Finlay 1986: 102). The renowned seventeenth-century surgeon Richard Wiseman advises:

> In some of those who have the Prepuce very short, the *fraenum* is also so strait, that upon erection of the *Penis*, the Glans is pulled downwards so they cannot endure coition. The remedy is by cutting the *fraenum* in pieces. If you suspect that the divided end may be troublesome, clip them off at the same time.
>
> (Wiseman 1696: 505)

However, it was not only a direct surgical assault upon the penis that might make a man fear for his virility. A number of other conditions also entailed a fearful proximity with the male organs of generation:

> Seeing that wee cannot otherwise help such men as have stones in their bladders, wee must com to the extreme remedie, to wit, cutting. … The patient shall bee placed upon a firm table or bench with a cloth manie times doubled under his buttocks, and a pillow under his loins and back, so that hee may lie half upright with his thighs lifted up, and his legs and heels drawn back to his buttocks. Then shall his feet bee bound with a ligature of three fingers breadth cast about his ankles, … [and] both his hands shall be bound to his knees.
>   The patient thus bound, it is fit you have four strong men at hand; that is, two to hold his arms, and other two who may so firmly and straightly hold the knee with one hand, and the foot with the other, that hee may neither move his lims, nor stir his buttocks, but bee forced to keep in the same posture with his whole bodie. Then shall the Surgeon thrust into the urinarie passage even to the bladder, a silver or iron and hollow *probe*, anointed with

oil, and opened or slit on the out-side, that the point of the knife may enter thereinto, and that it may guide the hand of the workman. ... He shall gently wrest the *probe*, beeing so thrust in, towards the left side, and also hee who standeth on the patient's right hand, shall with his left hand gently lift up his cods.

(Paré 1649: 427)

The illustration accompanying this passage (see Plate 2) is an astonishing revelation of masculine vulnerability in that the man occupies a position which we, in the twentieth century, have come to associate entirely with gynecological procedures. Thomas Laqueur remarks that in the nineteenth century "There are no pictures ... in which instead of men, scalpel in hand, seen poised over the body

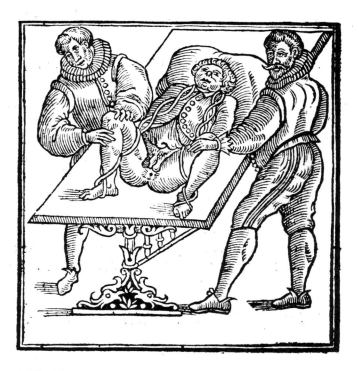

Plate 2 The Figure of a Man Lying Ready to be Cut for the Stone (*The Workes of that famous Chirurgion Ambrose Parey Translated out of Latin and compared with the French*, by Thomas Johnson (London 1634)). Reproduced by kind permission of the Folger Shakespeare Library.

of a woman, men (or more inconceivably yet, women) surgeons are preparing to castrate a man" (Laqueur 1990: 76). In early modern England almost the reverse is true. Though both Nicholas Culpeper's *Directory for Midwives* (1653) and Jane Sharp's *The Midwives Book* (1671) include directions for clitoridectomy for women who allegedly "suffer" from genital hypertrophy, all situate it as a distinctly foreign condition not to be found in England: "I never heard but of one in this country" (Sharp 1671: 45). English authored surgical texts are silent on the subject of female castration, while the German Johannes Scultetus lists "pincers to cut off the clitoris both streight and bent" in his inventory of surgical implements (Scultetus 1674: n. p.),[15] though he provides no record of the operation itself. However, Bulwer's encyclopedic compilation of all manner of what he regards as human depravity finds space to condemn female eunuchism discovered in foreign parts, though it is difficult to discern exactly what this entails:

> The extravagant invention of man hath run out so far as the Castration of women; Andramistes the king of Lydia, as the report goes, was the first that made women Eunuches, whom he used instead of Male Eunuches, after whose example the women of Egypt were sometimes spaded.
>
> (Bulwer 1653: 363)

Bulwer's meaning, in this instance, is something of a puzzle. Since the inference is that Andramistes's predilection is for anal copulation, it is possible that eunuchism here refers to ovariotomy, or hysterectomy, rather than clitoral and labial excision. Later in the text, however, he refers, without giving much detail, to the fact that "Many women both here and elsewhere have caused themselves to be cut, as being over-great, and exceeding nature" and suggests that such excision is the equivalent not of castration but of circumcision: "[I]t is done by cutting that part which answereth the Prepuce or Foreskin in a man" (Bulwer 1653: 381). Our author is more specific about an alleged English instance of female sexual mutilation, which clearly entails the removal of the womb and ovaries rather than the clitoris. He informs us that, unlike spaying a sow, drawing out a woman's womb, or castrating "by avulsion of their testicles," leads to grave endangerment of her life:

> For he must necessarily cut both the Flankes who would Castrate a woman, a work full of desperate hazard; yet it may be

done with little or no danger, if it be attempted in an Artfull hand. And a Friend of mine told me he knew a maid in *Northampton*-shire that was spaded by a Sow-gelder, and escaping the danger grew thereupon very fat.

(Bulwer 1653: 364)

In this apocryphal tale (completely unsubstantiated by criminal and gynecological evidence from the period),[16] the same man allegedly repeated the practise in Lincolnshire on one Margaret Brigstock: "But the Judges were much confounded how to give Sentence upon an Act against which they had no Law; for although the Castration of men was Felony by the Law, yet there was nothing enacted against spading of women." As a result, the perpetrator, one "Clearke," was hanged not for castrating his victim but for stealing "two penniworth of Apples from her apron" (Bulwer 1653: 365).

On balance, the evidence seems to indicate that female castration was exceedingly unusual and that male sexual organs were far more likely to be excised than female ones.[17] Indeed, while he takes emasculation (whether veterinary or human is ambiguous) as a cultural commonplace, Ambroise Paré waxes incredulous at the apparently alien phenomenon of clitoral excision: "Leo Africanus writes about it, assuring us in another place that in Africa, there are people who go through the city *like our castrators* ... and make a trade of cutting off such caruncles" (quoted from Parker 1994: 84, emphasis added).

Recent scholarship has advanced the importance of the Galenic theory's "one-sex" (paradigmatically male) model of sexual difference, in which women were understood to possess inverted male sexual organs, and therefore could, in certain circumstances such as vigorous exercise, turn into men (the reverse, however, appears to have been impossible) (Laqueur 1990: 125–30).[18] Yet, even within the one-sex model, the overwhelming cultural emphasis is on the genital sufficiency and deficiency of men rather than on female lack. The one-sex model is supported by Paré's fascinating tale of a woman, Marie, who one day developed the requisite genital equipment to shed her female identity and become the male, Germain. The story is tantamount to a compensatory fantasy about castration and reminds us that while the deprivation of male genitals through the surgical treatment of disease was a very regular occurrence, suddenly sprouting them as a result of violent exertions, in accordance with Galenic precept, was not (Laqueur 1990: 126).

Surgical procedures previously used only on animals were in early modern England routinely applied to humans, and specifically to men. Indeed, surgeon Thomas Gale (1507–87) was alarmed to find during an outbreak of venereal disease in the metropolis "sowgelders,"[19] among others, usurping the title and function of surgeons (Bishop 1960: 91). *The Husbandman, Farmer and Grasiers Compleat Instructor*, written in the late seventeenth century, describes veterinary castration, as it must have been practiced for hundreds of years:

> In Gelding, having slit the Cod, draw out the Stones with their sinews, as far as you can, without over-straining; clap the sinews into a cleft Stick, and so seer them off with a hot Iron, anoint them round with fresh Butter, and sow it up with very fine Silk, taking up no more than the outward Rim or Edge.
>
> (A. S. 1697)

This description reminds us that, though surgical procedures for male genitals were newly refined, they were not entirely remote from rural experience, and that the craft of "sowgelding" (and for that matter, butchery and barbery) might have been alarmingly similar to the skills of human surgery. The Act of 1540 uniting the Barbers and Surgeons resulted in part from the crisis in the organization of medicine provoked by outbreaks of pox and syphilis, and included the telling reservation that, in London, surgeons were not to "practice barbery, nor barbers surgery, except for toothdrawing" (Beier and Finlay 1986: 96).

Samuel Pepys's mention of his kidney stone operation, recorded in his diary for 26 March 1660, registers both the benefit and jeopardy of surgery in what can only be described as an instance of justifiable concern about his mortality: "This day is two years since it pleased God that I was cut for the stone at Mrs Turner's in Salisbury Court. And did resolve while I live to keep it as a festival, as I did the last year at my house." Despite its success, the operation, performed by Thomas Hollyer, ruptured the sperm ducts and rendered the diarist sterile, a common sequel to this operation at the time (Bishop 1960: 109–10). The incidental damage to Pepys's reproductive organs demonstrates the ever-present threat that the surgeon's hand might slip, causing the patient to die or lose his organs of increase, a possibility betrayed by the somewhat cavalier comments of surgeon John Vigo: "The wounds of the stones and the yard be not mortall, if it be not through the error of the Chyrurgio. Nevertheless, because they are necessarie to generation, they must be healed with all diligence" (Gale 1586: 162).

For all the persistent dangers of mortality in surgery of any sort, male genitals were both substitutable and dispensable – something the patient, however reluctantly, could live without. Johannes Scultetus's *The Chyrurgeons Store-House* (1674) includes the chapter heading "Of the taking off of a yard," while Bulwer laments those who are "not only gelt but have their Yards also cleane cut off" (Bulwer 1653: 359). We are in the realm here not of the excision of the testicles – the most common understanding of castration, and the one to which Freud pays negligible regard – but that of the penis itself. Scultetus instructs:

> In the Month of July 1653, a certain Citizen of *Ulme*, having his Yard mortified, I cut it off near the live part with a knife, … and to stop the Blood touched the Veins and Arteries with hot Irons till I had taken off all the Gangrene, and the Patient was sensible of the fire: the Operation being done, and a pipe … Put into the passage of urine: I applyed to the burnt place, the Egyptiacum Oyntment of *Mæsue*, to make the Eschar: which being taken away: I soon Consolidated the Ulcer with the ceratum divinum: and the patient was healed.
>
> (Scultetus 1674: 337–8)

Scultetus's patient was fitted with the device invented by Ambroise Paré, the "artificiall yard," to alleviate the suffering occasioned by urination in those who had been deprived, whether by surgery or accident, of their natural members (see Plate 3):

> Those that have their yards cut off close to their bellies, are greatly troubled in making of urine, so that they are constrained to sit down like women, for their eas. I have devised this pipe or conduit, having an hole through it as big as one finger, which may be made of wood, or rather of latin.
>
> (Johnson 1649: 583)

Deprived of his genitals, the man urinates like a woman, but he does not become one, in part, because a prosthetic can be substituted for the penis.

This potential for phallic metonymy is, as we saw in the induction to *Antonio and Mellida*, the source of humor. The interchangeability of the penis and power provides the comedy in the following anecdote about eunuchs in Persia and the Levant who gain great social advancement and "who therefore thinke they have a good bargaine in exchanging the naturall Conduit of their Urine for a Quill, which

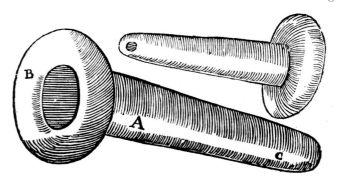

Plate 3 The description of a pipe, or conduit, serving instead of the yard in making of water, which therefore we may call an artificiall Yard (*The Workes of that famous Chirurgion Ambrose Parey Translated out of Latine and compared with the French*, by Thomas Johnson (London 1634)). Reproduced by kind permission of the Folger Shakespeare Library.

they weare in their hats in a way of a jolly orientation" (Bulwer 1653: 360). Jokes such as this one may well be a defensive reaction against the actual pain of venereal disease and the threat of castration as much as social satire on the follies of masculine ambition.

The potential loss of one's genitals was not merely a remote and foreign danger. Richard Wiseman, who has, ironically, been called the father of English surgery (G. Parker 1920: 113), provides a catalog of the putrid penises he encountered belonging to men of all ages and in all walks of life:

> A young fellow came to me with the Prepuce inflamed, and a mortification on the upper part of it, which had spread the compass of a broad Shilling on that part over the *Glans*. In scarifying the *Eschar* I found it had penetrated through: upon which consideration I made the separation of the Prepuce with a pair of Scissors cutting it off round. ... In making the extirpation of the Prepuce I had permitted him to bleed freely.
>
> (Wiseman (3rd ed.) 1696: 506)

Given the excruciating pain that accompanied this standard operation, it seems entirely plausible that castration was not as purely symbolic in early modern England as it is for us today. Whatever the statistical probability of losing one's penis (possibly on a par with a woman losing her breast today), as the techniques and instruments of surgery sharpened, anxiety about the loss of one's privy members likely became more acute, even as hopes against the loss of one's life increased. Although the surgical excision of male genitals was not literally used as a means of subjection, that is, as a threat, the history of surgery as we have learned from Foucault, can be linked to the discipline of the human subject in that London's barber-surgeons had the right to claim annually four bodies of persons executed for felony (Bishop 1960: 109, 111). Bodies cut down from the gallows and penises cut close to the belly established a visceral connection between social and sexual subjection and created a very concrete sense in which castration was located not only in the realm of the symbolic but in the ordinary business of surgical practise.

The vocal aesthetic

The physiological imperatives pursued in surgery were also vigorously articulated in contemporary considerations of the male voice. John Bulwer observes:

> [T]here arisith a Physicall question, whether the Testicles be required to the forming of the Voice? ... Castration is so experimentally known to advance the smallnesse and sweetnesse of the voice, that as an ingenious Traveller hath lately observed in Florence they are so given to musique of the Voice, that there the great ones keep their *Castrati*, whose Voices scandalize their breeches. Concerning the reason of this effect of Castration, the Conceit of Aristotle is pretty, although it agree not with the common opinion, who thinks the Heart is stretched by the Testicles, and therefore relaxed when they are cut away.
>
> (Bulwer 1653: 355–6)

That the voice might "scandalize the breeches" draws attention to the lack of genital equipment on which this vocal aesthetic is founded as well as to the vocal superiority of the castrato. Occasionally, less drastic measures were taken to preserve the voice: "Among the Antients, to prevent young effeminate Inamorato's, especially Comedians, from untimely Venery, and cracking their voices, they were wont to fasten a Ring or Buckle on the Foreskin of their Yard" (Bulwer 1653: 352).

In some of Bulwer's exotic anecdotes there is a complete displacement of the voice by direct and comic identification between music and the male genitals:

The inhabitants of *Ava* in the *West-Indies*, weare in their Yards betwixt the skin and flesh, bels of Gold, Silver or Brasse, of the bignesse of Nuts; which they put in when they are of age to use women, and in short time cure the place; and the men much please themselves to heare the sound of them as they go, these *Venus-Morris-Dancers* frisking often to the tune of their own Codpiece-musique.

(Bulwer 1653: 347)

The comic fascination here seems to lie in the notion of piercing the organ of penetration itself: "One Geographer gives in evidence against the *Peguans*, that they ... weare golden or silver bells, hanging at their virile members, to the end that they make a sound as they walk through the city" (Bulwer 1653: 348). Bulwer's commentary, however, indicates a curious combination of admiration and disgust for such practises. These "Bells of Siam," as "an ingenious Physician" has shown our author, consist of balls "an little bigger than a musket bullet, being about an inch in Diameter; the metall is of such a temper which we know not ... and yielding a very sweet sound, far above any of our hand Symbals, which this somewhat resembles" (Bulwer 1653: 349). Aesthetic considerations, it would seem, are capable of overcoming Bulwer's squeamishness about interfering with the work of nature.

When Bulwer attempts to divine the reason for eunuchism, he alights upon the notion of the castrating queen:

Many fantasticall reasons have been framed, and ends propounded to introduce Eunuchisme, and this way of degrading men from their manhood. Semiramis was the first that caused young male children to be made Eunuches, therein offering Violence to Nature, and turning her from her appointed course, by a tacite Law, as it were stopping the primigeniall Fountaines of Seed, and those ways which nature had assigned for the propagation of Posterity, that so she might make them have small voices and to be more womanish, that conjoined with her, she might better conceale her usurpation and counterfeit manhood.

(Bulwer 1653: 354)

This is a misogynist and startling commentary on female sovereignty, a sort of gender reversed *Totem and Taboo*, the mythic narrative of female supremacy. It reveals, however, that in phallic logic, there always lurks the possibility that women, precisely because they

do not have a penis and testicles, could castrate men without en-
dangering retaliation. In desiring men who are like herself,
Semiramis implicitly presents not only an aesthetic preference for
the castrato voice but also the possibility of an erotic preference for
a man devoid of the sexual use of his penis (see Campbell 1995:
30), a choice which threatens to make virility redundant. A further
possibility is that Semiramis's sexual predilection simultaneously
discovers and occludes the threat of tribadism beneath the sexual
oddity of the eunuch (Campbell 1995: 34).

In eunuchism, castration becomes a means of shaping masculinity in accordance with aesthetic precepts and runs counter to the
preference for uncut organs, which, as we have seen, is evident in
surgical manuals and anatomical treatises:

> And although this Castration of the Testicles being not done in an
> apparent part, causeth (of it selfe) no deformity, yet because when
> both the Testicles are cut out, other mischiefes follow, (especially if
> this be done while they are in the yeares of puberty,) which betray
> them to be Eunuches, as an effeminate voice, and the want of a
> beard, by this means it bringeth deformity upon them.
>
> (Bulwer 1653: 362–3)

The aesthetic qualities of eunuchism, that is, the "deformit[ies]" it
imposes on normative masculinity – namely, beardlessness and a
high voice – are characteristics that on stage were prized attributes
of the transvestite actor. Indeed, as Paré also observes, biological
eunuchism is the simulation of femininity, characterized by a
"smooth body and soft shirle [*sic*] voyce" that "doe[s] very much
assimulate women." Eunuchs, then, are understood as male *representations* of women: "The nature of Eunuches is to be *referred* to that
of weomen" (emphasis added) (cited in Jones and Stallybrass 1991:
85).

The aesthetics of eunuchism, indeed, are to be found in the use
of young male actors on the English stage:

> Welcome, good friends – O, my old friend! why thy face is val-
> anced since I saw thee last, com'st thou to beard me in Denmark?
> – What, my young lady and mistress! by'r lady, your lady-ship is
> nearer to heaven than when I saw you last by the altitude of a
> chopine. Pray God your voice, like a piece of uncurrent gold, be
> not cracked within the ring.
>
> (Jenkins 1982: *Hamlet*, II. ii. 418–25)

This passage, a sally in the war of the theatres, and premised on the idea that the actors are in Denmark because the boys' companies have taken over the English stage, is addressed to the boys in an adult company. Although the young actors who have come to Elsinore have acquired height and facial hair since their previous visit, it is principally their voices, explicitly made analogous to currency, that will affect their value.

As sources of precious revenue, boys must be closely and carefully kept. When the Duke of Stettin-Pomerania visited Blackfriars in 1602, he reported:

> [T]he Queen keeps a number of young boys who have to apply themselves zealously to the art of singing and to learn all the various musical instruments, and to pursue their studies at the same time. These boys have special præceptores in all the different arts, especially very good musicos.
>
> (quoted in Brinkley 1928: 22)

Such practises are reminiscent of contemporary reports of Moors who kidnap children "and not only cut off Virgia, but Parastrates also; such as escape death after this cutting, they educate them very delicately, and afterwards sell them to the *Persians*" (Bulwer 1653: 3). Aesthetic and economic values find their disturbing convergence here in the traffic in children.

While boys were hired out among the various acting companies, children in English theatre were, of course, neither castrated nor literally enslaved. Theatre as an institution was, however, implicitly based on the forced expropriation of child labor and the threat of sexual victimization. Further, these economic and sexual practises molded the boys, aesthetically, if not surgically, into the shape of eunuchs.

Though working conditions were nowhere ideal, children of the theatre were *more visibly* susceptible to exploitation than boys in other trades. In the adult companies, where wills often attest adult players' personal affection for and economic support of their junior colleagues (Bentley 1984: 129, 133), the ill-defined institutional status of the young performers left them nonetheless vulnerable to abuse. For neither the personal dimension of relationship between apprentice and master nor the economic one was as clear in the theatre as it was elsewhere in the early modern social order. G. E. Bentley points out that "the profession of player was never so well integrated into the established economic system as that of grocers, goldsmiths, merchant-tailors, or drapers" (Bentley 1984: 119; see also Austern 1992). When Nathan Field, who had spent his life in theatre since being impressed to it as a young boy, claims in his moving *Remonstrance* (1616) equality for his trade along with cobblers, smiths, and tailors, the effect is to suggest the incompatibility of acting with other trades, which had legally sanctioned guilds and their own courts to regulate practises and set durations of apprenticeship (Halliwell-Phillipps 1865: 12). In sum, while there were certain social advantages to becoming a player – principally access to education, culture, and to the hub of creativity in the metropolis – the specter of brutality and ostracism hung over these young performers.[20]

The situation of children in the boys' companies was different and evidently worse. Under the authority of a commission granted in 1597, the queen's choirmaster, Nathan Giles, was, in essence, given the right to abduct children for the Chapel Royal. Only when Robert Keyster took control of the boys on their move to Blackfriars was impressment replaced by an indenture system more like that used by the adult companies. This may not have resulted from concern about the boys' welfare, however, but the result of pressure on the master of the Revels to put boys' companies, whose juniority playwrights took as license to engage in biting social satire, under the same constraints that applied to other companies of players (Gurr 1992: 54–5).

The boys were apprehended without parental consent. Field was "taken up" one day on his way to school by Giles's deputy, James Robinson, as was Salmon Pavy (celebrated in Jonson's famous epitaph) (Brinkley 1928: 18). Giles was brought before the Star Chamber when Robinson kidnapped the son of a gentleman, one Henry Clifton of Tofttrees in Norfolk, who sought to deliver his boy, Thomas, from their clutches (Chambers 1923, Vol. 2: 43). The court proceedings of the Clifton case provide some insight into the violent seizure of these children. Both Field and Clifton were thirteen at the time they were captured, an age that would have spared their abductors most of the trouble and expense of their education. Thirteen is rather late in the day to commence a career as a chorister but not too late to play the virago, the hermaphrodite, or the lady. Indeed, the Clifton indictment records that the abducted boys were "noe way able or fitt for singing, nor by any [of] the said confederates endeavoured to be taught to sing" (Chambers 1923, Vol. 2: 43). The implication here is not simply that they were instead taught to act but that they were vulnerable to abuse.

As Clifton was "walking quietly from your subiect's sayd howse towards sayd schole" Robinson waylaid him and

> wth grete force & vyolence did seise & surprise, & him wth lyke force & vyolnce did, to the greate terror & hurte of jim the sayd Thomas Clifton, hall, pulle, dragge, and carrye awaye to the sayd playe howse in the black fryers aforesayd, threatening him that yf he, the sayd Thomas Clifton, would not obey him, the sayd Robinson, that he, the sayd Robinson, would chargdge the counstable wth him the sayd Thomas Clifton.

Once "committed to the said playhouse amongste a companie of lewd, & dissolute mercenary players," Thomas was threatened with whipping if he did not learn his lines by heart (Brinkley 1928: 19). No doubt the coercion and beating of children were not uncommon in early modern England, and no doubt children's sexuality was understood differently than it is today. For all that, abuse was more clearly visible in the theatre than elsewhere and, therefore, subject to condemnation, especially by Puritans, who had a particular concern for the welfare of children.[21]

There are insinuations of specifically sexual abuse in several plays of the period. Chapman's *Mayday* (1611) offers an exemplary instance of it: "Afore heaven, 'tis a sweet-fac't child: methinks he would show well in woman's attire ... Ile helpe thee to three crownes a week for him, and she can act well" (ed., Morris 1981: III. iii. 228) (Chapman 1970; Mann 1991: 115). The shift in pronouns here bespeaks not only histrionic femininity as a species of masculinity but also the commodification of the boy's sexuality as an object of trade. In the theatre the woman's part belongs to men and not, therefore, either to real women, who possess their parts merely by virtue of anatomical assignment, or to the young males who enact femininity. Thus the production of sexual difference in accordance with a male aesthetic does not privilege, or even necessarily benefit, the boys, who are open in theatre to direct abuse merely by virtue of being physically present, in a way women cannot be, simply by virtue of their absence.

Dekker's satire on theatre in *The Gull's Hornebook* (1609) advises his gull that by sitting onstage, he "may (with small cost) purchase the dear acquaintance of the boys," and in Jonson's *Bartholomew Fair* Cokes asks, "Ha' you none of your pretty impudent boys now, to bring stools, fill tobacco, fetch ale, and beg money, as they have at other houses?" (Jonson 1960; Dekker 1904 [1609]: V. iii. 60–2).

"Other houses" here connotes bawdy houses as much as other theatres. The boys are apparently made available for sexual titillation in an institutional configuration more akin to prostitution than indenture. This is similarly the case when in the induction scene to *The Taming of the Shrew* the Lord instructs:

> go you to Barthol'mew my page,
> And see him dress'd in all suits like a lady.
> …
> Tell him from me, as he will win my love,
> He bear himself with honorable action.
> Such as he hath observ'd in noble ladies
> Unto their lords, by them accomplished.
> Such duty to the drunkard let him do,
> With soft low tongue and lowly courtesy,
> And say, "What is't your honour will command,
> Wherein your lady and your humble wife
> May show her duty and make known her love?"
> And then with kind embracements, tempting kisses
> And then with declining head unto his bosom,
> Bid him shed tears.
> …
> Anon I'll give thee more instructions.
> I know the boy will well usurp the grace,
> Voice, gait, and action of a gentlewoman.
>
> (Induction i. 103–30)

This sort of sexual instruction illustrates the alarming proximity between the young actor's training in feminine wiles and an incitement to prostitution, a proximity exacerbated by the emphasis in the main plot on proper femininity as the abject submission to adult male authority. In the dressmaking scene this subjection takes upon itself the metaphor of castration: "snip and nip and cut and slish slash" (IV. iii. 90).[22] In its dimensions of panderism and prostitution, the *Shrew* induction becomes a sinister depiction of young male sexuality, as Marston's comic celebration of juvenile libido in *Antonio and Mellida* does not. Little wonder that when Henry Clifton voiced apprehension about the fate awaiting his son in the acting profession – "to exercyse the base trade of a mercenary enterlude player, to his uter lose of tyme, ruyne, and disparagment" (Chambers 1923, Vol. 2: 43) – he echoed the rhetoric that condemned prostitution as enticing youths "to their utter ruyne and decay" (cited in Ben-Amos 1994: 201).

The status of the boy player also became economically and aesthetically unstable at puberty when his voice broke. "Cracked within the ring" (*Hamlet*, II. ii. 440), a broken voice, more than any other aspect of masculine maturation, would spell a decline in profits as well the end of effective female impersonation. A famous alleged "exception" to the exclusion of English women from the public stage is a report by Richard Madox from 22 February 1583: "went to the theatre to see a scurvie play set out by one virgin, which proved a fyemartin without voice, so that we stayed not the matter." This is what one critic refers to as "the only unambiguous reference to a woman on the London stage" (Mann 1991: 246).[23] Since "virgin" can refer to both males and females, and since there is no gendered pronoun, it is hard to see why Madox should be seen as referring to a woman in any unequivocal fashion. More importantly, however, is that in this context, "fyemartin" is derogatory, meaning "freemartin" (not "pine marten," as critics suggest), a word used to describe hermaphroditism in cattle (Forbes 1966: 25; Mann 1991: 246).[24] The incident is, then, not about female performance but about poor masculine performance and demonstrates that an inadequate voice in the matter of female impersonation might well result in playgoers quitting the theatre, or, as Marston's players suggest, the actor being hissed from the stage.

Contrary to twentieth-century expectations, and despite the dissatisfactions we have noted with the sound of the performers, there are no recorded complaints about the *appearance* of male actresses in the Renaissance, only complaints about their sound. Henry Jackson's letter written in Latin about a performance of *Othello* in 1610 declares, "Indeed, Desdemona, killed by her husband, in death moved us especially when, as she lay in her bed, her face alone implored the pity of the audience" (quoted from Tillotson 1933: 494). Notably, the effectiveness of transvestite performance here is crucially connected with a moment of *silent* spectacle. In contrast, Restoration playgoers complained about the appearance of female characters. The dearth of young male actors arising from the closing of the theatres created a comic spectacle of femininity:

> For to speak the truth, men act that are between
> Forty and fifty, wenches of fifteen;
> With bone so large and nerve so incompliant,
> When you call Desdemona, enter giant.
>
> (Wickham 1959: vol. 2, part 1, 139)

As I have argued, the performance of femininity entails both an aural and a visual dimension as vital aspects of its aesthetic, or as Stephen Gosson put it, "not the apparell onely, but the gate, the gestures, the voyce, the passions of a woman," which, more than the mere imitation of the female voice, involves the substitution of an aesthetically superior male simulation.[25] Peter Stallybrass has asked what exactly the audience *saw* as Desdemona was "unpinned" by Emilia, revealing the body of the boy actor beneath.[26] But, just as important, we might consider what Jackson *heard* in that scene. Given the enormous emphasis on the dramatic aesthetics of vocality, Jacobean audiences surely did not hear the undersung renditions of the willow song that merely serve as the bland accompaniment to the visual impact of the female body in modern performances. The actor chosen to play Desdemona may well have been in late adolescence or early manhood in order to meet the demands of that taxing role (Field was twenty-nine when he was last heard of playing a "boy's" role) (Baker 1968: 68). Conceivably, then, as tragic tension mounted toward an absolute pitch, Shakespeare's audience heard either a falsetto willow song or the precarious beauty of an unbroken, adolescent male voice. The audience, by this stage in the performance, is desperate for release from the culminating and inexorable strain of tragic events. Simultaneously, they dread a premature vocal crisis that will forestall the full-fledged tragic crescendo of the final scene. The actor's voice sepulchrally breaks the tension that foreshadows the monumental silence of alabaster Desdemona's death. Willing the actor not to erupt into tenor or baritone, the audience also hopes for a reprieve from imminent tragic inevitability and relief from the present, excruciating pleasure, the piercing thrill of "Sing willow, willow, willow." (I take the liberty of imagining a sublime performance.) Soon, Desdemona's throat will be constricted forever, but the actor must not let it happen now. If he cannot sustain the aesthetic effect of this song, how will Emilia ever find her garrulous voice to reveal Iago's villainy? The actor playing Desdemona must have perfect control of breath and pitch; he must summon every tactic he can muster to circumvent the possibility of vocal crisis, which in full view of an audience is, like castration, "a physiological emergency, a bodily catastrophe" (Koestenbaum 1993: 127–8).[27]

Vocal crisis signals the interruption and rupture of seamless spectacle; cracked and raucous, it is "a rip in meaning, in coherence, in vocal consistency" (Austern 1994: 129). This vocal emergency is quite unlike the impotence of "drying up," the mere loss of words. It is also as distinct from the orgasmic cry as the crisis of *petit mort* is from death itself.[28]

When the problem of voice occurs again in the Restoration, it is in reference to the last of the boy actresses, Edward Kynaston, who, according to Pepys, "made the loveliest lady that ever I saw in my life, *only her voice was not very good* " (Jamiesen 1968: 77). In the Renaissance, it was overwhelmingly the vocal aspect of stage femininity that was found wanting, and contemporary accounts repeatedly refer to the auditory insufficiency, to the boy actor's "crackt organ pipes" (Hazlitt 1869: 263) and "squeaking" impersonations of femininity.[29]

Although the castrato represented the model of the fine operatic voice, invulnerable to the structural (as opposed to the spontaneous) vocal crises of male adolescence, castrati did not perform in England until 1667 when Thomas Killigrew, famous for bringing actresses to the stage, bought castrati to the stage also (see Ferris 1993: 15). The historical coincidence of these innovations is far from accidental, representing a shift in aesthetic as well as material conditions in English theatre. By the eighteenth century, castrati were all the rage. Women adored them (like Bulwer's Semiramis) because, as Jill Campbell argues, they "provided an occasion to isolate, and to literalize, to make explicit, the cultural significance of the phallus itself" (Campbell 1995: 29).[30] Male commentators nevertheless lamented that castrati could offer "ecstasy to the ear" while presenting only "an offence to the eye"–the exact opposite of the transvestite on the Renaissance stage. That male spectators did not enjoy castrati indicates that the earlier male performance of femininity had staved off the threat of castration that neither women nor castrated men could help these viewers to negotiate. Castrati were now understood to be male impersonators rather than actors whose objective was to impersonate femininity (Campbell 1995: 30, 193). Thus castrati made the threat of castration visible, "an offence to the eye."

In the history of castration-anxiety and its relation to spectatorship the castrato's voice helps us to recognize at once the radical alterity of all-male mimesis and its conceptual similarity to the present-day representational apparatus of patriarchy. That is, in twentieth-century representations that include women deficiency is insistently identified with femininity. In the acoustic and visual regimes of contemporary cinema, for example, female voices and bodies are relentlessly restricted to normative representations and functions (Silverman 1988: viii). In other words, it is women who are found wanting. In contrast, even though women were excluded from the Renaissance stage, castration referred to docked masculinity rather than innate female deficiency. Thus while the production of dramatic representation did not include women, it did not preclude, indeed may have enhanced, their pleasure in a spectacle that, in its production of sexual difference, exempted them from the cultural and symbolic violence of castration.

The Renaissance Englishwoman's pleasure as a spectator is roughly analogous to the pleasure that Laura Mulvey argues is offered to the male viewer of the classic Hollywood movie. The latter gets pleasure from women on the screen because they reassure him that they embody lack and, therefore, that he is not castrated. Alternatively, the female movie star becomes the phallus. In this scenario women on the screen are fetish objects that can plug the gap (the anxiety, the insecurity) in the viewer's masculine subjectivity. There is, however, a crucial difference between the early modern female spectator and the male spectator of the Hollywood classic, namely, that he is absolved from castration anxiety without being excluded from mimesis.[31]

In early modern theatre there was less ideological occlusion of the absolute restrictions imposed on women by culture, no insistence that the symbolic order included women when it patently did not. That is, the illusion that women are fully represented is harder to penetrate both in Lacanian theory and in a world where images of "real" women are everywhere. The point is not that representations of women in early modern theatre were "better" than they are today (some were, some were not – it depended on the play) but that the marginalization of women was more obvious there, one is tempted to say more honest.

In my deliberate, literal-minded violation of the Lacanian injunction that one must *never ever* confuse the phallus with its somatic analogue, I have endeavored in the above analysis to dislocate historically the analogy and to expose it as a problem of women's exclusion from the symbolic. On the Renaissance stage, where there were no women, it was very clear that the production of difference was all about "men, men, men … ."

3
"Othello was a white man"
Properties of race on Shakespeare's stage

At James VI's marriage to Anne of Denmark in 1589, four young black men danced naked in the snow in front of the royal carriage (Hall 1991: 4; 1995: 128–41). In 1554 five black men from Guinea were brought to London by traders, and one of the men fathered a child who became the object of intense scrutiny because, even though his mother was English, he was "in all respects as black as his father" (Jordan 1968: 6; Tokson 1982: 1). In 1577 an "Eskimo" couple captured by Martin Frobisher's expedition to Meta Incognita were brought to London where they could be found on the banks of the Thames with their English-born child, fishing and hunting swans and ducks by royal license (Mullaney 1988: 65). In 1596 Elizabeth (unsuccessfully) issued a warrant ordering that all "blackamoors," black servants, exotic signs of their masters' wealth, be rounded up so that Caspar Van Senden, a merchant of Lubeck, could trade them for English prisoners held captive on the Iberian peninsula (Hill 1984: 8; Cowhig 1995: 6). Between 1585 and 1692, numerous civic pageants, *tableaux vivants* devoid of action and dialogue, specify the inclusion of "Negroe boys" or "beautiful Raven-black negroes" (not just English people in blackface), sitting astride effigies of lions, camels, griffins and unicorns (Barthelemy 1987: 50, 47). These are not representations of racial otherness performed by the English (or, in the first instance, the Norwegians, since the royal couple were married in Oslo) but rather the display of people from Africa and the New World motivated by curiosity and profit.

If, as James Walvin claims, Africans, who were by far the most numerous and conspicuous racial others in early modern England, were an everyday sight in London (Walvin 1971: 61–3; Shyllon 1977: 3; Drake 1990: 274) and participated in the forms of cultural exhibition outlined above, why is it that an African never trod the boards of a Renaissance stage? Given that Africans and representations of them were so popular in exhibitions and such a potential box-office attraction, one might expect some venturesome theatre-owner or playwright to have included an actual African in his group of players, problems of training and apprenticing a foreign actor notwithstanding. Shakespeare was in fact more enterprising in this regard than most of his contemporaries, incorporating a role for the Prince of Morocco in a plot that did not originally require one and, in the case of Othello and Aaron, elaborating extensively on the nameless prototypes in his sources (Gillies 1994: 102). Despite the intensive use of "exotic" characters in the plays, however, they were always depicted by white actors. Yet, as the above instances of an African presence in England indicate, there was no paucity of Africans in England, a fact that bespeaks complexities of racial impersonation unaccounted for in our habitual assumptions that there were no blacks in Shakespeare's England. This chapter will investigate the obvious – but nonetheless – curious fact that in Shakespeare's plays there are histrionic depictions of negritude, but there are, to use Coleridge's infamous phrase, no "veritable negroes." There are, indeed, no authentic "others" – raced or gendered – of any kind, only their representations.

The first part of the chapter will address the histrionic mechanisms of racial impersonation and their attendant social dynamics, while the latter part will attempt to grasp the striking but ineluctable discrepancy between the cultural performance of alterity on the one hand and its lived condition on the other, positioning it as a function of the representational systems required by emergent capitalism.[1] I will insist throughout, though not in the sense meant by the critic I quote, that "Othello *was* a *white* man" (Ridley 1958: li).[2] This proposition was put forward by one Miss Preston, writing in the notoriously racist pre-Civil Rights South. Preston, doubtless, would be less enthusiastic about endorsing the notion, equally true, that if Othello was a white man, so was Desdemona.

All representation is predicated upon the absence of the thing represented, but in the instances of race and gender on the public stage there is a perfect coincidence between social exclusion and exclusion at the level of dramatic representation. Neither Africans nor women performed on the public stage in Elizabethan and Jacobean England,[3] although both were present in other forms of cultural display: Africans were involved in civic presentations and women in nonmimetic performances of the court masque. While neither court nor public theatres employed racial others, in civic pageants racial impersonation seems to have persisted alongside the actual exhibition of alien peoples (Barthelemy 1987: 50). However, the representation of Africans is far from being neatly analogous to the question of female impersonation. In fact, it troubles the paradigm of gender representation most clearly when we consider that white women are never exhibited as such, and we do not find them dancing naked before the royal coach.

In what follows I will describe the operations of two distinct, though connected, systems of representation crucially at work in the culture's preoccuption with racial others and singularly constitutive of its articulation of racial difference: the display of black people themselves (exhibition) and the simulation of negritude (mimesis). These phenomena are the poles of the representational spectrum of early modern England, and their respective mechanisms can be defined as follows: in exhibition, people are set forth for display as objects, passive and inert before the active scrutiny of the spectator, without any control over, or even necessarily consent to, the representational apparatus in which they are placed. Mimesis, on the other hand, entails an imitation of otherness, and its dynamism results from the absence of the actual bodies of those it depicts, whose access to the scene of representation, therefore, needs no further restriction or containment. Theatrical mimesis, however, involves the active manipulation of the actor's body in the process of representation, and regardless of the power of the theatre owner, the director, the patron, or the playwright, acting finally involves an embodied performance, which manifests the actor's interpretation of the role (Gurr 1992: 99). By contrast, in the forms of attention which constellate the representational mechanisms of exhibition, power resides almost entirely with the spectator. The actor, then, at least in the context of early modern society, has more power than the exhibit. For all that, the actor cannot control the meanings ascribed to his performance, as we will see in the historically subsequent instances of AfricanAmerican and female actors.

Here mimesis and exhibition tend to overlap because the actor is always already construed as an exhibition in a representational context that severely curtails the actor's creative control. Traversing intricate structural continuities and discontinuities between exhibition and mimesis in the complex representational economy of Renaissance England, femininity (rather than actual women) is itself used to trope racial difference – whiteness – and plays a pivotal if problematic role in the relation of race and sexuality (Doanne 1991: 243, 245; Neely 1995: 302–15). For race, crucially *both* black *and* white, is articulated onstage as an opposition principally by means of cosmetics: burnt-cork negritude projects racial difference against white Pan-Cake. The elaboration of cosmetic practises will, I hope, bring into sharper focus the relation between race and gender in drama, showing how whiteness becomes visible in an exaggerated white and, crucially, feminine identity.[4]

I

Racial difference on its most visible theatrical surface requires makeup. The representation of race on the Renaissance stage is fundamentally a matter of stage properties (Bristol 1990: 7). Because it is closer to the body of the actor, blackface is a less superficial theatrical integument than the black mask and gloves sometimes used in popular festivities (Jones 1965: 30). In village theatricals, blackface consisted of soot while performances at court and in the theatre used charred cork mixed with a little oil, "the oil of hell" as it is referred to in *Lust's Dominion* (1599) (see Jones 1965: 60–8). To complete the representation of negritude, "Cappes made with Cowrse budge" – that is, stiff lambskin fur – "Corled hed sculles of blacke laune" (Jones 1965: 30,123), served for African hair. More striking than all other features and accoutrements of alterity, such as nakedness or sartorial splendor, the definitive characteristic of the racial other both on and offstage remained skin color. Black skin persisted as the most conspicuous marker of racial difference despite burgeoning distinctions between peoples of other races, such as "white Moors," "blackamoors," "tawny Moors," and "savage m[e]n of Inde."[5] As the primary histrionic signification of racial otherness in Renaissance court and public theatre, blackface concealed under the sign of negritude a host of ethnicities ranging from Eskimo to Guinean.[6] Indeed, in regimes of cultural representation, negritude became the *sine qua non* of Renaissance alterity. The capacity of blackness simultaneously to intensify, subsume, and absorb all aspects of otherness is a specifically Renaissance configuration of othering. Later, with the tawny Restoration heroes such as those of Behn and Dryden, the exotic would part company with blackness (Gillies 1994: 33). But on Shakespeare's stage, blackness marked sheer difference. As the polar opposite of absolute coincidence in the period's antithetical episteme, the culture's construction of its own "unmarked" (male) identity, black skin was preeminent as an integer of a starkly demarcated racial difference.

Blackness, whether actual or cosmetic, was defined by an anterior whiteness just as the exotic in Renaissance systems of representation functioned as accident rather than essence. That is, the not-yet-systematic distinction between white and black finds itself expressed as ornament, as an overlay of whiteness, not, in Winthrop Jordan's famous phrase, "white over black," but precisely its opposite, black over white. This understanding of negritude as an augmentation of whiteness stresses blackness *as representation* – that is, as an (anti) aesthetic as opposed to an essence – and was corroborated in the period by a climatic theory of racial difference, which proposed that blackness was an extreme form of sunburn. In *The Merchant of Venice*, for example, the Prince of Morocco uses this theory in order to forestall objections to what the Venetians regard as a monstrous bid to secure a union with a wealthy white woman:

> Mislike me not for my complexion,
> The shadow'd livery of the burnish'd sun,
> To whom I am a neighbour and near bred.
> (II. i. 1–3)[7]

Rehearsing the latitudinal aetiology of race does not, of course, bring the Prince his hoped for success, and Portia, relieved of him, says, "A gentle riddance … / Let all of his complexion choose me so" (II. vii. 78–9). Climate theory both coexisted with and contradicted competing theological and empirical understandings of race (black skin did not fade when Africans were shipped to England), neither of which were entirely discrete or coherent. In crediting the make-up artist of *The Gypsies Metamorphosed* (1621), Ben Jonson ironizes a range of Renaissance theories of racial origin from the mark of Ham to Phaeton's chariot flying too close to the sun:

> Knowe, that what dide our faces was an oyntmen[t]
> Made and laid on by Mr Woolf's appointment.
> (Herford and Simpson 1941: vol. VII, 615, lines 1481–5)

The nature of dark skin as an indelible tincture is conveyed in the Renaissance commonplace that one cannot wash an Ethiop white (see Newman 1987). Black skin becomes at once immutable *and* superficial, analogous to blackface that cannot be washed off.[8] Skin color thus bears an arbitrary rather than necessary relation to the essential racial identity negritude is assigned to express. It is precisely this inessential status that made negritude vulnerable to the obsessive economy of the visual.[9] For example, when, in *Titus Andronicus*, Aaron asserts the indelibility of blackness, he focuses the audience's attention not only on the conceptual priority of whiteness, but also on the fact that he is a white actor whose black veneer is stage make-up:

> Ye white-lim'd walls! ye alehouse painted signs!
> Coal black is better than another hue,
> In that it scorns to bear another hue;
> For all the water in the ocean
> Can never turn the swan's black legs to white,
> Although she lave them hourly in the flood.
>
> (IV. ii. 100–5)

Elsewhere in the play, Aaron rehearses cultural commonplaces about the demonic quintessence of negritude, but here he posits a monstrous inversion of racial identity: whiteness is merely a temporary emulsion ("white-lim'd" suggests that whiteness is not intrinsic but consists only of paint) in contrast to a fast and permanent black identity. Black, says Aaron, is better than white because white is characteristically subject to black inscription: it can be defaced. Black, in contrast, can neither be written on, nor can it be returned to white. In arguing for the positive specificity of negritude, Aaron counters the dominant idea of an originary whiteness.

Whiteness, especially when complemented by red, was "the color of perfect human beauty, especially *female* beauty" (Jordan 1968: 8).[10] That is, in its chromic opposition to blackness, what allows whiteness to be represented at all is "a certain conceptualization of sexual difference" (Doanne 1991: 224). Race – black *and* white – thus becomes not only cosmeticized but, in the case of whiteness, also feminized.

Both negritude and whiteness are, on the Renaissance stage, the cosmetic, though far from superficial, surfaces of difference (Copjec 1994: 13). In practical terms, "fair" femininity consisted of a wash for blanching the complexion and rouge for cheeks and lips. Whiteface was a lethal concoction of ceruse or white lead, sometimes mixed with sublimate of mercury and ground orris; occasionally it included slightly less noxious ingredients such as ground hogs' bones, powdered borax, beaten egg whites, and lemon juice. Rouge consisted of red ochre and mercuric sulphide, vermillion, or cochineal (see Garner 1989: 132; Drew-Bear 1981: 75). Rather less deadly preparations made of powdered brick, cuttle bone, coral, and eggshell were available as tooth whiteners. Blackface thus found its practical equivalent in cosmeticized femininity, "white and red." Both were referred to as "face-painting," a derogated species of art. Stage directions for Richard Brome's *The English Moor* (1637), for example, specify that "A Box of black painting" is required (Jones 1965: 122). William Carleton who witnessed a performance of Jonson's *The Masque of Blackness* also provides evidence that racial difference was conceptualized as a species of comparative cosmetology: The ladies,

> as a part of greatness, are privileged by custom to deface their carcasses. Instead of Vizzards, their Faces, and Arms up to the Elbows, were painted black, which was disguise sufficient, for they were hard to be known; but it became them nothing so well as their red and white, and you cannot imagine a more ugly Sight, than a Troop of lean-cheek'd Moors.
>
> (Jonson 1969: 4)

While blackface was traditionally an aspect of the grotesque in popular entertainments (Jones 1965: 28), one senses that Queen Anne and her ladies intended an erotic presentation of themselves, which Carleton reads, contrary to their intention, as defilement of the pure aristocratic body. For Carleton the ladies' impersonation is a failure, implausible (they are lean-cheeked) and inappropriate because their dress is "too light and Curtizan-like for such great ones." There is a tension here between diaphanous raiment and the impenetrable cosmetic, the opacity of the latter perhaps licensing the transparency of the former. Dense black painting (which, because of the practical difficulty of washing it off, meant that the transformation from black to white promised at the end had to wait until the *Masque of Beauty*) thus becomes congruent with the unveiling of the aristocratic female body and produces the exotic as sexually charged.

Jonson wrote the masque at the request of Queen Anne, who specifically wanted to perform in blackface.[11] That she chose to exercise this degree of creative control is significant in a culture that did not permit women to act on the public stage or even to speak in court entertainments. By engaging with the fascinations of alien femininity, the ladies of the court do not involve themselves in the mimetic performance of the type found on the public stage because they are always, to some degree, representing themselves. Nonetheless, such representation is, as Carleton is quick to point out, a form of privilege. Yet, in refusing "their red and white," which in the context of the masque at least would be entirely conventional, the queen and her ladies resist the orthodox model of female beauty. Contrary to cultural propriety, they, the mute referents of culture, endeavored, "as a part of greatness," to possess their own representation (see Rogin 1987: 224). Seen from this perspective, Carleton's disapproval of blackface and costume is less the product of a racist repulsion than it is part of the general censure of women's power over cultural representation.

The printed text informs us that *Blackness* was "*Personated* at the court at Whitehall on the Twelfth Night, 1605." While this term was sometimes used synonymously with "acting," *personate* has more the force of "bearing the character of."[12] One might imagine the court lady almost ritualistically bringing to the stage, as a precious and perhaps fragile object, her own character, in its most highly stylized and emblematic form. This requires a more passive enactment than the active characterization we associate with mimesis, where a character, not the actor's own, has to be "brought to life" onstage. "Personate," which, as Andrew Gurr argues, indicates a relatively new theatrical development (Gurr 1992: 99), is perhaps closer to our modern word *impersonate*, a simulation whose contours are fully visible rather than hidden and naturalized in the manner of a theatrical *trompe l'oeil* (see Parry 1990: 103). Blackface, then, by far the most popular way women represented themselves in masques (see Barthelemy 1987: 41), takes the place of acting in *Blackness*, standing in not only for what is not there – black women – but also for the limits of female cultural production. Interestingly, these limits remain visible after the Restoration when actresses were not permitted to use blackface.[13]

That cosmetic adornment registered as an act of cultural representation, a species of theatricality, is apparent in the "highly artificial, mask-like appearance" produced by cosmetics of the Elizabethan and Jacobean era (Garner 1989: 133). Elizabeth I, of course, not only concealed her smallpox scars but also exercised her power behind a mask of whiteness. Sovereignty became the art both of occlusion and display. Little wonder, then, that an impetus to restrict women's cultural self-representation informs the period's misogynist invective against *women's* use of cosmetics. (Men, like Benedick in *Much Ado About Nothing*, also used cosmetics, and while they were subjected to a certain amount of ridicule, they were spared the fierce invective unleashed upon women.)[14] Ostensibly, it was because of their power to beautify that the red and white were assumed to be a form of hypocrisy, misleading men by feigning a beauty that women did not really possess. Cosmetics were associated with prostitutes, as in Hamlet's reference to "The harlot's cheek, beautied with plast'ring art" (III. i. 51). Women's use of cosmetics was roundly condemned, often by the same people who fulminated against theatre and associated all manner of artifice with femininity. In his *Treatise Against Painting and Tincturing of Men and Women*, Thomas Tuke condemns "painting" as an interference with nature (Garner 1989: 124), while Philip Stubbes argues that the use of cosmetics impugns God, "for if he could not have made them faire, then hee is not almightie" (quoted in Garner 1989: 133; see also Dolan 1993: 224–39). This condemnation of cosmetics as a barbaric practise is also to be found in relation to exotic peoples. Celts, of course, ornamented their bodies with blue woad, and New World peoples engaged in body painting as well as more permanent forms of cosmetic mutilation (such as piercing). John Nicholl records the Olive Branch expedition encountering the inhabitants of Santa Lucia in 1605:

> These Carrebyes at their first coming in our sight, did seem most strange and ugly, by reason they are all naked, with long black hair hanging down their shoulders, their bodies all painted with red, and from their ears to their eyes, they do make three strokes with red, which makes them look like devils or Anticke faces, wherein they take a great pride.
>
> (quoted in Hulme 1992: 129)

The natives' childish pride seems to align them with the vanity of English women. The objection to painting here presents itself merely as an aesthetic objection, while the objection to women's conventional red and white painting is more often a moral one. That the problem is not merely one of cosmetics as an extension of costume but with cosmeticizing as a low-level mimetic practise becomes apparent when we consider male appropriations of female beauty. Shirley Nelson Garner remarks:

In the picture of beauty drawn in poetry from the Middle Ages through the Renaissance and after – and even still imprinted in the Western imagination – women were admired for their golden hair, high foreheads, blue eyes, lily-white skin, rosy cheeks, cherry lips, and teeth of pearl. The marked white and red of the makeup available allowed them to imitate literally if they wished, the beauty praised in the sonnets.

(Garner 1989: 132–3)

It is striking that precisely the qualities admired in verse, the rhetorical devices that constitute femininity in poetry – ruby lips, rosy cheeks, white flesh – are condemned when they are the result of cosmetic artifice. The male-controlled discursive display of women in the blazon tradition is culturally valorized, while women's hold on even the lowest reaches of the representational apparatus, cosmetics, is condemned.[15] Women's use of cosmetics might be seen as a sort of writing on the body, but even when it is practised in conformity with male definitions and fantasies of female beauty, because it is performed by women, as Frances Dolan has argued, it enacts transgressive femininity. What is art in the hands of a poet and presumes a superiority of imitation over nature becomes vanity and artifice in the hands of a woman (Dolan 1993).

Red and white, like blackface, is both racial and mimetic (see Hall 1994: 179). That is, anxiety over the use of cosmetics by women betrays itself as an endeavor to exclude women from even the most lowly and personal representational practise and thus discloses their marginal relation to, or, more accurately, exclusion from, mimesis. The theatrical depiction of women through cosmetics, on the other hand, uncovers the pivotal role of white femininity in the cultural production of race.

Onstage, whiteface was probably the primary way of signifying femininity. It was an impersonation, just like blackface.[16] Not only does female characters' use of cosmetics become a recurrent issue in plays of the period (see Garner 1989 and Dolan 1993), but also, as Annette Drew-Bear has shown in her splendid study of the moral significance of face-painting on the stage, there is a wealth of specific evidence for players' whitening their faces in, for example, the account books of touring companies in Coventry, Cambridge, and Chester. The boy playing Ganymede in Ben Jonson's *Poetaster* is admonished that he "should have rub'd [his] face, with whites of egges ... till [his] browes had shone like our sooty brothers here [i.e., Vulcan, whose face is 'collied' or blackened] as sleeke as a hornbooke" (Drew-Bear 1994: 32–3, 34). Although race is not directly at issue here, the reflective surfaces and textures of difference, "sleeke" and "shone," refer to emergent, if displaced, concepts of race, which they help frame, co-ordinate, and unify.[17] The sensous difference between black and white here is reminiscent of Olivier's blackened body, silk-buffed to a sheen for his performance of Othello. Olivier played opposite Billie Whitelaw, as Desdemona, who was covered from head to toe with white Pan-Cake.

> Olivier was blacked up to the nines, of course. Only the part covered by his jockstrap wasn't. It took him about four hours to get himself buffed up. Jack, his dresser, put rich browny-black pancake onto his body and buffed him up with silk so that he really shone. Olivier was a master of make-up and he really looked magnificent. …
>
> To make my own skin look "as white as alabaster" as the bard says, I had alabaster make-up all over my body. Once, as I knelt down at his feet, I put my hand on his knee. He glared down at me: there was a white mark on his black knee! Some of my white alabaster had come off on his beautiful shiny black make-up.
>
> (Whitelaw 1995: 13)

In contrast to *Poetaster*, where we see, in the endeavor to make whiteface aesthetically superior to blackface, spectacles of difference becoming racialized for the first time, Olivier and Whitelaw cosmetically enhance already-instantiated racial and gender aesthetics.

In the process of early modern theatrical impersonation the dominant group, white men, take on the characteristics of subordinate groups, namely Africans and women. Because women cannot impersonate a femininity they already embody, offstage, women's use of make-up is not impersonation, but an attempt both to "normalize," to blend in, and a transgression of the boundary that marks subordination. Women's use of cosmetics was at once an attempt to meet an ideal standard of beauty (sometimes, for instance, in an attempt to hide smallpox scars) and a breech of the restrictions on women's representation.

The obverse of impersonation is "passing," a twentieth-century term, one of whose principal connotations is the imitation of whites by blacks in an attempt to gain access to social privilege from which blacks are excluded (see Robinson 1994). The representational *mechanisms* inherent in women's cosmetic practises (though not their social significance) bear a resemblance to the subordinate's imitation of the dominant found in twentieth century "passing." They do so in that both passing and impersonation raise hermeneutic problems of knowledge, identity, and concealment (see Doanne 1991: 234; Robinson 1994). These issues, central to *Othello*, are articulated with reference to female beauty by Iago, who manipulates Petrarchan tropes about dark and fair female beauty as the play's *blazoner manqué*: "What an eye she has, / A parley to provocation." By way of entertaining the ladies, he rhymes his praise of women at the dockside, surveys and evaluates their parts:

> *Iago*:   If she be fair and wise, fairness and wit;
>   The one's for use, the other using it.
> *Desdemona*: Well prais'd! How if she be black and witty?
> *Iago*:   If she be black, and thereto have a wit,
>   She'll find a white, that shall her blackness hit
>   (II. i. 129–33)

Possible glosses on Iago's puns are that the dark lady will find a partner like herself, that she will conceal her lack of virtue, or become sexually "covered" by a man of a lighter complexion, or transform her blackness with white cosmetics. That this is not merely a primordial opposition between fair and dark supremely apposite for Shakespeare's purposes may be glimpsed in Kim Hall's compelling argument that the use of *fair* to connote light complexion dates back only to the mid-sixteenth century (Hall 1994: 179). In using cosmetics, women attempt by morally dubious means to assume an ethically and aesthetically irreproachable racial identity.

In the Renaissance the disturbing spectacle of absolute racial otherness is staged via the trope of gender difference. That is, by means of stage cosmetics, the marriage of Othello and Desdemona presents itself as the union of absolute antitheses, black and white. While racial intermarriage in *Othello* symbolically overturns racial hierarchy in terms of the mimetic process itself, it does so not by inverting but by exactly replicating of the performance of negritude. Miscegenation in the play consists precisely of "black over white" (Jordan 1968: 38) and has its parallel in the techniques of Renaissance theatricality – white skin *under* black make-up. Further, the coincidences between miscegenation and the practise of blackface could never be entirely expunged in performance because black always evoked its underlying antithesis, whiteness: "One of the marveylous thynges that god useth in the composition of man, is coloure: whiche doubtlesse can not bee consydered withowte great admiration in beholding one to be white and an other blacke, beinge coloures utterlye contrary" (Peter Martyr, quoted in Jordan 1968: 7; see also Little 1993). No other colors were so frequently used to denote polarization. By the time of Edmund Kean's tawny Moor, there is literally a toning down, using make-up, of what is constructed all along as an irreducible disproportion between Othello's "begrim'd" countenance and "sooty bosom" and Desdemona's "whiter skin of hers than snow."

The double impersonation of Othello – the white actor playing a Moor who is trying to assimilate in Venice – focuses the structural ambivalence on which impersonation is founded (Neill 1984: 115). Othello's appearance before the Senate is a defensive simulation of dominant racial and sexual mores. He duplicates the tropes of civilization – deference and decorum: "Most potent grave, and reverened signiors. My very noble and approv'd good masters" (I. iii. 76–7). Having probably (depending on the time sequence) just committed what may be regarded by the Venetian citizenry as gross miscegenation with Desdemona, he attempts to play white and straight, against the aberration signified both by his blackness and by his sexual transgression (see Silverman 1992a: 148–50; Neill 1989: 391–2). What Othello self-deprecatingly describes as his "Rude ... speech" and "round unvarnish'd" story turns out to be not so much the plain tale he promises but a compelling and flagrant rendition of the exotic, replete with proper names, marvels, and geographical specificity (Gillies 1994: 31). That his tale would win the Duke's daughter, too, is indicative not of assimilation but of the sexual potency of racial alterity. While Othello's appearance before the Senate articulates difference at the level of the visual, and then his narrative obsessively refers us, even in its most compellingly aural aspects (the famous "Othello music" caricatured by Iago as grotesque "bombast," and "horribly stuff'd") to the *spectacle of tactility* Jonson urged in *Poetaster*; to the "rude" (i.e., stark), "round" surfaces of a difference we might touch.

Michael Bristol has argued that, for Shakespeare's playgoers, Othello in the blackface familiar from carnival "would confront the audience with a comic spectacle of abjection rather than with the grand opera of misdirected passion" (Bristol 1990: 10). There is, he claims, a burlesque element to *Othello* which critics have been reluctant to notice because of their desire to recuperate Othello as tragic hero. As a result, Bristol powerfully contends, critics have ignored the fact that

Othello is "a text of racial and sexual persecution" doing the cultural work of *charivari* and employing many of its methods – impersonation, ridicule and social control, a ritual unmarrying of the couple whose marriage represents the erotic grotesque – beauty and the beast, so to speak. Bristol does not, however, attempt to reduce *Othello* to *charivari* but to show the elements of punitive exhibition inherent in it. Similarly, in a brilliant analysis François Laroque has shown "the potential note of farce" throughout the play which is far too complex to be read according to a single ideological line (Laroque 1993: 283).

Building on the recognition of these critically suppressed dimensions of the play, it is also important to consider how the dramatic form of theatre *does more than* "make an exhibition" of the culprits who have violated social norms, which is the object of popular rituals such as *charivari*. Because it can negotiate the entire representational register from exhibition to mimesis, and the racial register from deficiency (Moors as subhuman) to excess (libidinous, "extravagant and wheeling stranger[s]"), theatre allows for more nuanced depictions – that is, more finely calibrated productions of difference – even while working with thoroughly emblematic depictions of Moors and a polarized concept of woman.

Desdemona, probably in whiteface, is, after all, as potentially comic as Othello. Although she would have been the principal object of ritual punishment in *charivari*, Desdemona is not the carnivalesque feminine of the play. Rather, the alabaster Desdemona is a plausible impersonation of transgressive femininity, certain formations of which are both punished and valorized in tragedy (Callaghan 1989: 34–73). Indeed, Desdemona, "smooth, as monumental alabaster" (V. ii. 5) is aligned with the conventional representations of the sepulchre. Bianca, who, as her name indicates, is the play's contrasting rendition of ultra-white womanhood, is associated with the derogated cosmetic arts. As a Cypriot her histrionic femininity may also entail an element of racial impersonation in that she is "passing" as a white Venetian beauty.[18] Bianca is probably heavily made up, grotesque, depicting the hyper-femininity that registers the proximity between transvestism and prostitution:

> She was here even now, she haunts me in every place. I was t'other day talking on the sea-bank with certain Venetians; thither comes this bauble; by this hand, falls me thus about my neck … So hangs, and lolls, and weeps upon me; so hales, and pulls me: ha, ha, ha!
>
> (IV. i. 132–7 ff)

Bianca, the "bauble" who has made her chastity a gaudy plaything, constitutes a commentary on the construction of Desdemona's absolute virtue, that is on the production of difference among women and the elision of polarized categories of femininity. Bianca thus displaces Desdemona, who, because she has made an improper marriage, would be the proper object of ritual subjection. As an "impersonation" both of Desdemona in particular and of women in general, Bianca enacts the difference between resemblance to and correspondence with "the thing itself," thus marking out the space of referentiality inherent in dramatic representation. In this play, of course, "the thing itself" is figured not as the real women absent from the stage but as female chastity, a reified and essentialized femininity, whose fundamental characteristic is an inherent vulnerability to gross dissimulation, such as that practiced by Iago.

If, in subsequent historical moments, blackness is always visible and whiteness invisible, so that white women have been able to claim the dominant group's privilege of denying their racial identity, this is not so on the Renaissance stage. This subsequent development is what Mary Ann Doane calls "the exercise of whiteness *rather than its representation*" (1991: 245, emphasis added). In Shakespeare's theatre, however, in the figure of woman – in alabaster Desdemona and the racially not-quite-white but cosmetically ultra-white Cypriot Bianca – we have precisely the representation of the dominant race.

II

In the theatre, the exotic, as John Gillies has argued, expresses a relation of exclusion from the commonwealth (Gillies 1994: 99–100), a condition whose spectacular liminality might be identified with femininity. There is perhaps more of a continuity among the various representational registers of the culture and between economics and the stage than is suggested by Anthony Barthelemy's nonetheless acute perception that "If the politics of otherness and exclusion are the primary forces in determining the portrayal of blacks in the masque, the economics of colonialism play an essential role in creating the black stereotypes found in Lord Mayor's Pageants" (Barthelemy 1987: 42). In a burgeoning market economy liminality inheres in the alienated status of the commodity. Exotics in civic pageants, for instance, literally celebrate the opulence of an alterity accessible through trade. At the London Draper's pageant in 1522, along with the obligatory integumentary blackness, the Moor was costumed in a "turban of white feathers and black satin, sylver paper for his shoes, &c.," while at a Henrician court festivity, torchbearers were appareled in "Crymosyn satyne and grene, lyke Moreskoes, their faces blacke," and six ladies had their "heads rouled in plesauntes and typpers lyke the Egipcians, embroudered with gold. Their faces, neckes, armes and handes, covered with fyne plesaunce blacke ... so that the same ladies seemed to be nigrost or blacke Mores"(quoted in Jones 1965: 28, 29).[19] In civic and stage simulations, then, "exotics" could be identified by an almost grotesque "spectacle of strangeness" (as Jonson refers to it in the *Queens* antimasque) – feathers, gaudy satins, gold embroidery, silver shoes. Such splendid accoutrements reflect the fact that in nondramatic presentations the function of African characters was primarily (rather than merely) "decorative." Indeed, as another image of racial difference reproduced on the stage, its superficiality belies its complexity. More than simply a representation of the exploitation of foreign resources and labor, the exotic (which might even be said to be the originary commodity) instantiates the representational apparatus necessary for the advent of the commodity proper. The dehumanization of Africans required in order to rationalize slavery and the alienation intrinsic to commodification (which makes the products of human labor seem to exist independently of it) have their origins at the same historical moment and in the same representational nexus. The "appetite for the wonderful" which has been seen as a natural facet of Western culture (Jordan 1968: 25), was fueled, if not itself produced by, the mechanisms of alienation that are simultaneously representational and economic.

Commodities now appeared to have an objective, "real" existence, independent of the relations of production from which they were made. This fuller development of the mechanisms of alienation constitutive of the commodity, most crucially enabled by the slave trade, made possible as never before an elision between the representational and the real (see Appleby 1978: 243–79). So when the American Ira Aldridge played Othello in London in April of 1833, one critic opined:

> In the name of propriety and decency, we protest against an interesting actress and lady-like girl, like Miss Ellen Tree, being subjected by the manager of the theatre to the indignity of being pawed about by Mr. Henry Wallack's black servant; and finally,

in the name of consistency, if this exhibition is to be continued, we protest against acting being any longer dignified by the name of art.

(quoted in Cowhig 1995: 20)

Importantly, neither Ellen Tree nor Ira Aldridge is here understood to be acting: they are seen to be merely playing themselves.[20] The critic objects to seeing the figure of pure womanhood literally in the "gross clasps of a lascivious Moor." For this critic, when the distance between Shakespeare's Othello and Ira Aldridge is diminished by being performed by an African American, the performance becomes an exhibition as opposed to "art"; it ceases to be acting, becoming not the *representation* of the-thing-itself but, instead, *the-thing-in-itself*. Comparison with Shakespeare's stage is instructive: Unlike Aldridge, Burbage could not have been understood as a barbarian *prior* to the fact of mimesis, whatever his interpretation of Othello. That is, the physical presence of a black man is always already an exhibition of monstrosity, whereas his absence on Shakespeare's stage allowed the sign of negritude, that emblem of barbaric alterity beyond the parameters of civilization, to represent tragic humanity.

But before determining whether representations of racial otherness in the Renaissance were relatively benign when compared with the regimes of racial representation that succeeded them, it is worth considering the ideological work of subsequent instances of racial impersonation, such as D. W. Griffith's negrophobic film *Birth of A Nation* (1915). In Griffith's "classic," members of the Ku Klux Klan revivify a post-Civil War South, where freed slaves allegedly pose a threat to civilization. No AfricanAmerican actors were given major parts, and none of the hundreds used as extras throughout the film appeared in the list of credits (Rogin 1987: 224). There was a great deal of doubling, too, with white bit-part actors playing "renegade colored people" one moment and the whites pursuing them in Klan robes the next. Gus, the black rapist in *Birth of A Nation* is played by a white actor since "no black could be allowed to manhandle Lillian Gish" (Rogin 1987: 225). Griffith claimed that blackface enabled whites to "impersonate" both sides. However, as Michael Rogin has argued, white control over the cultural production of racial difference also propelled white America's economic hegemony by making readily available for foreign and domestic policy an image of the demonized other which, in its paradigmatic form, bears a black face (see Rogin 1987: ch. 1).

The progenitor of Griffith's movie is of course the minstrel show. In antebellum America people of African ancestry were condemned to a system of hereditary slavery in order to provide free labor for a plantation-based economy. Despite the fact that they existed in sufficient numbers to represent themselves, blacks were imitated by white men who donned blackface to do so. Ridicule can only have been part of the motivation; such derision seems superfluous in light of the daily humiliation and degradation of black labor. Writing in the *North Star* on 27 October 1848, Frederick Douglass denounced blackface imitators as "the filthy scum of white society, who have stolen from us a complexion denied to them by nature, in which to make money, and pander to the corrupt taste of their white fellow citizens" (quoted in Lott 1993). For Douglass such travesties marked the expropriation of both black labor and culture, a phenomenon already incipient, as we have seen, in early modern instances of racial impersonation.[21]

It would be anachronistic to suggest direct parallels between the early modern use of blackface in England and later constructions of white supremacy not fully instantiated in early modern England. But that the practise of blackface flourished when there was no practical necessity for it serves to demonstrate that the ideological and cultural motor of black impersonation has no alliance with the practical necessity we habitually assume in relation to Renaissance theatre.[22] Shakespeare's audience would have witnessed in Othello and Desdemona the spectacle of two men, one young with his face whitened and one older with his face blackened. While culturally blackness and femininity become identified with one another, literally, as I have argued above, it is not blackness and femininity that are the same but the extra-diegetic white masculinity that underlies them both. Although the history of *Othello* criticism from Coleridge onwards occludes, rationalizes, and temporizes about race, the theatrical necessity of Shakespeare's stage was to *produce* racial difference *and to control it nevertheless*.

III

Both Africans and white women present the peculiar practical and conceptual obstacles inherent in the dramatic depiction of those categories of persons whose cultural alterity, for different reasons, requires their exclusion.[23] Despite significant differences between both the representation and the exclusion of women and Africans from the stage, members of neither group are understood to be capable of mimesis, even though Moors were thought to be suitable objects of exhibition. In discursive exhibitions of femininity, as when women's "private parts" are displayed in graphic detail in medical treatises of the period, the oversized labia and clitorises of alien races excite the greatest interest and curiosity (see Parker 1994: 84–91). White women themselves, however, were not thought of as exhibits until the Restoration. The privilege of becoming an actress was somewhat tainted by the fact that women were understood not to be exercising the thespian arts but engaging in a species of natural self-display (see Howe 1992a).[24]

The difference between representations of Africans and women is, I believe, a result of the difference between their roles in emergent capitalism, which uniquely expropriates the labor of both groups. Africans and women supply "free" labor – women in the domestic sphere and black men and women as slaves.[25] As the *ideology* of the gendered division of labor intensified, women, newly relegated to the domestic sphere, became objects of intense scrutiny at close quarters, which cultural representation reflected accordingly. Increasingly seen to embody the qualities of the private, English and other European women were, for example, uniquely probed by the new scopic practises of anatomy (see Parker 1994; Traub 1995: 85–6).

In the gendered division of labor, a naturalized rationale for the expropriation of female labor was already established. In contrast, no such rationale for the expropriation of black labor existed: one had to be invented. Slavery, practiced on the unprecedented scale required by burgeoning capitalism, had comparatively weak ideological foundations, relying on fairly inchoate connections between black skin and the Prince of Darkness and on a hazy history of the marvelous as the benchmark of alterity.[26] In the representational register, the rationalization of slavery had to extrapolate a discourse of the marvelous. Negritude demanded, then, not the furtive disclosures appropriate to white femininity but the "full scale" exposure of discovery, marked so vividly in the public display of naked Africans at James's wedding.[27] In that instance representation became quite literally *exposure*, a condition of which the Africans died within days of the event (Hall 1991: 4).

In the public theatre, where blackness and femininity were both performed rather than simply exhibited, the stage properties ("props") used to represent them secured the etymological and material connection between *property* (possession) and *expropriation* (dispossession). Theatrical integuments of black and white thus marked the production of a difference that could not possess itself.

IV

Margo Hendricks has recently argued that, in the Renaissance, people did not equate race with color as people today do in the United States and Western Europe, and that feminist and cultural scholars cannot limit their readings to seeing the "whiteness" of Renaissance Studies:

> Such a move will only make more precise the ideological binarism produced by racial categories, not undo it. Rather than marking "whiteness," the imperative that faces cultural and feminist scholarship is theoretically and historically to map the discursive and social practices that prompted seventeenth-century Englishmen and women to define themselves not only in terms of nationalism but also increasingly, in terms of color.
>
> (Hendricks and Parker 1994: 226)

Because *Othello* is a paradigmatic instance of race/gender representation, topics that come into focus most sharply on the issues of miscegenation, the play has become the locus of feminist attempts to deal with the problems elucidated by Hendricks. Karen Newman's seminal essay, "'And wash the Ethiop White': Femininity and the Monstrous in *Othello*," argues that it is not the dissimilarity but the equivalent monstrosity of Africans and women in the Renaissance that makes miscegenation doubly fearful. By these means Newman interrogates the cultural tendency to assume a natural antithesis between race and gender.

Taking issue with Newman's position, which she sees as symptomatic of the way Western feminism collapses categories of difference and assumes a common history of marginalization, Jyotsna Singh contends that while there are certain parallels in Renaissance attitudes toward racial and sexual difference, we cannot elide the condition of black masculinity with that of white femininity:

> Historically we know the taboo of miscegenation was not so much based on fear of the femininity of the white woman as it was on

the potential phallic threat of black men, who, incidentally, bore
the brunt of the punishment for violating this taboo.

(Singh 1994: 290–1)

Seen in the context of feminist politics, however, these essays reflect
urgent debates and are perhaps less incompatible than at first they
might seem: Newman emphasizes the investment white women and
people of color share in overturning patriarchal precepts, while
Singh shows how cultural constructions of white women as the victims of black men buttress patriarchy.

Virginia Mason Vaughan's wonderfully comprehensive
contextualization of *Othello* similarly insists that "race was (and is)
integrally tied to the concept of gender and sexuality"and details
this connection in the play's performance history (Vaughan 1994:
5).[28] When William Charles Macready toured America, playing
Othello in blackface and African costume, he recorded in his dia-
ries his horror at the treatment of the slave population, though he
makes no connection between slavery and his own performance.
In this respect, Vaughan observes, he is just like his white slave-
owning audiences, who conveniently severed art from life, and
who "could accept a black Othello on stage where they would not
welcome a genuine Negro" (Vaughan 1994: 155). Although there
was never a regulation prohibiting black performance in Britain,
black actors, most notably Ira Aldridge, were not permitted to
perform at the prime professional London theatres in Drury Lane
and Covent Garden. This uncodified color bar persisted until Paul
Robeson broke it in 1930 in the face of a barrage of racism from
the play's producers as well as audiences. Even those who liked
the first performances considered Robeson better suited to the
part because they thought he possessed primitive black emotions
(Vaughan 1994: 188).

The up-hill struggle for black representation in elite culture and,
perhaps more crucially, for recognition of people of African ancestry's capacity to engage in mimetic performance should not be
underestimated. Racially mixed casting has recently become more
common in British and American theatre. African American director Hal Scott used African American actors to play both Othello
and Iago because he does not believe in casting "solely on the basis
of someone's skin color" (Vaughan 1994: 198). Vaughan is critical
of this maneuver because, she argues, this helps to explain why
Othello is so willing to believe Iago but obscures Iago's racism as his

motivation for ruining Othello. Whatever the merits and failures of this particular production, Scott's comments indicate that the issue turns on understanding the relation between blacks and their mimetic capacity. The point is not that society has reached a stage of enlightenment such that it can now afford to be color blind, but that an AfricanAmerican actor can perform white racism (see also Orkin 1987; Salway 1991).

V

In his powerful examinations of contemporary racism, Immanuel Wallerstein suggests that xenophobia becomes the ideological formation of racism with the development of capitalism, only then developing its "symbiotic relationship" with sexism to produce free and cheap labor (Wallerstein 1991: 34). In all prior historical systems xenophobia meant the ejection of the other from the community, but with the advent of capitalism and its need for constant expansion and cheap labor, ejection becomes counterproductive. Racism is the magic solution to the capitalist objective of minimizing production costs and the resistance of the labor force to that process (Wallerstein ibid.: 33). The boundaries of race definition within this system must to be flexible enough to meet specific and changing economic needs. Racism is constant in form and in venom, but somewhat fluid in boundary lines (Wallerstein ibid.: 34). The theatrical evolution from inhuman Mully Mahomet in George Peele's *The Battle of Alcazar* (*c.*1588) to Othello, the humanized Moor, indicates precisely the origins of such ideological flexibility. *Othello* dramatizes the possible consequences of not excluding the racial other from the community and so presents the dazzling spectacle of someone who is, like Caliban, both monster and man. Yet even as it does so, the play reenacts the exclusionary privilege on which such representations were founded. Othello was a white man.

4
Irish memories in
The Tempest

I often wondered why the history of the English in the Americas was so different from that of either the Spanish or the Portuguese. The English fought a war of total extermination against us, with a virulent xenophobia, a disgust at the idea of intermarriage, and a mind-boggling self-righteousness that fueled an endless discourse. It is in large part simply because the English had accustomed themselves to such monstrosity, and had founded their new economic culture upon it, through their experience with Ireland.

(Durham 1993: 15)

I am informed by an honest young man of Captaine *Morris* Company, in Lieutenant Generall *Iretons* Regiment, that at Cashell in the County of *Tipperary*, in the Province of *Munster*, in *Carrick Patrick* Church, seated on a hill or rock, stormed by the Lord *Inchequine*, and where there were neare seven hundred put to the Sword, and none saved but the Mayors Wife, and his Son; there were found among the slaine of the *Irish*, when they were stripped, divers that had Tailes near a quarter of a yard long the Relator being very diffident of the truth of this Story, after enquiry, was ensured of the certainty thereof by forty Souldiers that testified upon their oaths that they were eye-witnesses, being present at the Action.

(Bulwer 1653: 411)

In this extraordinary reconstruction of the slaughter of the Irish by parliamentary troops at Cashel in 1647, the desecrated corpses of the victims are adduced as testimony of their monstrosity. The butchered cadavers become the demonic and bestial detritus of Gaelic popery. The story is a misrepresentation that the dead are in no position to counter, a rhetorical disfigurement of the victims produced by the asymmetrical power of Cromwellian reconquest.[1] Subjugation provides the structure and rhetoric of distortion integral to the colonial agenda and projects its own deformity onto the Irish. The alleged evidence of memory thus serves to rationalize and reinforce atrocity.

This chapter is about the misrepresentations of colonial memory and about what colonial memory chooses to forget, namely cultural representations from the perspective of the colonized themselves.

There is a disturbing continuity between the Cashel massacre and earlier blunt ideological instruments such as John Derricke's *The Image of Irelande* (1578) and Spenser's *Veue of the Present State of Ireland* (registered with the Stationers' Company in 1598).[2] These texts produce the monstrous exotic through the prism of the generic expectations of travel writings and, by dint of brute force, endow irredeemably lopsided "testimony" with the status of history. "For there is no historian of all those who have written on Ireland … that has not continuously sought to cast reproach and blame both on the old foreign settlers and on the native Irish," complained historian Seathrún Céitinn (Geoffrey Keating) in the most widely read and disseminated book ever written in Irish, *Foras Feasa ar Éirinn* (*The History of Ireland*) (*c.* 1634): "Whereof the *testimony* given by Cambrensis, Spenser, Stanihurst, Hanmer, Camden, Barckly, Moryson, Davies, Campion, and every other new foreigner who has written on Ireland … should [not] have the repute of an historian" (Keating quoted in Maxwell 1923: 321–2, emphasis added).[3]

What made the Irish particularly irksome in the matter of cultural representation was that they could, like Keating, represent themselves. Possessed of an unusually rich oral tradition and a powerfully literate indigenous culture, the Irish were far from being devoid of their own representational apparatus. Since Irish was the oldest vernacular language in Europe, its literature already a thousand years old by the reign of Elizabeth, it was impossible

SHAKSPERIAN SKETCHES, BY W. G. BAXTER.
No. 2.
CALIBAN.——"THE TEMPEST."
" As wicked dew as e'er my mother brush'd
With raven's feather from unwholesome fen
Drop on you. "

Plate 4 "Caliban." Uncataloged black box, Folger Shakespeare Library. Reproduced by kind permission of the Folger Library.

to sustain the fantasy, widely held in relation to American Indians, for example, that they were without speech.[4] Indeed, such was the threat of Gaelic cultural expression that all of its manifestations, from poetry to music, were vigorously suppressed. There is for Ireland, as there is not for the English colonies in America, an extensive chirographic culture from the other side of the asymmetrical colonizing process, a body of written discourse contesting English imperial expansion. Yet, despite the capacity to represent themselves, the Irish could neither seize control of representation nor reverse the inexorable momentum of conquest and colonization.[5]

In what follows I want to explore this phenomenon, the struggle for representation in relation to *The Tempest*.[6] Ireland provides the richest historical analog for the play's colonial theme.[7] Like the isle of *The Tempest*, Ireland was a hazardous voyage away across the sea, the demiparadise of the Old World, as even its detractors, such as Edmund Spenser, were compelled to acknowledge: "a most beautiful and sweet country as any is under heaven." On the edge of Europe, in the semiperiphery of the Atlantic world, Ireland occupied an unspecified conceptual space, somewhere between the Old World and the New. Ireland was a foothold to power, a place whose resources would fuel imperial ambition: "[S]eamed throughout with many goodly rivers, replenished with all sorts of fish, most abundantly sprinkled with many sweet islands and goodly lakes, like little inland seas, that will carry even ships upon their waters, adorned with goodly woods fit for building of houses and ships, so commodiously, as that if some princes in the world had them, they would soon hope to be lords of all the seas, and ere long of all the world" (Spenser quoted in Maxwell 1923: 313–14). In his ostensibly objective description Spenser forgets what was to be the major obstacle to ambitions of the kind he articulates, namely the Irish themselves. In contrast, Shakespeare's play draws attention precisely to omission, slippage, occlusion, and prevarication whose accretions constitute the deep contours of colonial recollection. What is at stake in relating Ireland to *The Tempest*, is not, then, a matter of direct and specific correspondence between Ireland and the isle, but precisely the play's resolute nonspecificity, its haziness and imprecision on matters of both geography and, especially, as we shall see, of history; its deliberately bad memory.[8]

This heightened attention to memory as the active process of constructing history for posterity imparts the irresistible impression of a repressed, negated alterity. Indeed, the play has a critical tradition of being the basis on which some of the most eminent writers of our century have "written back" their responses to the structures and situations of colonialism. Such responses are generated (and, arguably, invited) by the subversive energies immanent in the text itself. More than any other Shakespearean drama, Stephen Orgel cautions, "More even than *Hamlet*, the play tempts us to fill in its blanks, to create a history that will account for its action, and most of all for its hero" (Orgel 1987: 11). Following the dictum coined by that notorious Anglo-Irishman Oscar Wilde, that the only way to get rid of temptation is to succumb to it, my purpose here is precisely to fill in these blanks by tracing the echoes of suppressed Irish culture and the secret whispers of repressed hybridity within Shakespeare's play and beyond it, to the other side of colonial representation.

My strategy is conceptually and politically distinct from "writing back" and reflects my own temporally and geographically dislocated relation to English colonialism. What follows is an attempt to grasp, to remember, a cultural history that has shaped my own identity and which entails an "unreading" of the assumptions of colonial logic. I will focus in particular on struggles over land (which the English reduce to property), poetry, music, and language – the very foundation of cultural memory and, crucially, the structure of personal identity. Finally, I will argue that the key to these formations is the absent Sycorax, the figure who is most palpably under erasure though absent from the text in any straightforward, positivist sense (see Chedgzoy 1995: 94–134). Through her and through the reverberations of her relationships, *The Tempest* registers those disfigurations of colonial memory that prepare the ground for the *tabula rasa* of colonized space.[9] And this process, eloquently described in the epigraph to this chapter, by Jimmie Durham (himself a Cherokee artist who has used *The Tempest* to "write back"), is instantiated and uniquely exacerbated in the English relation to Ireland (see Allen 1994: 52–70).

I begin this attempt to give substance to indigenous cultural representations razed by colonialism with Ariel, whose aesthetic offices, in contrast to the brute material labors of Caliban, do not seem to endow him with sufficient material solidity to inhabit the earth let alone stake a territorial claim on it. A bifurcated model of colonial subjection constitutes Ariel as an airy spirit who flits about "this bare island" (Epilogue, l. 8) at Prospero's behest, while Caliban is confined to arid ground – "You sty me in this hard rock" – so that even the most arduous of his physical labors will not sustain him independently of his colonial master. However, to understand the difference between Caliban and Ariel as that between the bestial and the ethereal is to take colonial mystification on its own terms.

The difference in their roles may be better understood as a distinction of class. Indeed, the elision of class differences by the processes of English historiography is one of the principal sources of Keating's somewhat elitist critique of English racism:

> Whoever should determine to make a minute search for ill customs, or an investigation into the faults of inferior people, it would be easy to fill a book with them; for there is no country in the world without a rabble. Let us consider the rough folk of Scotland, the rabble-rout of Great Britain, the plebeians of Flanders, the insignificant fellows of France, the poor wretches of Spain, the ignoble caste of Italy, and the unfree tribe of every country besides, and a multitude of ill-conditioned evil ways will be found in them; howbeit, the entire country is not to be disparaged on their account.
>
> (quoted in Maxwell 1923: 322)[10]

In class terms, then, Caliban clearly occupies the category of rabble/plebeian/rough folk, while Ariel belongs to the cultured, lettered echelons of Irish society. Though racism homogenized the Irish in most accounts, the English were keenly aware of the existence of an influential cultural stratum of Gaelic society and understood Irish cultural heritage, especially in the form of bardic poetry, as part of a powerful cultural apparatus that could be mobilized to incite insurrection. Cu Chonnacht O Dalaigh's *Poem Before Leaving Aodh Ruadh* (*c.* 1598), records the parlous position of the cultural classes in the face of a vigorous campaign not merely to censor but to annihilate Gaelic language and culture, both by force and by statute:

> An chéadchoir chuirfid ruinne
> fian Ghall, gasriadh Londainne,
> mé re hathaidh i nUltaibh;
> dár rachoir é d'fhionnachtain.
>
> Is sé adéarthaoi arís rinne
> Aodh Ruadh, díobhadh Duibhlinne-
> ní baothrogha, an té dan toil –
> gurbh é m'aonchara d'Ultaibh.
>
> Gá dám acht adéardaois Goill
> go mbeinnse i mbaile 'I Dhomhnaill –
> sgéal oirn a fhionnachtain d'fhior –
> fa mhoirn iomarcraidh aimsear.

Dá n-éistinn orfhuighle Gall
do bhiadh dá n-eagla oram
go séanfainn méid mo mhoirne
ó ghéig mhéarchuirr Mhodhairne. …

Adéardaois más díobh meise,
aos cuma mo cheirdise
do-bheir i nGaoidhealaibh gomh
's neimh ré saoirfhearaibh Saxan:–

'Maoidhid orra uaisle a sean;
reacaid re macaibh Míleadh
Banbha gurab dóibh dleaghair,
labhra ar nach cóir creideamhain.

The first charge the English warriors, the Londoners,
will bring against me is that I was for a time in Ulster;
it is a part of my great crime to have it discovered.

Again I would be told that Aodh Ruadh, scourge of
Dublin, was my special friend among Ulstermen – a
wise choice, whoever wishes it.

Besides, the English would say that I was honoured in
O'Donnell's abode for many periods – I am reported
to have told someone so.

Were I to heed the speech of the English, for fear of
them I would deny the measure of the honour shown
me by the slender-fingered scion of the Mourne. …

They would say, if it is the case, that I belong to those
practitioners of my art who excite bitterness in Irish-
men and enmity against Saxon nobles: –

…'They extol the nobility of their forebears to the
descendants of Míl. They declare to them that Ireland
is their due inheritance – words that ought not to be
believed.'

(Breatnach 1989: 39–40)

The poet records here the dynamics of colonial encounter, specifically the threat that Irish culture poses to English hegemony and
the struggle against endless misrepresentation generated by the
colonizer. That O'Donnell has been his patron, that he has been

closely involved with resistance in Ulster, are seen by the English as marks of sedition. Indeed, these are concrete political ties, and the poet's invocation of the idea that the Irish are descendants of the mythological Mil, the genealogy of indigenous cultural memory, is a very significant element in the composition of verse histories. Sir Thomas Smith in his enumeration of the septs of "rhymers," the Irish cultural classes, refers to

> the "Shankee" (Senachie) [*seanchuidhe*], an historian, genealogist, storyteller] which is to say in English, the "petigrer" (genealogist). They have also great plenty of cattle, wherewithal they do succour the rebels. They make the ignorant men of the country to believe they be descended of Alexander the Great, or of Darius, or of Caesar, or of some other notable prince; which makes the ignorant people to run mad, and caring not what they do; the which is very hurtful to the Realm.
>
> (Smith quoted in Maxwell 1923: 341)

The dangers of Irish culture were not confined to the native population but presented the problem of the Gaelicization of English settlers. For this reason the Articles of Plantation forbade undertakers to "receive into their habitations, retain or lodge any Irish rhymers, bards, harpers or such idle persons" (Henley 1928: 106).

In response to the perceived threat of Gaelic culture, English policy on the practises of indigenous cultural history became increasingly vicious. In 1571 a statute against "rhymers" (often used by the English as the generic name for the cultural classes) declared that they were all to be put to the stocks. Subsequently, more severe restrictions included an order issued by the Lord Chancellor and Council of Ireland in 1579 that harpers, bards, and rhymers (whose repertoire, because of its oral performance, was not confined to the cultural and political elite) were to be executed by martial law (*Calendar of State Papers Ireland*, 1574–85: 179).[11] The 1582 address to Elizabeth by the then Lord Lieutenant, Sir John Perrot, which urged the summary execution of all "Brehons, Carraghes, Bardes, and Rhymers that infect the people," suggests that the law was not, perhaps, as vigorously enforced as he would have wished.[12] That the cultural class was not singled out for executable offenses as the order demanded may not, however, be the result of leniency on the part of the English but may instead indicate that periodic indiscriminate assaults on the native populace combined with ineffective government outside the Pale did not allow for such careful distinctions.

The English were especially perturbed by the prospect of the dissemination of indigenous history in the tradition of bardic poetry, which they routinely dismissed as "lies." Barnaby Rich inveighs against the indigenous historians: "There is nothing that hath more led the Irish into error, than lying historiographers, their chroniclers, their bards, their rhymers, and such other their lying poets; in whose writings they do more rely, than they do in the Holy Scriptures" (Rich quoted in Maxwell 1923: 340).

"Thou liest, malignant thing!" roars Prospero before coercing Ariel into a narrative about the island's history:

> hast thou forgot
> The foul witch Sycorax. ... Hast thou forgot her?
> *Ariel*: No, sir.
> *Prospero*: Thou hast. Where was she born? Speak; tell me.
> *Ariel*: Sir, in Algiers.
> *Prospero*: O, was she so? I must
> Once in a month recount what thou hast been,
> Which thou forget'st.
>
> (I. ii. 259–64)

By means of these formal interrogatives, Prospero seeks to inculcate ideology on specifically catechistical (and therefore Catholic) lines. The "unremembering" he seeks to effect is thus also an act of appropriation and resonates with the same Catholic practises Protestantism intended to supplant. While this latter process occurred in England, too, it was painfully protracted in Ireland, where in fact the Reformation never actually took hold.[13]

Since Ariel is apparently the source of all information about the island before Prospero arrived there, Prospero's allegations about the spirit's faulty memory seem rather wide of the mark. There is an extraordinary sense in this passage that it is not Ariel who is the source of the oral history Prospero insists on having him perform but Prospero himself. Repetition will serve to reinscribe Ariel's memory with Prospero's version of events. Memory, representation, and reenactment, as Judith Anderson points out, are basic to Prospero's power (Anderson 1996: 163). In his interrogation of Ariel, Prospero may resemble his usurping brother, who has also played tricks with memory:

> Who having into truth, by telling oft,
> Made such a sinner of his memory
> To credit his own lie
>
> (I. ii. 100–2)

Now that Prospero speaks for him, or rather through him, monthly reiterating the "official" history of the isle, Ariel as the native historiographer is barred from relating his own past.

Instead of trying to denigrate or annihilate Gaelic culture, another strategy was to discount it altogether. Sir John Davies, for example, argues that the Irish have achieved culture *without* civilization:

> For, though the Irishry be a nation of great antiquity, … and were lovers of music, poetry, and all kinds of learning … yet which is strange to be related, they did never build any houses of brick or stone … plant any gardens or orchards, enclose or improve their lands, live together in settled villages or towns, nor made any provision for posterity; which being against all common sense and reason, must needs be imputed to those unreasonable customs which made their estates so uncertain and transitory in their possessions.
>
> (Davies quoted in Maxwell 1923: 353)

The implication here is both that the Irish, despite the contrary evidence of their scholarship, are not really civilized, and that they do not have a grasp on the materiality of their environment. In a profound way, then, the plan to exploit Ireland's material resources denies and negates the existence of the indigenous populations. Devoid of the entrepreneurial spirit, having no interest in exploiting resources and establishing towns, the pastoral Irish become vague figures on an alien horizon, as "uncertain" and "transitory" as the property they fail to possess. Notably, there is no attempt to denigrate the Irish in this passage but only an effort to register the apparently puzzling contradiction posed by the acquisition of culture without a concomitant acquisition of property.

The cultural classes, comprised of the repositors and guardians of indigenous oral and written cultural memory – the poets, the musicians, the genealogists, the historians, the keepers of legal and fiscal records – were, nonetheless, key to the attainment of English imperial goals. Attempts to eradicate the Brehon Code, such as a 1571 statute decreeing "All Irish laws called Brehon Law to be of no force," a measure that conveniently invalidated Gaelic titles to land recorded by the sept of genealogists, the Shanahas, paved the way for the establishment of an English legal infrastructure (English Common Law).[14] English common law was, as J.G.A. Pocock has demonstrated, crucially and paradoxically dependent on the memory of forgetfulness: "[A]ll English law was common law, common law was custom, custom rested on the presumption of immemoriality; property, social structure, and government existed as defined by the law and were therefore presumed to be immemorial" (Pocock 1975: 340–1).

An analog to Prospero's re-education of Ariel may be glimpsed in Sir John Davies's account of how he coerced and intimidated "a very ancient Brehon" (an old man of the Irish lawyer class) in the Maguire territory of Fermanagh into handing over documents that would enable the English to divide the spoils of their conquered territory:

> The poor old man, fetching a deep sigh, confessed that he knew where the roll was, but that it was dearer to him than his life; and therefore he would never deliver it out of his hands, unless my lord Chancellor would take the like oath, that the roll should be restored unto him again; my Lord Chancellor smiling, gave him his word and his hand that he should have the roll re-delivered unto him, if he would suffer us to take a view and copy thereof; and thereupon the old Brehon drew the roll out of his bosom, where he did continually bear it about him: it was not very large, but it was written on both sides in a fair Irish character; howbeit, some part of the writing was worn and defaced with time and ill-keeping: we caused it forthwith to be translated into English.
>
> (Keating quoted in Maxwell 1923: 326)

In a comparatively benign act of appropriation – translation – Davies accesses the distribution of land and tribute the better to exploit the country's resources. Thus cultural labor, which depends on the very class distinctions among the native populace the English sought to deny, becomes indispensable in the exercise of colonial authority, especially in the project to replace the structures of indigenous memory with English history.

In Prospero's regime the only form of cultural expression left to Ariel is music. Significantly, there is more music in *The Tempest* and more varieties of music than in any other play in the Shakespearean canon (see Orgel 1987: 220). Critics typically misattribute the music to Prospero,[15] despite the fact that Ariel and his fellow spirits are its primary performers. When roused at the prospect of the liberty to which he has so long aspired, he spontaneously bursts into song: "Where the bee sucks, there suck I." Whatever Prospero's role in the play's music, Ariel is here the instrumentalist: the music emanates from his tabor and pipe and from unspecified strange, "twangling" (i.e., stringed) instruments. Harp music, in particular, perhaps because it was associated with the upper echelons of Irish society, was felt to be so powerful that the English, as we have noted, tried to eradicate it in 1571; and as late as July 1698, there is a presentment to the grand Jury that Tadhg Dash had a harper playing in his house contrary to the Act.

Caliban's aesthetic sensibility may, likewise be an appreciation not of one of Prospero's entertainments but of the indigenous music of the isle:

> the isle is full of noises,
> Sounds, and sweet airs, that give delight and hurt not.
> Sometimes a thousand twangling instruments
> Will hum about mine ears. ...

(III. ii. 132–5)

Ireland was quite literally full of noises, a culture of sound. "You shall find but very few of their gentry, either man or woman, but can play on the harp," observed a contemporary, writing *c*. 1610; "also you shall not find a house of any account without one or two of those instruments and they always keep a harper to play for them at their meals" (quoted in MacLysaght 1950: 111). A very explicit reference to harping is to "the miraculous harp" of Amphion who raised the walls of Thebes by music. The "sweet Harp" of Orpheus, "so musically strung," is conventionally associated with civility, as in Drayton's *Poly-Olbion* (1622), drawing "The stony, blockish rout, that nought but rudeness knew, / T'imbrace a civil life." Antonio and his companions use this classical reference to the materiality of culture to belittle Gonzalo before he articulates his utopian fantasy. When Gonzalo shows some confusion about matters of classical history and geography, he is further disparaged as "a lord of weak remembrance." In Gonzalo, then, a member of the lower orders of Italian society, who identifies himself with an oral culture ("Letters should not be known", II. i. 148), the colonial mnemonic has not taken hold; and he is identified with the harp, which in relation to Ireland is the emblem of the music and memory of alterity (Drayton 1622: 31; see also Berger 1969: 253–83).

Harp music was the traditional accompaniment to bardic poetry, which, as we have seen, served to establish genealogical links between contemporary leaders and classical heroes by way of a legitimating panegyric. When Caliban hears a voice that would bestow riches on him, he is listening to the aestheticized rendition of his own earlier genealogical declaration: "This island's mine by Sycorax my mother":

> ... and sometime voices,
> That if then had waked after long sleep,
> Will make me sleep again, and then in dreaming
> The clouds methought would open and show riches
> Ready to drop upon me, that when I waked
> I cried to dream again
>
> (III. ii. 132–41)

While the oral performance of verse histories in Ireland was accompanied with music, the process of composition was an astonishing mental exercise that took place when the poet retired to a darkened room. The work would not be committed to manuscript until much later, and the practise of nonwritten composition persisted despite the fact that Ireland was a highly literate culture. There was a sharp and hierarchical distinction between the composer, the *file*, and the performer, who was usually one of the lower grades of rhymers. Although the process of composition itself was an isolated aesthetic activity, bardic poetry from conception to performance was nonetheless very politically charged. The pleasure and reverie that constituted Gaelic poetic practise combined to promote the dynastic ambitions of patrons, and the bard, rigorously trained in prosody and history, was responsible not only for promoting and authorizing his lord's status via eulogy but also actively intervening in affairs on his patron's behalf as negotiator and propagandist (Canny 1982: 91–116). Ironically, the Irish bard, who, as Spenser observed in *A View*, was held in "so high regard and estimation" and whose verses were "taken up with a generall applause," represented all that an English poet might aspire to be, namely, as Jonson put it: "the interpreter and arbiter of nature, a teacher of things divine no less than human, a master in manners; and can alone, or with a few, effect the business of mankind" (Spenser 1997: 75).[16]

The bards' exalted position, and indeed that of the Gaelic literati in general, was, however, as we have seen, under threat from the systematic erosion of the society that produced it (Canny 1982: 94). The sense of inconsolable loss in Caliban's dream in the wake of former glory, "that when I waked / I cried to dream again," is strangely reminiscent of the body of Irish poetry which laments the decline of the race brought about by the advent of "the foreigner." The content of the following poem, for instance, is, like Caliban's lament, a sort of cultural mourning:

> Anocht as uaigneach Éire
> do bheir fógra a firfhréimhe
> gruaidhe a fear sa fionnbhan fliuch
> treabh is iongnadh go huaigneach. …
>
> Gan gáire fa ghníomhraibh leinbh
> cosg ar cheól glas ar Ghaoidheilg
> meic ríogh mar nár dhual don dream
> gan luadh ar fhíon nó aithfreann. …
>
> Gan rádha rithlearg molta
> gan sgaoileadh sgeóil chodalta
> gan œidh ar fhaicsin leabhair
> gan chlaistin ghlœin ghenealaigh.
>
> Lonely is Ireland to-night: the outlawry of her native stock fills with tears the cheeks of her men and her fair women: that the land should be desolate is unusual.
>
> No laughter at children's play: an end to music: Gaelic is silenced: sons of kings un-honoured: no mention of wine-feast or of Mass.
>
> No reciting of panegyrics: no telling of sleep-inducing story: no wish to examine a volume, nor hear a roll of genealogy.

These stanzas (1, 5, and 7) are from *The Sorrows of Éire* by one of the foremost poets of the period, Eóghan Ruadh Mac An Bhaird, the bard of Tir Conaill (Walsh 1957: 118–25). In this poem it is not merely that sorrow prevents the former gaiety of the people, their poetry, and their prayers, but that their language, customs, and religion are suppressed. This vein of "adverse destiny," "immense calamity," and "piercing regret" is precisely what led Matthew Arnold to attribute, somewhat nostalgically, the turn of melancholy in English literature to Celtic sources and motivated Victor Hugo in the introduction to his French translation of *The Tempest* to claim that Shakespeare had given shape in this play to the ancient dogmas of the druids, whose influence in Ireland was never erased by Christianity, but rather blended with it (Barton: 1919: 229).

The voices Caliban hears are like the strains of a cultural unconscious that, given the pervasive fulminations against Gaelic culture, make it unlikely that even the English could have been unaware (Bradshaw 1978: 65–8; Canny 1982: 91–116).[17] Indeed, despite the official English view of those cultural practises lumped together as "harping," appreciation of Irish music and poetry and, simultaneously, its appropriation were also to be found among the English. Sir John Davies's use of the harp as a metaphor for harmonious English law and order in *The Discovery* (1612), endeavored, exactly like Prospero, to appropriate indigenous culture. Such an appropriation is, perhaps, analogous to the present dislocation of black music which, as Paul Gilroy argues, though "produced out of the racial slavery which made modern western civilisation possible, now dominates its popular cultures" (Gilroy 1993: 80). So, despite the English ban on bards and rhymers, when James I came to the throne, two bards composed poems for him, Eochaidh-hEodhusa and Fearghal-gMac an Bhaird. James was portrayed in traditional terms as the legitimate spouse of Ireland who had been predicted by prophecy. Such praise seems to have ensured -hEodhusa's survival. He had been chief poet to the Maguires of Fermanagh, and upon the demise of the bardic order was found to be one of the surviving Irish who were allotted land in the Ulster plantation. Thus, even though the bard was a figure who in other contexts was the very hallmark of recalcitrant Gaelic culture, in *The Irish Masque* Jonson has an Irish bard offer a eulogy to James:

> Advance, immortall Bard, come vp and view
> The gladding face of that great king, in whom
> So many prophecies of thine are knit.
> That is that IAMES of which long since thou sung'st,
> Should end our countreyes most vunnaturall broyles
> …

Jonson's move here is in line with a spate of nostalgic antiquarianism about Celtic culture provoked by the Scottish king's accession to the English throne. Nostalgia is another form of memory (one gestured to in the title of this chapter) whereby indigenous history can be recognized and perhaps contained.

Though the point here is not to establish direct causal connections but to suggest the relevance of cultural difference to the English production of alterity, it remains true that Shakespeare himself, though he could not read Gaelic, had probably, like Jonson, some knowledge of bardic poetry. He certainly knew and admired Welsh manifestations of Celtic culture, as we see in *Henry IV* when Glendower's wife sings a song in her native Welsh; and in *Richard III* the Irish bard is assoicated with the prophetic powers of druidism: "I started, / Because a bard of Ireland told me once I should not live long after I saw Richmond" (IV. iii. 109–11). In *The Tempest*, echoes and specters of the Irish may not be a result of the conscious intention of the playwright, but they constitute the repressed knowledge of a people whose simultaneous propinquity and estrangement in relation to the English had become so exacerbated by the processes of Stuart colonialism that its rupture into consciousness was imminent if not actual.[18]

When Ferdinand hears the music of the isle, he harkens to the rhythms of a different mode of existence. Indeed, music and memory are closely connected in the play, evoking the traces and fragments of a past that Prospero has endeavored either to suppress or appropriate:

> (*Burden Ding dong*).
> Hark, now I hear them, ding dong bell.
> This ditty does remember my drowned father.
> This is no mortal busines, nor no sound
> That the earth owes I hear it now above me.
> (I. ii. 403–6)

Paradoxically, those aspects of Irish cultural practise that were most pleasurable to the English – impenetrable, quasimagical, and exotic – were probably also most threatening. The English were emotionally susceptible to the aesthetic productions they witnessed in Ireland but did not much understand. While for the Irish the pleasure of music is integral to the pleasure of history, for the English pleasure is disturbingly severed from narrative even as they attended to it.

> Where should this music be? i'th'air or th'earth?
> …
> This music crept by me upon the waters,

> Allaying both their fury and my passion
> With its sweet air.
>
> (I. ii. 388–94)

This passage describes the powerful emotional impact – in this case grief and consolation – evoked by such music. Spenser, in his description of the harps in the Masque of Cupid describes their effects upon the senses in not dissimilar terms:

> The whiles a most delitious harmony
> In ful straunge notes was sweetly heard to sound
> The feeble sences wholy did confound
> And the frayle soule in deepe delight nigh drownd.
> (*Faerie Queen*, Bk III, *c*.xii)[19]

Again, there is considerable emphasis on the exoticism of the music, its "ful straunge notes" and almost druglike effect. "Strange music" in *The Tempest* constitutes an auditory nostalgia for the repressed and almost erased culture of alterity.

The aspect of Irish music more disturbing to English memory than the purely aesthetic pleasure of harp music was the belief that, like Ariel, the Irish expressed in music their desire for liberty. This was true of the elite and peasant classes alike. Fynes Moryson (secretary to Mountjoy) complained:

> This idleness also makes them to love liberty above all things, and likewise naturally to delight in music, so as the Irish harpers are excellent, and their solemn music is much liked of strangers; and the women of some parts of Munster, as they wear Turkish heads and are thought to have come first out of those parts, so they have pleasant tunes of Moresco dance.
>
> (Moryson in Falkiner 1904: 312)

The class demarcations that are both articulated and occluded in relation to Ireland emerge here specifically in terms of music, that of the lower orders being allied with Turks and Moors. A rustic Irish melody would not have been unsuitable for Caliban's own rude music:

> 'Ban,'Ban, CaCaliban
> has a new master get a new man!
> Freedom, highday! Highday, freedom! Freedom,
> highday, freedom!
>
> (II. ii. 179–81)

There is no mistaking the source of energy from whence proceeds Caliban's rousing refrain.

Barnaby Rich read Irish culture as a form of political resistance:

> [T]he songs that they use to sing are usually in the commenda-
> tion of theft, of murder, of rebellion, of treason, and the most of
> them lying fictions of their own collections, invented but of pur-
> pose to stir up their hearts to imitation of their ancestors, making
> repetition … how many times they had rebelled against their
> Prince, and what spoils and outrages they had done against the
> English.
>
> (Rich quoted in Maxwell 1923: 341)

Yet the only audible discord in the play that Prospero has not choreographed in advance is the "[*S*]*trange hollow, and confused noise*" (IV. i. SD) that erupts not from Caliban, the island's native, but from Prospero's masque and even from his person as he remem-bers Caliban: "*Prospero starts suddenly and speaks*." At this point in *The Tempest* memory works to register the space of non represen-tation as well as mere distortion, which admits nothing of the anti-aesthetic of disproportion and incongruous hybridity embod-ied by Caliban, recollection of whom dissolves the myth of colo-nial harmony into the dissonance of alterity.[20] Prospero may indeed be trying to employ "the arts of music, poetry, and spectacle to civilize his subjects and restore harmony to his kingdom," but he is singularly unsuccessful in doing so (see Wells 1994: 63–80). In Jacobean England the masque was the most exalted form of cul-tural representation. The spectacular vision of courtly harmony it was the masque's business to effect was typically preceded by the comic mayhem of the antimasque, which further enhanced the beauty and propriety of the masque itself. Yet Prospero's masque, his grand spectacle to impress the visitors from Milan, instead of progressing from the disorder of the antimasque to the orchestrated harmony and perfect control of the masque, reverses the process, dissolving into an eerie cacophony when "Nymphs and reapers heavily vanish." Prospero's masque denies all knowl-edge of the colonial venture, and his antimasque, if we can call it that, is compressed into this abrupt moment of recollection: "I had forgot that foul conspiracy / Of the beast Caliban"(IV. i. 139–40). His mnemonic crisis, not Caliban's rebellion, thus triggers the play's major aesthetic disruption.

In contrast, Ben Jonson's *The Irish Masque at Court*, staged only

months after *The Tempest* had been performed as part of the wedding festivities for James' daughter Elizabeth and the Elector Palatine
in February 1613, followed the conventional trajectory from chaos
to order. Though the masque itself consisted of a display of dancing
performed primarily by Scottish aristocrats, the text that has come
down to us is actually that of the antimasque, performed by professional actors, the King's men, rather than the masque itself, which,
presumably would not have required "text" as such. The antimasque,
something akin to a photographic negative of courtly civility, per-
mits the invention of the stage Irishman, that tamed barbarian whose
defining characteristic is stupidity.

The comic possibilities entailed in colonial subjection are outlined in Shakespeare's play in the entrepreneurial scheme to sell
Caliban to a court menagerie, where his relation to Prospero as
recalcitrant and bestial slave will be refigured as obedient domestic
beast "if I can recover him, and keep him tame, and get to Naples
with him" (II. ii. 667). Caliban's slave status pitches him somewhere
between beast of burden and humanity as well as between two models
of subjection – relatively pliant slave and intractable indigenous
inhabitant. In this construction the unpresentable, foul-smelling
Caliban is a perfect commodity for exhibition and sale. Caliban,
then, deprived of his indigenous history and powers of cultural memory,
can be represented all too easily. However, such representation in
no way constitutes enfranchisement because, above all, it denies
Caliban his own capacity for representation.

Caliban's extraordinary powers of self-representation become an
issue in the play around the problem of language as the transcrip-
tion of memory. Language, that uniquely human capacity to represent
thoughts, needs, and desires is the foundation of culture as the re-
pository of memory; and, like Caliban, the allegedly bestial Irish
are said by the English to be incapable of it. Just as the music of the
isle is typically handed over to Prospero, critics – traditional and
postcolonial alike – typically attribute Caliban's eloquence entirely
to a colonial education.[21] Yet the beauty of Caliban's language
emanates from his autochthonous identity:

> I'll show thee the best springs; I'll pluck thee berries;
> I'll fish for thee, and get thee wood enough.
> … I prithee let me bring thee where crabs grow,
> And with my long nails will dig thee pignuts,
> Show thee a jay's nest, and instruct thee how

> To snare the nimble marmoset. I'll bring thee
> To clust'ring filberts, and sometimes I'll get thee
> Young scamels from the rock.
>
> (II. ii. 162–6)

Far from being merely descriptive, Caliban's account of his indigenous habitat shows a lived relation with his environment. The difference between the colonists and the Irish on this matter was in large measure due to the fact that land was not just an economic resource in Gaelic Ireland. While in England schemes for enclosure and drainage increasingly subjected the peasant population to the economic discipline of efficiency, Ireland was a traditional society with a deep and ancient bond to place. Like the Native American landscape, the Irish land offered a kind of sacred, readable topography devoid of the English sense of proprietorship (see Collins 1990: 48). It is Caliban's distinctive relation to place, the fact that his personal history belongs to the island, that allows him the ability to represent himself and in terms quite distinct from those available to other characters despite the linguistic homogeneity among them (they all speak English).

Unable to determine the meaning of "scamel," critics speculate that it is a word adopted from or misunderstood in a foreign language, French and Italian, *squama*, meaning "small fish" (see Orgel 1987: 151). The dialect dictionary, however, defines *scamel* unequivocally as a bar-tailed godwit, a marsh bird. *Scallachan* is also an Irish word that means an unfledged bird (Armstrong 1825; Wright 1904). "Scamel" may register quasi-provincial culinary practises as alien, while its etymological perplexity highlights the problem of the linguistic integrity of English itself. Fynes Moryson, rejecting outright the possibility of the hybridity of the English language, projects it onto Irish:

> Touching the Irish language. It is a peculiar language, not derived from any other radical tongue (that ever I could hear, for myself neither have nor ever sought to have any skill therein); but as the land, as I have showed, hath been peopled by divers nations besides the first inhabitants, so hath the tongue received many new words from them, especially Spanish words from the people coming thence to inhabit the west parts. But all I have said hereof might well be spared, as if no such tongue were in the world I think it would never be missed either for pleasure or necessity.
>
> (Moryson in Falkiner 1904: 317)

Irish, the language that allows access to indigenous cultural memory, was, in short, "gabble," which none of the New English spokesmen like Spenser, Davies, or Rich even troubled to learn. "Gabble" is of course precisely the pejorative used by Miranda to describe Caliban's linguistic capacities before she taught him the language, if not the behaviors, of civility:

> … thou didst not, savage,
> Know thine own meaning, but wouldst gabble like
> A thing most brutish.
>
> (I. ii. 354–6)

The first use of the word *gabble* recorded in the *OED* is from Palesman Richard Stanihurst's *Description of Ireland* in Holinshed's *Chronicles* (I. iv.), a text which argues that three things should accompany conquest, law, *language*, and clothing where it is used to describe loquacity: "[H]e that dooth not perceyve, what is fitting or decent for every season, or gabbleth more than he hath commission to do." Stanihurst's position as English colonialism's instrument of overwriting and erasure was, however, decidedly problematic.[22] Attacked for denigrating a language of which he had himself no knowledge, Stanihurst countered defensively, "Indeed on the contrary, I have long been convinced on the authority of scholars that the speech of the Irish is rich in vocabulary, elegance and wit. Moreover the language is directly descended from Hebrew" (Lennon 1981: 100). Despite his ignorance of Irish, Stanihurst must have been influenced by it, because *gabble* is not an English word but, to quote Spenser, "a word mingled out of Irish and English together" (Spenser 1997: 43), deriving from *gobaireachd*, which means loquacity or impertinent tattle (exactly the sense in which Stanihurst uses "gabble"). When the non-Gaelic-speaking Stanihurst went to the Inns of Court, he was ridiculed for his brogue as "pogue morris." Perhaps, like Stanihurst, Caliban is completely monolingual and still bears the stigma of an alien tongue. There is a deliberate indeterminacy about Caliban's primal babble/gabble, which, like the etymology of *scamel*, is caught somewhere between an English dialect and an Irish tongue. Whatever the case, gabble offers a vivid instance of the way colonialism overwrites the representations and historical record of alterity and linguistic hybridity, scrambling and unremembering what it cannot yet quite fully erase.

Whether the Irish spoke Gaelic, English, or Latin, and regardless of the fluency with which they spoke, they were still understood to be gabbling rather than speaking. Thomas Campion, for instance, disparaged Irish intellectualism, especially the use of Latin (the European common language of cultural memory) in place of the vernacular: "Without either the precepts or observation of congruity they speak Latin like a vulgar language, learned in their common schools of leechcraft and law" (Campion quoted in Maxwell 1923: 315).

In the Irish context, Trinculo's question about Caliban, "Where the devil should he learn our language?"(II. 66–71), displays staggering naiveté about the coercive requirement that indigenous cultural memory be erased by establishing English as the only tongue that constitutes a language. The impetus to enforce English linguistic hegemony, and thereby English history, in Ireland is a means to exercise power fully, flatly, and evenly on all regions within its jurisdiction (see Elias 1982). In 1537 an Act for the English Order, Habit, and Language urges "a conformity, concordance, and familiarity in language, tongue, in manners, order and apparel, with them that be civil people, and do profess and acknowledge Christ's religion, and civil and politic orders, laws and directions, as his Grace's subjects of this part of this his land of Ireland, that is called the English Pale, doth … [and] that there is again nothing which doth more contain and keep many of his subjects of this his said land, in a certain savage and wild kind and manner of living, than the diversity that is betwixt them in tongue, language, order and habit …" (quoted in Maxwell 1923: 112–13). The preservation of difference in this document, in other words, Irish cultural integrity (that which "doth … contain and keep"), is registered as lamentable; difference is to be first marked, then annihilated: "And be it enacted that every person or persons, the King's true subjects, inhabiting this land of Ireland, of what estate, condition or degree he or they be, or shall be, to the uttermost of their power, cunning and knowledge, shall use and speak commonly the English tongue and language … [and] shall bring up … his … children in such places, where they shall or may have occasion to learn the English tongue, language, order and condition" (quoted in Maxwell 1923: 113). Prospero has been very diligent in the exercise of this duty prompted, of course, by the fear that the English settlers will, as they had after the Anglo-Norman conquest, "degenerate" into the use of Gaelic.

Miranda's claims about Caliban's use of language in light of the Irish context may offer more in the way of evidence of her racism, her participation in the colonial erasure of indigenous memory, than of his linguistic ineptitude:

> I pitied thee,
> Took pains to make thee speak, taught thee each hour
> One thing or other.

(I. ii. 352–4)

Caliban's language or lack thereof directs us, then, once again to the problem of colonial memory, this time Miranda's recollections of a Caliban who once had something of the status of an adopted sibling. If we interject a certain skepticism about Miranda's memory, where did Caliban's English come from, and did it supplant an indigenous "gabble"? English is clearly Caliban's primary language even if it is not his mother tongue. Jacobean ideas of language acquisition included the notion that a child isolated from human society would speak Hebrew or Phrygian as a sort of default option. Montaigne (whose father brought him up speaking Latin as his first language and did not introduce him to French until later in his childhood) noted: "And yet I believe (though it would be difficult to assay it) that if a child, before learning to talk, were brought up in total solitude, then he would have some sort of speech to express his concepts. ... But we do not know what language an isolated child would actually speak and all the guesses made about it seem improbable" (Screech 1993: 512–13).[23] It is possible that, like the child Montaigne speculates about, Caliban acquires language as the means of communicating with others (as opposed to the innate human capacity for speech) for the first time from Prospero and Miranda and was, before their appearance, merely too young to know his own meaning.

The problem of language also leads us back to Prospero's colonial version of history. The only person who has had an adult's memory since his arrival on the island, he has the longest memory one which has conveniently obscured the history of Caliban's mother tongue and even of Caliban's mother. Indeed, language as the instrument of memory, thematized as the problem of Caliban's mother tongue, is intimately related to the problem of mothers more generally in the play. Nowhere embodied and persisting in only hazy and distorted memories, mothers, who have been erased from the colonial scene of the play, represent the highly racialized problem of origin and identity, as well as the repressed alternative to Prospero's resolutely patriarchal history. Mothers in *The Tempest* are not well remembered. Miranda's unnamed mother and Sycorax constitute not only an alternative but also an implicit threat to patriarchal history, which Prospero recounts immediately after the shipwreck. This is European memory, of dukedoms taken and lost, the history of cultural and racial purity secured by female sexual integrity: "Thy mother was a piece of virtue." Reassured that Miranda has no memory of her own and recollects only her former female attendants "far off, /And rather like a dream." Prospero anxiously proceeds to imprint the history of their race: "I pray thee mark me" (I. ii. 67/87); "Dost thou attend me?" (I. ii.78); "thou attend's not!" (I. ii. 86). The process induces a hypnotic effect: "The strangeness of your story put/ Heaviness in me" (I. ii. 306–7), and by Act III scene i, in conversation with Ferdinand, she can assure that her memory is devoid of maternal imprint; that she can "no woman's face remember" (III. i. 49).

The Tempest is an absolutely male realm, founded on the exile of Sycorax – who invisibly represents indigenous femininity in the colonial situation, and who leaves her traces in a story we hear only from Prospero's perspective, and on the polarization of the mothers: Miranda's "piece of virtue" and Caliban's "wicked dam" (I. ii. 320).[24] Recounting her arrival on the isle, Prospero describes Sycorax with an adjective that is more neutral than the derogatory noun that follows it: Sycorax we are told is "a blue-eyed hag" (I. ii. 269). Editors gloss the term as referring not to the color of Sycorax's eyes – blue as opposed to brown – but to the notion that (empirical evidence to the contrary notwithstanding) the eyelids were thought to go blue during pregnancy. This curious report, compressing physical characteristics that span from her reproductive years to her old age ("hag"), is the most concrete description of Sycorax in the play. In fact, as Leah Marcus has shown, her blue eyes link Sycorax with Athena, with a decidedly Caucasian image of female alterity (Marcus 1996: 5–17). Thus at the very moment when the awesome supernatural power of Sycorax becomes physically substantive, though not, crucially, dramatically embodied, she is summoned up with the image of the face, that unique stamp of personal identity.

Prospero is the only character in the play who tenders a description of Sycorax, although he claims never to have seen her. Sycorax, like her son, is described by Prospero with the vituperative rhetoric of deformity: "The foul witch Sycorax, who with age and envy / Was grown into a hoop" (I. ii. 257–8). Sycorax's body, deformed, decrepit, or monstrously pregnant, remains invisible, alluded to but never directly represented. She is the personification of negative space: "Sycorax, as a symbol of a landscape and a changing human situation, is a memory, an absence, and a silence …"(Paquet 1992: xxii). Deprived now of any access to self-representation, razed from the island's landscape, she has also veered beyond the horizons of visual representation altogether. Less detectable than occlusion, nonrepresentation is inscrutable and unreadable.

Indeed, around Sycorax the lacunae in colonial memory yawns wide. The absence that shrouds Sycorax is such that, intially, my strategy of "filling in" the gaps of colonial memory faltered. For, as Richard Halpern has so acutely observed in the context of American Indians: "[T]he fact remains that the 'repressed' forgotten history remains irreducibly speculative" (Halpern 1994: 289). Despite the enormous conceptual and methodological difficulties here, such moments also offer the opportunity to resist the way in which conventional reading practises reenact the erasures for which they cannot account. In reading cultural erasures, we are compelled to confront what is not, perforce, *present* in the text, or as Halpern puts it, the repressed "cannot be (or at least has not been) definitively produced" (Halpern ibid.).

In the history of Stuart colonialism Irish women are remembered, like Sycorax, by a record of negative perceptions about their political power. As Christopher Highley has argued, "resistance to English expansionism is figured in terms of a monstrous and emasculating Gaelic femininity" (Highley 1997: 112). In a similar vein, William Palmer points out: "[R]acial and gender prejudices intersected as English men fused their images of disorderly women and rebellious Irish men, and blamed Irish women in part for why Ireland was so difficult to govern. The gender prejudices of English men may have been intensified by the fact that women actually did assume active political roles …" (Palmer 1992: 699–712; see also Highley ibid.: 101–3). Rumors about the activities of one such unnamed woman, who claimed to have been born in Spain, were reported to Burghley by John Jonson in 1581: "great murmurs here and secret talk among the common mariners and masters of ships that she has brought over certain money and packets of letters which is to be suspected, and it is to be thought that she is a fit instrument for such a purpose as she can speak as good Spanish as if she had been born in Spain; [and] good Irish and English"(Palmer ibid.: 703). Other women were similarly indicted. Finola, known as the "Dark Daughter" of Turough Liuneach O'Neill, who later became the wife of another Ulster chief,

Hugh O'Donnell, was accused along with her Scottish mother, Lady Agnes Campbell, of being "conveyors of all mischief against the English Pale" (quoted in Palmer ibid.: 703). Palmer points out that while misogyny in the period was widespread, "there does seem to be something excessive about … [English] hostility toward Irish women. They do not seem to have held Scottish or Welsh women in quite as low esteem" (Palmer ibid.: 712).

Remembering the history of colonialism which shaped *The Tempest* involves, then, a reiteration of the overwhelmingly negative and uncannily Prospero-like accounts of Irish women. Nowhere mentioned by the Irish annalists, though very well known in oral tradition, Granuaile (Grace O'Malley, 1530–1603), chief of the seafaring O'Malley clan in county Mayo, paradoxically becomes visible, registered for good or ill on the historical record, in the documents of empire (see John Appleby 1991: 56). In the *Calendar for State Papers*, she is described as "a woman that hath impudently passed the part of womanhood and been a great spoiler, and chief commander and director of thieves and murderers at sea to spoille this province" (quoted in Chambers 1998: 87), a woman who "subdued the whole country from Asgalan in the West … to Ballinrobe" (quoted in Chambers ibid.: 92).[25] A "notorious offender" against the Crown in Ireland, according to the Privy Council yet "famous for her stoutness of courage and person, and for her sundry exploits done by her by sea" (quoted in Chambers ibid.: 85, 95).

In July 1593, accompanied by Sir Murrough – né Doe – O'Flaherty, then over sixty, Granuaile set sail for London for an audience with Elizabeth I, where she was to represent her own interests on her own behalf. In her long battle and negotiation with the English, it is her surprising domestic supremacy that contemporaries focus on, as in Sir Henry Sidney's report of his encounter with Granuaile:

> There came to me also a most famous feminine sea captain called Grany Imallye … she brought with her her husband, for she was as well by sea as by land well more than Mrs Mate with him. He was of the Nether Burkes and now [in 1583] as I hear MackWilliam Euter and called by the nickname Richard in Iron. This was a notorious woman in all the coasts of Ireland. … This woman did Sir Phillip Sydney see and speak withal, he can more at large inform you of her.
>
> (Sir Henry Sidney quoted in Chambers 1998: 85)

The fascination Granuaile exerts, like Prospero's description of

Sycorax, is freighted with a certain libidinal energy. Unlike Granuaile, Sycorax is not, of course, a native of the isle but an immigrant from Algiers, thus bequeathing her son an identity that is hybridized by even more than his contact with Prospero. It is against this complex backdrop that the integrity of European racial identity is set and to which, as we shall see, the sexuality of women posed the supreme threat.

Sixteenth-century English historians of Ireland, aware of the absolute failure of the first colonists to segregate themselves from the native population, stressed the racial purity of English settlers. Richard Stanihurst, in his contribution to Holinshed's *Chronicles*, for instance, commended the refusal of the social elite in the Pale to intermarry with the Irish (Bradshaw 1993: 180). Writing in a direct riposte to such history, Geoffrey Keating stakes his claim to history not only as an objective assessment of the past but also as a defense of Irish hybridity:

> It is not for hatred nor for love of any set of people beyond another, nor at the instigation of anyone, nor with the expectation of obtaining profit from it, that I set forth to write the history of Ireland, but because I deemed it was not fitting that a country so honourable as Ireland, and races so noble as those who have inhabited it, should go into oblivion without mention or narration being left of them: and I think that my estimate in the account I give concerning the Irish ought rather to be accepted, because it is of the Gaels (native Irish) I chiefly treat. Whoever thinks it much I say for them, it is not to be considered that I should deliver judgment through favour, giving them much praise beyond what they have deserved, being myself of the old Galls (foreigners) as regards my origin.
>
> (Keating quoted in Maxwell 1923: 322–3)

Keating defended racial intermingling, a phenomenon that others deplore as degeneration, and used *Eireannaigh* (the Irish) to designate both the Old English and the Gaelic Irish (Bradshaw 1993: 182). Himself descended from the original Anglo-Norman settlers in the twelfth century, Keating, writing with a commitment to Counter-Reformation ideology, thus responds to a long-standing tradition of cultural and racial hostility in this crucial recognition of the stakes of representation, namely that English historiography has assigned the Gaels "into oblivion without mention or narration being left of them" (see Bradshaw ibid.: 180).

What the colonial mnemonic insists on, in contrast to Keating's conception of the validity of hybridity, is the specifically sexual segregation of the truly English from the taint of Gaelicization, that is, assimilation through marriage and other forms of social intercourse, such as habit and language.[26] Sexual commingling threatens to redress the oppressive imbalances of colonial history. Moryson writes approvingly: "For marriage I will only say of the English-Irish that they keep it orderly as in England, save that in respect of the law forbidding them to marry with the mere Irish, the citizens taking wives within their own walls were grown to be all of kindred one with another, and so forced to marry those of near kindred" (Moryson in Falkiner 1904: 317–18). This passage is fraught with contradictions. On the one hand, the English in Ireland are orderly because they keep to themselves. On the other hand, there seems to be an implicit impurity about the inhabitants of the Pale in that they are "English-Irish" rather than simply the English in Ireland. Further, they are tainted because they are incestuous. The image of "taking wives within their own walls" is especially resonant, since the English were segregated from the Gaelic population not merely by the invisible workings of an ideology of racial segregation but by the great defensive bulwark, comprised of banks and ditches, a palisade, guard towers, and castles which separated the Pale from the surrounding community (Collins 1990: 14). When Miranda wonders if Ferdinand is her brother, she does so in a colonial context in which such a suspicion might be all too plausible.

Fear of miscegenation and thence cultural degeneration was so rampant in Ireland that it overwhelmed any concern about inbreeding. Spenser warns against "licentious conversinge with the Irishe or marrying and fosteringe with them" (Gottfried 1949: 117). Fynes Moryson declared:

> the posterities of the English planted in Ireland do each descent grow more and more Irish, in nature, manners and customs, so as we found in the last rebellion divers of the most ancient English families, planted of old in Ireland, to be turned as rude and barbarous as any of the mere Irish lords. Partly because the manners and customs of the mere Irish … of old overtopped the English-Irish in number, and nothing is more natural – yea, necessary – than for the less number to accom-

modate itself to the greater. And especially because the English are naturally inclined to apply themselves to the manners and customs of any foreign nations with whom they live and converse, whereas the mere Irish by nature have singular and obstinate pertinacity in retaining their old manners and customs, so as they could never be drawn, by the laws, gentle government, and free conversation of the English, to any civility in manners or reformation in religion.

(Moryson in Falkiner 1904: 310–11)

In this piece of deft ideological maneuvering, Moryson argues that coercion is necessary because the relation between the English and the Irish is indeed one-sided, and it is the Irish who are at fault in the asymmetry. In contrast, the English generously make concession to the cultural habits of the Irish. He does not, of course, explain what possible impetus the Irish would have to Anglicize themselves.

The marital arrangements of the Irish were notoriously irregular: polygamy was common and divorce very easy, marriages often being for a period of one year (MacLysaght 1950: 48). In 1634 it was found necessary to pass a law to enforce monogamy, and "this was only carried after determined opposition in both Houses, which at that time were composed of Catholics as well as Protestants, and six years after the Bill became law the Lords made an unsuccessful attempt to get it repealed" (MacLysaght ibid.: 49). That there were also charges that the English in Ireland also kept more than one wife indicates that Gaelic sexual practises and marital arrangements often proved more attractive than repugnant. In Ulster:

The King being informed that divers of the Undertakers, especially the Scottish, marry with the Irish, by which they will degenerate and become altogether Irish, His Majesty requires him to restrain all Undertakers from marrying with the Irish, and to call before him [Lord Chichester] all such as have offended herein, and to reprove them severely intil order be taken for their further punishment.

(*CSPI 1611–14*: 482–3)[27]

Arthur Chichester, who planned the plantation, supported the view that marriage with the Irish should be forbidden because "that would be a means to link the Undertakers and their issue together in marriage and affection, and to strengthen them against a common enemy. The English language and customs would thus be presented pure and neat to posterity; and without it he accounted it no good plantation nor any great honour to them to induce people thither" (*CSPI 1611–14*: xvii–xix). A major practical fear caused by intermarriage was the subsequent dilution of English political power. Once the English were connected to one another by marriage, their political, financial, and religious interests came into far clearer alignment.

In *The Tempest* the prospect of sexual desegregation is figured specifically as the threat of rape. The source of racial purity so well primed by Prospero's history lesson is, of course, the female body:

Prospero: Thou most lying slave,
Whom stripes may move, not kindness, I have used thee
Filth as thou art with humane care, and lodged thee
In mine own cell, till thou didst seek to violate the honor of my child.
Caliban: O, ho, O, ho! Would't had been done!
Thou didst prevent me. I had peopled else
This isle with Calibans.

(I. ii. 34–48)

Caliban does not deny the allegation that he tried to rape Miranda. The threat of rape, of course, was to became a standard colonialist trope that thus presented miscegenation as always already an act of sexual violation. In the context of the rabid fear of miscegenation with the Irish, Caliban's apparent guilt warrants, at the very least, a certain skepticism. What is suppressed by Prospero and Miranda's version of history is the reality of colonial desire, here transformed into and demonized as rape:

Even if I were guiltless, I think that because of their evil disposition I would not dare to make it known; that is a part of my great perplexity.

If I were among them I well believe they would accuse me of more offences; all the more is it better not to go near them.

"You yourself like all of them are pleased to praise their crimes. If it should harm you … it is fitting; inciting evil doings is part of your nature. …"

The fearsome English of Ireland would say finally to me: "Your offences are more numerous than all the charges brought". – Who ought to go into their jurisdiction?

(Breatnach 1989: 39–42)

From the perspective deliniated in Cu Chonnacht O Dalaigh's *Poem Before Leaving Aodh Ruadh*, the veracity and justice of the English are highly questionable. Within the colonial dynamic of accusation and denial, guilt becomes inevitable and justice impossible.[28]

The distortions and erasures of the colonial mnemonic require a considerable material investment in an apparently abstract concept of racial purity and the purity of English women. Racialization in Ireland, as elsewhere, was underscored by practises alien to the native culture, especially that of ensuring the transmission of unbroken parcels of property through primogeniture. In contrast, the Irish custom was to divide land among the surviving kin.[29] Sir John Davies opined that Irish inheritance practises, though of a kind with other European societies, were deleterious to the accumulation of wealth:

> Again, in England, and all well-ordered commonweals, men have certain estates in their lands and possessions, and their inheritances descend from father to son, which doth give them encouragement to build, and to plant, and to improve their lands, and to make them better for their posterities … [whereas the Irish] made all their possessions uncertain being shuffled, and changed, and removed so often from one to another, by new elections and partitions; which uncertainty of estates, hath been the true cause of such desolation and barbarism in this land, as the like was never seen in any country that professed the name of Christ.

(Davies quoted in Maxwell 1923: 352, 353)

While the Gaelic social order was often violent and should not be casually idealized, its communitarian tribalism posed an enormous practical obstacle to the imposition of emergent capitalism. That English proto-capitalist ideas of property were alien to the Irish is perhaps evident even in the structure of the Irish language: there is no verb "to have."[30]

Gonzalo's utopian fantasies, transposed from Montaigne, about how he would govern "Had [he] plantation of this isle" (II. i. 142) may refer to the tangible existence of a society adjacent to England in all the disturbing propinquity of Ireland, where there was so little

that comported with English understandings of property, ownership, and government: "And use of service, none; contract, succession,
/ Bourn, bound of land, tilth, vineyard, none" (II. i. 149–50).[31]

These differences in the conceptualization and distribution of
property and power become coded as racial impurity. The discourse
of racial, cultural, and religious purity both naturalized and rationalized the expropriation and reproduction of human and material
resources. Prospero has justified Caliban's enslavement and the di-
vestment of his native terrain on grounds of his allegedly natural
rapacity. That Caliban is confined like an animal, "here you sty
me" (I. ii. 342), resonates with the Irish context, where miscegenation is frequently configured in terms of bestiality; To commingle
with the Irish is to copulate with people who live like animals: "The
custom of these savages is to live as the brute beasts among the
mountains."[32] Rationalization for the appropriation of Irish land
was the idea that the Irish dwelt as beasts, that their practises, such
as seasonal migration with cattle (known as booleying), constituted
something closer to grazing than human habitation:

> like the nomads removing their dwellings, according to the com-
> modity of pastures for their cows, sleep under the canopy of
> Heaven, or in a poor house of clay, or in a cabin made of the
> boughs of trees, and covered with turf, for such are the dwellings
> of the very lords among them. And in such places, they make a
> fire in the midst of the room, and round about it they sleep upon
> the ground, without straw or other thing under them, ... they
> cover their heads and upper parts with their mantles ...
>
> (Moryson quoted in Maxwell 1923: 317–18)

This description bears more than a passing resemblance to the shel-
tering Caliban discovered by Stephano and Trinculo in II. i. Just as
Caliban's dwelling cannot be defined by a building but only by a
place, the hard rock, the Irish were considered to live in the open:
"[T]hese wild Irish are not much unlike to wild beasts," claimed
Fynes Moryson, "in whose caves a beast passing that way might
perhaps find meat, but not without danger to be ill-entertained,
perhaps devoured of his insatiable host" (Moryson quoted in
Maxwell 1923: 318). Conflicting with reports of Irish hospitality:
"If you except the port towns, there are no hotels or lodging houses
to be found in the island. Every traveller sets up in the first house
he meets, and there is provided with whatever he desires,"[33] is the
description of Sir John Davies, who (predictably) feared theft and

Plate 5 W. Holler, *Irish Costumes*. Reproduced by kind permission of the Folger Shakespeare Library.

rapacity: "No man could enjoy his life, his wife, his lands or goods in safety if a mightier man than himself had an appetite to take the same from him. Wherein they were little better than cannibals" (quoted in Baker 1997a: 93).

English attacks on Irish habits of dress also correspond with the representation of Caliban as misshapen and inhuman. While indigenous peoples of the New World were marked by their undress, by their nakedness, rather than by the peculiarity of their clothing, the Irish look like beasts "over all mantles or shaggy rugs. … [T]hey clothe themselves, according to their habit, with tight trousers, and short loose coats of very coarse goats' hair. They cover themselves with mantas (blankets) and wear their hair down to their eyes" (William Camden quoted in Maxwell 1923: 320). As crypto-civilized beings, the Irish and Caliban exert the fascination required to impose the discipline of colonial mores: "The inhabitants of cities and corporate towns shall wear no mantles … Irish coats, or great shirts, nor suffer their hair to grow to glib, but to wear clerks gowns, jackets, jerkins, and some civil garments" (Maxwell 1923: 167).

When the storm comes, Caliban covers himself with his cloak only to have Trinculo and Stephano come along to gape at his alleged monstrosity and "creep under his gabardine" (II. ii. 37). In doing so, the lower orders of Europe show their affinity with Caliban's alleged bestiality. Michael Neill has pointed out that, despite a profound anxiety about mantles, caused by a belief in their ability to make the Irish invisible and therefore impervious to the disciplinary colonizing gaze, mantles became an item of fashion in England, and thus attest to the fascination and repulsion simultaneously exerted by the vestmentary aspects of alterity. In the Rainbow Portrait of the queen, Neill contends, Elizabeth appropriates the mantle and reverses the trope of invisibility for the purposes of discipline by posing in a cloak covered with eyes (Neill 1994b: 31). Just such a gesture of appropriation becomes visible when Prospero renounces his magic. He divests himself of his mantle of power, "his magic robes," which have been, like the queen's cloak, imbued with the apparatus of surveillance. But Prospero's mantle differs from Elizabeth's in that it is the sign that he both appropriated native power and that disturbingly, in doing so, he himself, unlike Elizabeth, did not fully retain his civility but actually "went native": "Fetch me the hat and rapier in my cell: / I will discase me, and myself present / As I was sometime in Milan" (V. i. 84–6). Act V, scene i requires an elaborate transformation of a degenerate Prospero *back* into a civil subject.

"If we consider the nature of the Irish customs," Sir John Davies expounds, "we shall find that the people which doth use them, must of necessity be enemies to all good government ... and bring barbarism and desolation upon the richest and most fruitful land of the world" (Davies quoted in Maxwell 1923: 351–2). This logic, the ideological motor of social and sexual segregation, culminated in the idea of the erasure not just of indigenous history and cultural memory but of the indigenous inhabitants altogether. Depopulation frequently proved an impractical colonial fantasy. Sir Arthur Chichester recognized fundamental flaws in such an extremist plan to dispossess and remove "the great mass of the common people": "If the natives be removed according to the project, it will be impossible for the undertakers to perform their work, for when the natives are gone there will be neither victuals nor carriage within twenty miles and in some counties more" (*CSPI 1611–14*: 357). Torn between the expropriation of Irish labor on the one hand and Irish resources on the other, English policy toward Ireland vacillated between the objectives of annihilation and subjection.

Depopulation might be successfully accomplished by starvation, for example, as Spenser's *Vuew* pointed out, and this tactic had been tried in Munster. Though it must be noted that Spenser, like the other colonists, also paid lip service to humanist principles of reformation – a noble ideology designed to fail – other policy measures were then assayed: "The English and Scottish Undertakers were forbidden to have Irish tenants; in recollection, according to Sir Arthur Chichester, of the Munster plantation, where it was thought good policy to scatter and divide the Irish amongst the English Undertakers, hoping that by cohabitation they would become civilized; but instead of imitating the Undertakers, they scorned them, envied them, and longed to be masters of what they possessed" (*CSPI 1611–14*: xviii).[34]

Irish masters in the Gaelic system, might have supremely obedient servants. Sir John Harington observed at the household of Hugh O'Neill, where he read from his translation of Ariosto's *Orlando Furioso* and gave a copy to O'Neill's sons: "His guard, for the most part, were beardless boys without shirts; who in the frost, wade as familiarly through rivers as water spaniels. With what charm such a master makes them love him I know not, but if he bid come, they come; if go, they do go; if he say they do this, they do it ..." (*CSPI 1611–14*: xviii). It was not, one must surmise, hierarchy intrinsic to the master–servant relationship in general, but colonial masters in particular that were the cause of Irish rancor. Thus the problem of the Irish became not one of their inability to adopt civil ways but of the necessity to secure them in a position of malleable servitude to English masters unable to "charm" them, as Prospero coercively charms Ariel by having him recount the history of the isle.

Sexual and social segregation exacerbated rather than allayed the friction between the Irish and the English. In the scene in which Caliban is accused of rape in *The Tempest* and amid the flurry of mutual recrimination, we glean that Caliban was once a member of Prospero's household "lodged … / In mine own cell, till thou didst seek to violate the honor of my child" (I. ii. 341–2). *The Tempest* gives us a sense that Caliban has, in violation of orders against social segregation, enjoyed not only domestic proximity with Prospero and Miranda but also familial intimacy.[35] If Caliban was more than a servant, what status did Caliban actually have in Prospero's household? There are a number of suggestive cultural possibilities. One such possibility is that Caliban has the status of a foster child. Fostering was a practise that caused consternation and alarm among the English in Ireland, once again because it threatened English systems of inheritance, as Sir John Davies notes:

> [T]here were two other customs proper and peculiar to the Irishry … the one was fostering, the other gossiped both which have ever been of greater estimation among this people, than with any other nation in the Christian world. … They put away their children to fosterers: the potent and rich men selling, the meaner sort buying the alterage [fostering or rearing] of their children; and the reason is, because in the opinion of this people, fostering hath always been a stronger alliance than blood, and the foster children do love and are beloved of their foster fathers and their sept, more than their own natural parents and kindred. … Such a general custom in a Kingdom giving, and taking children to foster, making such a firm alliance as it doth in Ireland, was never seen or heard of, in any other country of the world besides.
>
> (Davies quoted in Maxwell 1923: 353–4)

Fostering and prestation had thus been an instrument of Gaelicization. According to Spenser, the taking of Irish milk and the simultaneous acquisition of Irish speech leads to the foster child in some sense literally becoming Irish (Spenser 1997: 87). Ireland thus figures as a powerful, quasi-magical maternal influence, who, like Sycorax, becomes an immensely powerful and symbolic rather than a literal, biological agent of maternity. The English, however, took Irish children from noble families in the hopes of Anglicizing them. Thomas Fleming, "a gent of thenglish [*sic*] Pale," was a foster brother to Turlough Luineach O'Neill. This reverse maneuver didn't always work: Hugh O'Neill, for instance, was fluent in English language and habits, having been brought up with the Sidneys, and yet proved well capable of temporizing with and manipulating the English (Fumerton 1991: 478).[36] Similarly, Tibbot-na-Long of the Burke's (Theobald of the Ships) was fostered in Ireland by the brother of the governor of Connaught, whom Elizabeth described as "one that hath been brought up civilly with your brother and can speak English" (Chambers 1988: 133). That Tibbot's status was more that of hostage than adopted child might be attested by the fact that he was subsequently arrested by his foster uncle for supporting the Ulster chieftains. Thus fostering was an Irish practise unsuccessfully appropriated by the English.

A stronger possibility in terms of Prospero's cultural contact than having been involved in the practise of fostering is the sense that his life has diverged from the past he narrates. *The Tempest* begins with Prospero's history, and it is a history, that as we have seen, insists on racial purity, continually striving to banish to the sphere of radical alterity the culture of hybridity so powerfully manifested in Caliban's eloquence. Prospero says he came to the island with Miranda and that Caliban taught him how to survive. With a perverse sense of symmetry, Prospero then took Caliban as his slave, and he and Miranda taught their slave language. Miranda, however, betrays a telling uncertainty about her father's past, an uncertainty that sounds like the uncanny echo of repressed memory: "Sir, are you not my father?" Yet they have agreed between them, father and daughter, to a collective amnesia, "more to know / did never meddle with my thoughts" (I. ii. 212), which seems to best suit Prospero's emotional block about the past: "You have often / Begun to tell me what I am, but stopped … / Concluding, 'Stay, not yet'" (I. ii. 336). Miranda's complicity in Prospero's willful forgetfulness is telling: "I not rememb'ring how I cried out then/ Will cry o'er it again" (I. ii. 1345).

As the description of Irish corpses with tails at Cashel demonstrates, the colonial memory tells compelling lies. Stephen Orgel points out: "Sycorax died some time before Prospero's arrival; Prospero never saw her, and everything he knows about her he has learned from Ariel. Nevertheless, she is insistently present in his memory –

far more present than his own wife" (Orgel 1987: 19–20).[37] Of course,
Sycorax is a threat to Prospero in that she is the basis of Caliban's
all-too-solid claim to sovereignty of the island. Yet Prospero's astonishing affinity with Sycorax as a fellow-sorcerer far exceeds this
motivation for his obsession (Orgel 1987: 212). This affinity bears
all the characteristics of what Robert Young has called "colonial
desire," for which Prospero's orthodox history about Sycorax arriv-
ing pregnant on an uninhabited isle leaves no room. Colonial desire,
what Prospero's history has forgotten, is the sexually overcharged
production of racial difference that simultaneously prohibits and
provokes erotic contact with the other.

The intensity of Prospero's colonial desire for the unrepresentable
Sycorax and his venomous paternalism in relation to Caliban expose the possibility that Caliban might be the misshapen progeny
of Prospero himself.

> These three have robb'd me; and this demi-devil –
> For he's a bastard one – had plotted with them
> To take my life. Two of these fellows you
> Must know and own; this thing of darkness I
> Acknowledge mine.
>
> (V. i. 271–6)

Prospero's claim that Caliban was fathered by Satan obscures the
fact that "this thing of darkness I / Acknowledge mine" connotes
an admission of paternity.[38] Oddly, Prospero's assertion that Caliban
is his is never read by critics as an admission of paternity, whereas
the fact that Caliban fails to deny the charge of attempted rape is
always read as a clear confession to it. As Orgel points out, "we
have no way of distinguishing the facts about Caliban and Sycorax
from Prospero's invective about them" (Orgel 1986: 55), any more
than we have a way of distinguishing the facts about the Irish from
racist English invective about them. My point is not so much the
bald assertion that Caliban *is* Prospero's son but that Shakespeare's
plot is deliberately vague and thus deliberately inclusive about "the
facts" of the sexual and seignorial relationships on the island. The
master–servant relationship in the colonial situation, which in this
case has persisted some fourteen years, is so aberrant that it forces
this repressed reading to the surface, a reading that clearly does not
pertain to the far more straightforward relation between Antonio
and his servants – one of knowing and owning: "Two of these fel-
lows you / Must know and own." As witchcraft accusations and

records of village turmoil amply demonstrate, people in early modern England regularly slandered others with such suggestions about the paternity of illegitimate offspring, not so unreasonable a proposition in a scheme of thought where such violations of order were unequivocally aligned with the forces of darkness. Caliban, a dispossessed bastard, is the monstrous obverse of the lost, legitimate child of the other late plays and the comedies. He is, as Frances Dolan notes, a "dangerous familiar," who threatens domestic as well as colonial rebellion (Dolan 1994: 60–71).[39] In the Irish context Prospero's charge of bastardy has particular resonance. O'Neill was advanced to the earldom of Tyrone on the basis of his being the illegitimate son of Turlough Luineach; and a further consequence of instigating legal reforms, most persuasively argued by Davies, is that Irish landlords, products of ostensibly irregular marital practises, could be dispossessed for being bastards.

The idea that Prospero could be Caliban's father, however, more than merely a plausible suggestion within the structure of colonial encounter, is the logical, though repressed, destination of that encounter. In the notoriously propagandistic verse tract, *The Image of Ireland*, John Derricke claims that the offspring of intermarriages are beasts in human guise, "Transformed now and then: / From Bores to beares, and yet sometyme, / resemblying honest men" (Harington in Maxwell 1923: 33–89). Similarly, Spenser, who insists that Irish women are inherently repugnant and yet feels it necessary to deter English men from sexual congress with them, argues: "How cane suche matchinge but bring forthe an evil race seinge that Comonlye the Childe taketh the moste of his nature of the mother besides speache, manners, inclynacion … for by them are firste framed and fashioned soe as what they receave once from them they will hardly ever after forgoe" (Spenser 1997: 87). Such a match would certainly explain Caliban's allegedly obstinate nature as well as his apparently grotesque physiognomy. For hybridity becomes mongrelity in Caliban. "Shallow monster, weak monster, credulous monster, most perfidious and drunken monster, puppyheaded monster, scurvy monster, abominable monster, ridiculous monster, howling monster, brave monster, ignorant monster, lost monster, poor monster, servant monster, lieutenant monster", "[A] freckled whelp," and "mooncalf" (see Vaughan and Vaughan 1991: 14; and Hulme 1992: 114). In the array of racist epithets, the latter at least provides some variety among the otherwise monotonous vicious and derogatory and intimates a corpselike grotesquerie, being, according to Pliny,

THE IRISH CALIBAN.
(*Not to be Confounded with the True Irishman.*)
Caliban.—THIS ISLAND'S MINE . . . WHICH THOU TAK'ST FROM ME.—Tempest, *Act* 1, *sc* 2.

Plate 6 "The Irish Caliban." Uncataloged black box, Folger Shakespeare Library. Reproduced by kind permission of the Folger Library.

"a lumpe of flesh without shape, without life, … Howbeit, a kind of moving it hath" (see Vaughan and Vaughan 1991: 15).[40]

That memory and representation are the constitutive powers of history becomes vividly apparent when we compare Caliban, "a salvage [*sic*] and deformed slave," with Othello. The latter's memory, his control of his own history from slave to warrior, is the source of both his erotic and military prowess, "the dangers I have passed."

Othello has a history of his passage into civilization – a journey that allows him, by virtue of fully developed powers of adult recollection, a historicized consciousness. In contrast, Caliban has acquired language and therefore memory from Prospero, and his tender recollections, the most moving lines in the play, are deeply reminiscent of those of infant intimacy with a parent:

> Thou strok'st me and made much of me; wouldst give
>   me
> Water with berries in't; and teach me how
> To name the bigger light, and how the less,
> That burn by day and night:, … And then I loved
>   thee.
>
> (I. ii. 332–6)

When Caliban says he showed Prospero "all the qualities o'th'isle, / The fresh springs, brine pits, barren place and fertile" (I. ii. 389), he suggests territorial as much as temporal priority, the sense of a child showing his discoveries to a parent. While this passage fits a scheme of colonists and childlike natives, it is possible to put pressure on this reading to reveal the repressed sexual and familial relations that constitute colonial paternalism. Whether literally and biologically or simply metaphorically and culturally, Caliban is the miscegenated product of colonial relations on the island.

Ireland, I have argued, might be understood as the sublimated context for colonial relations in *The Tempest*, whose presence can be figured in the dense imprint of memory. Indeed, the negative space it occupies – the bare isle – while indiscernible in the field of the visible, can be felt only in the heavy texture of impressions left by memory and music. Finally, the project of colonization proves unsuccessful on Prospero's island, and he must go home, *sans* cloak, staff, and all the things that formerly gave him power. The power he has left, however, is that of having history on his side:

> No more yet of this:
> For 'tis a chronicle of day by day,
> Nor a relation for a breakfast, nor
> Befitting this first meeting.
>
> (V. i. 162–6)

Nostalgically, he is eager to entertain the tempest-tossed visitors with "the story of my life, / And the particular accidents gone by" (V. i. 304–5). Prospero has never relinquished his power to tell history, and the play ends, appropriately, with him preparing to repeat his monologue, this time without interruption: "Please you, draw near" (V. i. 318). In Prospero's "Irish memories" Caliban has acquired a confabulatory tail/tale.[41]

5
What is an audience?

William Alabaster's *Roxana*, performed at Cambridge in 1592 (first published in 1632), was a lurid revenge tale crammed with acts of violence and atrocity ranging from cannibalism to murder. Perhaps most shocking of all, the eponymous heroine, Roxana, is forced to kill her own children and is tortured to death on stage. The play was a rip-roaring success, its author described in *The History of the Worthies of England* by Thomas Fuller as

> A most rare Poet as any our Age or Nation hath produced: witnesse his tragedy of *Roxana* admirably acted in that Colledge [Trinity], and so *pathetically;* that a Gentlewoman present thereat (Reader I had it from an Author whose credit it is sin with me to suspect), at the hearing of the last words thereof, *sequar, sequar,* so *hideously* pronounced, fell distracted and never after fully recovered her senses.
>
> (Fuller 1662: I. ii 3v, emphasis added)

Although both women and townspeople did indeed attend Latin performances at the universities along with the all-male faculty and student body, Fuller's account has all the features of an apocryphal tale, especially the parenthetical gesture of authenticity: "I had it from an Author whose credit it is sin with me to suspect." However, whether the Cambridge gentlewoman exists merely as a rhetorical trope or as a real person, what is significant here is that she is used

Plate 7 William Alabaster, *Roxana*, 1632. Frontispiece and title page. Reproduced by permission of the Syndics of Cambridge University Library.

as a figure to demonstrate the violent potency of mimetic operations to which only men, and in this case only relatively privileged men, had access.

In the all-male context of the university, the woman's condition is conspicuously erotic. Overpowered by emotions induced by dramatic spectacle, the figure of the "distracted" gentlewoman becomes a vividly gendered and, crucially, class-marked index not of the play's ineffectiveness but of its success.[1] Fuller attributes the play's triumph to the performers almost as much as to the playwright: the woman is driven to insanity by "pathetic" and "hideous" acting. Unusually, we can glean some idea of the style of performance (in other words, its "hideous," or histrionic, pronouncement) that is alleged to have driven the woman at Trinity out of her senses. In his prefatory material to the printed version of the play, Alabaster pleads for the lines to be declaimed in a ranting, grandiose, and inflated manner: "*cum spuma soni, ut solent poetae tragoedias suas, quia in grandius quodammodo excoluntur, quae cumampulla oris leguntur* (... with a foaming sound, in the manner in which poets are accustomed to recite their tragedies, because works which are read in a bombastic voice are somehow brought to a more grand style)" (quoted in Binns 1990: 132). If this note is any indication of the actual performance, the traumatized female spectator did not lose her wits in the face of disturbingly realistic horror. Rather, a student in drag executing his role with blatant artifice and in a histrionic manner is the source of her perturbation. The exaggerated aesthetic *effects* of theatrical representation become visible as *affect* in the figure of the overwrought gentlewoman. She serves as the object of theatrical reception who is "worked over" by the performance, and her changed psychological condition is the means whereby mimetic powers of transformation are proven upon and extended into the audience. Rather surprisingly, perhaps, there is no suggestion in Fuller's account that the Cambridge gentlewoman either did not understand the nature of dramatic spectacle or the Latin in which it was performed. On the contrary, it is precisely her comprehension of the final, "hideous" pronouncement that precipitates her distraction.

Fuller voices an understanding of spectatorship whose relation to the historical circumstances of women in the audience is no less significant in perhaps partaking more of fiction than fact. For just as "the audience" is a construct that bears upon – though it is not identical with – the heterogeneous playgoers who attended performances at venues as diverse as the court, the university, the public theatre, the private theatre, the inns of court, and even makeshift locations in the provinces, the Cambridge spectator is not so much a person as a cultural phenomena crucially located at the intersection of gender and class. Indeed, Fuller's account bespeaks the conceptual dimension of spectatorship, which is the subject of this chapter.

Specifically, I am concerned to address the cultural construction of particular groups of spectators – women (especially gentlewomen) and the lower orders – and their relation to theatrical mimesis on the one hand and to political representation on the other. I will argue that women and lower-class men are defined in relation to each other and are granted particular contrasting affects – hypersensibility and hyposensibility respectively – that remove them from the privileged category of upper-class male response.

Finally, I will demonstrate my case for the intersection between gender and class in early modern concepts of spectatorship in the specific context of *A Midsummer Night's Dream*. Here the mechanicals deform (denaturalize as well as bungle) mimetic operations with the marks of their labor "conned with cruel pain" (V. i. 80) and thereby mark their own exclusion from dramatic representation. Focused on the gendered division of theatrical labor (male performance versus female spectatorship) and in terror about frightening "the ladies" (I. ii. 68) the mechanicals, who have "never laboured in their minds till now" (V. i. 73) are oblivious to the division of intellectual and manual labor which their performance makes painfully and comically visible.[2] The play celebrates the inclusiveness of the theatrical experience, which, at its most powerful, confounds even fundamental distinctions between actors and audience, performance and perception, even as it rehearses theatrical divisions of labor and the fantasy of feminine perception possessed by all-male mimesis.

Women re/acting

Accounts of their reactions in the playhouse charge that women and, notably, always women of some social standing, far from being merely passive consumers of events portrayed before them, *produce* affect to such an excessive extent that they themselves become spectacles to rival the plays. Thomas Heywood in *An Apology for Actors* records two incidents where bourgeois women confess to murder after seeing a dramatic enactment of crimes alarmingly similar to their own. In the first "a towneswoman (till then of good estimation and report) ... suddenly skritched and cryd out Oh my husband, my husband! I see the ghost of my husband fiercely threatning and menacing me" while in the second "a woman of great gravity" becomes "strangely amazed" and "with a distracted & troubled braine oft sighed out these words: Oh my husband, my husband!" (quoted in Rackin 1996: 34; see also Armstrong 1996: 216–37). In contrast, women who neither lost their senses nor became besieged with paroxysms of guilt during performances were thought nonetheless to be morally as well as psychologically vulnerable in the theatre:

> Credite me, there can be found no stronger engine to batter the honestie as wel of wedded wiues, as the chastitie of vnmarried maides and widowes, than are the hearing of common plaies. ... insomuch that it is a miracle, if there be fou[n]d anie either woman, or maide, which with these spectacles of strange lust, is not oftentimes inflamed euen vnto furie.
>
> (Munday quoted in Cook 1981: 157–8)

Here, women's pleasure in the theatre is construed as sexual receptivity, as a function of her impressionable nature rather than her perceptual acuity.

Much of the attention paid to female spectatorship as a distinct phenomenon stems from the pervasive belief that women in general (not just drabs, doxies, trulls, and harlots) go to the theatre with lewd intent, and even those who do not may still become the hapless targets of men. Anthony Munday reports:

> Alas, saie they to their familiar by them, Gentlewoman, is it not pittie this passioned louer should be so martyred. And if he find her inclining to foolish pittie, as commonlie such women are, then he applies the matter to himselfe, and saies that he is likewise caried awaie with the liking of her; crauing that pittie to be extended vp[on] him, as she seemed to showe toward the afflicted amorous stager.
>
> (Munday quoted in Cook 1981: 157)

Though there remains an important distinction between the female spectator who is overpowered by her desires and emotions in the theatre and the naive spectator who takes mimesis literally, Munday's female spectator accepts her would-be seducer as an approximation of the martyred lover on the stage.[3] Thomas May's *The Heir* (1620) reports female playgoers response (again, with appropriately willing suspension of disbelief) to Burbage's great performances:

> Ladies in the boxes
> Kept time with sighs, and teares to his sad accents
> As had he truely been the man he seem'd.
>
> (May quoted in Gurr 1987: 44)

The range of emotional reactions to drama included sighs, tears, psychological trauma, and guilty confessions, all of which were recorded as specifically female. Even the production of affect in men was, as Phyllis Rackin has argued, insistently characterized as feminine.[4] In a theatre where (some) men act and women (over)react, women become both hypervisible and exemplary spectators – THE audience – as men do not by virtue of being represented onstage as well as in the auditorium. This produces a heavily gender-coded dichotomy between performance and perception. The cultural construction of women as exemplary spectators simultaneously incorporates the audience as feminine and allows femininity to instigate crucial problems, practical as well as philosophical, in both the performative and perceptual dimensions of mimesis. Overendowed with affect, then, women figure the general human susceptibility to the operations of mimesis.[5]

Plebeian spectators

The female spectator is the primary but not the only object of my analysis. She cannot be understood in isolation because she is constructed only in relation to that other hypervisible, marked category of spectatorship, the plebeian audience (see Mayne 1993: 33). In fact, the oversensitive citizen-gentlewoman serves as a figure for the culture's ideal of spectatorship, and her antithesis is the "barren" spectator (*Hamlet*, III. ii. 41), the young apprentice or "the ruder hanicrafts seruant." The barrenness of plebeian men contrasts the excessive production of sexualized affect associated with the female spectator. Indeed, it is *in definitive contrast to women* that the blunted sensibilities, uncouth behavior, and allegedly diminished intellectual capacities of plebeian spectators serve to insulate them from rather than expose them to mimetic power. These conceptual categories are thus irreducibly distinct but contiguous.

While we have no way of knowing about the actual processes of aesthetic cognition belonging to this group, "barren" spectators are not necessarily naive. Indeed, nowhere in the records of early modern drama does the naive spectator constitute a specific spectatorial identity (Thomson 1996: 96–104), even though the generally naive mechanicals of *A Midsummer Night's Dream* attribute naive spectatorship to women. Nor does the category of barren spectatorship seem to include plebeian women; rather it completely subsumes those applewives, fishwives, and other female playgoers about whom we know so little.

These "barren" members of the audience are associated with a disparaged anal eroticism: "the *Foeces*, or grounds of your people, that sit in the oblique caves and wedges of your house, your sinfull six-penny Mechanicks" (Dekker, *If This Be not a Good Play*, quoted in Cook 1981: 217). However, unlike either women or the disruptive aristocratic spectators we see in *Love's Labour's Lost* or *A Midsummer Night's Dream*, when "the rude raskall rabble" disrupted performances, they did not do so in response to what they had seen onstage. Their disruptive behavior always constituted *action* rather than *reaction* and, more than anything, expressed a resistance to theatrical performance, if not a resolute insensibility to mimesis as well as the exercise of direct and coercive control over theatrical performance:

> if it be on Holy dayes, when Saylers, Water-men, Shoomakers, Butchers and Apprentices are at leisure, then it is good policy to amaze those violent spirits, with some tearing Tragaedy … the spectators frequently mounting the stage, and making a more bloody Catastrophe amongst themselves, then the Players did. I have known upon one of these *Festivals*, but especially at *Shrove-tide*, where the Players have been appointed, notwithstanding their bils to the contrary, to act what the major part of the company had a mind to: sometimes *Tamerlane*, sometimes *Jugurth*, sometimes the Jew of *Malta*, and sometimes parts of all these, and at last, none of the three taking, they were forc'd to undresse and put off their Tragick habits, and conclude the day with the merry milk-maides. And unless this were done, and the popular humour satisfied, as sometimes it so fortun'd, that the Players were refractory; the Benches, the tiles, the laths, the stones, Oranges, Apples, Nuts, flew about most liberally, and as there were Mechanicks of all professions, who fell every one to his owne trade, and dissolved a house in and instant, and made a ruine of a stately Fabrick.
>
> (Edmund Gayton quoted in Cook 1981: 227; Gurr 1992: 225)

Initial attempts to placate these vulgar spectators involve "tearing Tragaedy," bombastic Marlovian rhetoric, precisely the type of performance alleged to have driven women to insanity. In this, lower-class male spectators constitute the obdurate, impervious antithesis of the impressionable, receptive female spectator. While the aristocratic female spectator is understood as psychologically, emotionally, and morally vulnerable to the powers of mimesis as a function of what was believed to be her physiological impressionability, lower-class male spectators are aligned not with affective production and sexual (re)production but, as we have seen, with the degraded functions of defecation, "the *Foeces*, or grounds of your people," and represent the potentially torrential eliminations of the social body.

A Midsummer Night's Dream

With "take your places, ladies" (V. i. 84) in *A Midsummer Night's Dream*, Theseus commands the women to position themselves in the audience for the mechanicals' entertainment. The lines incorporate a stage direction and specify the ladies in a way that may even suggest that this small audience, though close enough to talk, is nonetheless gender segregated. Alternatively, Theseus's direction may signal that the ladies seat themselves while the men stand, or may indicate any number of other possibilities for the physical arrangement of the actors.[6] Whatever blocking cue is imparted by the line, Theseus's words mark in literal terms what the play elsewhere explores in conceptual ones, namely, the place of the women in relation to dramatic spectacle. The duke's instruction may even serve to remind his audience of possible correlations between theatre architecture and gender, with primarily men in the yard ("groundlings" and "six-penny Mechanics") and women perhaps confined to the seated galleries.

Certainly, however, when Theseus singles out the women, his attention to them connotes an idea that is already in cultural circulation, that is, that theatre, allegedly a site of women's intense and often specifically erotic pleasure is also a place where women in particular are subject to what antitheatrical pamphleteers such as Stephen Gosson regarded as "a kind of rape of the mind, a 'ravishing' of the senses" (Gosson quoted in Levine 1996: 210).[7] For example, when William Gager argued that "no hurt could come to any by the passions that were moved in your plays," Puritan academic John Rainolds reminded him: "your generall proposition do faule in the wemen" (Rainolds quoted in Binns 1974: 110–20, esp. 113). If dramatic representation is essentially the power men have over women – in Quince's telling definition the power "to disfigure, or to present" (III. i. 56–7) – then dramatic enactment becomes a kind of violent misrepresentation directed at women.

In the context of the exemplary violence that Laura Levine has argued is shown toward women in the play, the solicitous concern of the lower orders about offending female sensibilities provides a grotesque parody of the cultural postulate that women are ravishable either on grounds of cognitive delicacy or constitutional fragility. They have chosen, after all, a spectacle that seems calculated to fright rather than delight, a play about a woman who is pursued by a "grizzly beast" (V. i. 138). "[L]adies," or "Fair ladies, I would wish you," or "I would request you," or "I would entreat you not to fear, nor to tremble" (III. i. 36–8).[8] The ironies of the workmen's sensibilities about the female audience surface in particular when we witness the play's central spectacle of female sexual appetite, one whose overtly bestial eroticism, as Bruce Boehrer has argued, "comes as close to enacted sexual intercourse as any scene in Shakespearean comedy" (Boehrer 1994: 132). Titania's liaison with Bottom offers an ironic commentary on the notion that "There are things in this comedy of Pyramus and Thisbe that will never please ... which the ladies cannot abide" (III. i. 8–10). A possible source for Shakespeare's parody of tragic love drama is the manuscript version of Thomas Moffett's unintentionally hilarious rendition of the story in *The Silkwormes and Their Flies*.[9] Moffett casts silkworms in the romantic roles of Pyramis and Thisbe, whose plights he imagines will elicit compassion from his women readers. Moreover, Moffett proposes that women's pleasure in raising silkworms will be enhanced by the "hurring" and the "churring" of silkworms acting out "hot *Priapus* loue" (Moffett 1599: L1). Such quasi-pornographic speculation about the production of female desire and affect correlates with the notion that what should, ostensibly, terrify Titania is comically and pornographically displayed as at some level what she really wants.

The fact that Bottom, even in his metamorphosed condition, is hardly a figure to inspire terror places the monstrosity of this union firmly with Titania, in whom the play rehearses the problem of both *female* perception and performance. Titania's enchantment at the hands of Puck and Oberon ("with the juice of this I'll streak her eyes, / And make her full of hateful fantasies" (II. i. 257–8)), often dramatized so as to make her reminiscent of an amorous inebriate, offers a vivid instance of the problem of disorderly spectatorship more generally. She is making a spectacle of herself, which, as Mary Russo points out in her discussion of the female grotesque, has to do with "a kind of inadvertency and loss of boundaries" (Russo 1997: 318). While Titania as *Venus Vulgaris*, "aroused by Bottom's 'beastliness,' " may offer Bottom, the male spectator who watches her, "a reflection and a presentiment of the Celestial Venus," and certainly events in the bower ultimately exalt him to the status of visionary, these same events are clearly intended by Oberon only to humiliate Titania (Kott 1987: 39, 38).

The degradation of an aristocratic woman contrasts sharply with, for instance, a citizen comedy of the period, Thomas Heywood's *The Wise Woman of Hogsdon*. Jean Howard points out, "This play's climactic scene presents the highly entertaining spectacle of a man observed, manipulated, and humiliated by the women he has tried to wrong. And this male is ultimately made subject to the desire of the woman who has most aggressively and transgressively sought him" (Howard 1994: 90). No doubt citizens' wives, applewives, and fishwives identified with Heywood's female characters and enjoyed a spectacle of female power, but those same women might equally have enjoyed the spectacle of the humiliation of an aristocratic woman, which Leonard Tennenhouse has shown to be a central ingredient of Elizabethan drama (Tennenhouse 1989: 77–97).

Titania's gross desires (both repellent and exaggerated) overspill the boundaries of feminine decorum. Bottom's diminutive phallic implements, his "cock" and "quill" (III. i. 118,121) now become exaggerated and perhaps enlarged by Titania's attention.

> Sleep thou, and I will wind thee in my arms.
> Fairies, be gone, and be always away.
> So doth the woodbine the sweet honeysuckle
> Gently entwist; the female ivy so
> Enrings the barky fingers of the elm.
>   (IV. i. 39–43)

In this sexually explicit imagery the play's running joke about Bottom's penis (his "barky finger") continues. That Bottom possesses certain bestial sexual features has already been established when Pyramus's fidelity is compared to that of a horse: "As true as truest horse that yet would never tire" (III. i. 90). The bawdy joke is that "never tire" here refers to an infinitely sustainable erection.[10] The equine connotation implies a phallic disproportion that is not so much a sign of power or hypervirility as one of comic monstrosity, which in relation to Bottom, whose very name insists upon his nether parts, connotes the fecal phallus. It is with this "barky" (rough) phallus that Titania, taking the sexual initiative, "enrings" (penetrates) herself.[11] We may infer, then, particularly since Bottom's metamorphosis alludes to the scandalous liaison in William

Adlington's translation of Lucius Apuleius's *The Golden Ass* (1566), that in the process of his satyr-like transformation, Bottom's penis has been enlarged, either in fact or in Titania's fancy, in comic proportion with his ears. Love, after all, "looks not with the eyes, but with the mind" (I. i. 234). The purported hyperphallicity of men who, whether by virtue of race (as in the case of Othello as "barbary horse") class, or physical deformity, constitute unsuitable sexual partners and the equation of such liaisons with both anality and bestiality are culturally pervasive notions resonant in Puck's gloating commentary on Titania's misplaced desire: "My mistress with a monster is in love" (III. ii. 6).

In Book X of *The Golden Ass*, an Athenian matron is, in an archetypal fantasy about female receptivity, and despite anatomical incommensurability, penetrated by an ass. There is no uncertainty here about how to delight the ladies. Phallic hypertrophy is the sexual fantasy projected onto women:

> Then she put off all her Garments to her naked skinne, and taking the Lampe that stood next to her, began to annoint all her body with balme, and mine likewise, but especially my nose, which done, she kissed me, not as they accustome to doe at the stewes, or in brothell houses, or in the Curtiant Schooles for gaine of money, but purely, sincerely, and with great affection, casting out these and like loving words: Thou art he whom I love, thou art he whom I onely desire, without thee I cannot live … Then she tooke me by the halter and cast me downe upon the bed, which was nothing strange unto me, considering that she was so beautifull a Matron and I so wel boldened out with wine, and perfumed with balme, whereby I was readily prepared for the purpose: But nothing grieved me so much as to think, how I should with my huge and great legs imbrace so faire a Matron, or how I should touch her fine, dainty, and silken skinne, with my hard hoofes, or how it was possible to kisse her soft, pretty and ruddy lips, with my monstrous mouth and stony teeth, or how she, who was young and tender, could be able to receive me. … she eftsoones imbraced my body round about, and had her pleasure with me, whereby I thought the mother of Minotarus did not causelesse quench her inordinate desire with a Bull.
>
> (Apuleius 1893 [1566]: 219–29)

The interest in female pain, the woman's rupture by the enlarged phallic object, presents itself as a concern for female pleasure, a concern that is completely belied by ensuing events. When word of his exploits reaches Lucius's master, the master plans to "shew before the face of all the people, what I could doe." Because of her elevated class status, the spectacle cannot be staged with the matron, so "at length they obtained for money a poore woman, which was condemned to be eaten of wilde beasts, with whom I should openly have to doe" (Apuleius 1893 [1566]: 219).

> But I, beside the shame to commit this horrible fact, and to pollute my body with this wicked harlot did greatly feare the danger of death: for I thought in my selfe, that when she and I were together, the savage beast appointed to devoure the woman, was not so instructed and taught, or would so temper his greedinesse, as that hee would teare her in peeces lying under mee, and spare mee with a regard of mine innocency.
>
> (Apuleius 1893 [1566]: 226)

That which gave the matron perverse pleasure would constitute only an additional torment for an already condemned woman. Indeed, the proposed reenactment of bestial intercourse with a lower-class woman signals a status difference among women and their relation to pleasure that we do not see in Shakespeare's play, where women of the plebeian class are quite out of sight. Fortunately, Lucius runs away, having resisted, as it were, the temptation to become an actor.

While in one sense the liaison in Titania's bower constitutes a purely male fantasy of female desire, perception, and receptivity, it is also clear that within the economy of all-male mimesis, the pleasure of the female spectator can be articulated only in terms of that fantasy. When Bottom is "translated" (III. i. 113) into an ass, he is in rehearsals and has just missed his cue. The parody of a female spectator, Titania thus becomes enamored of an actor:

> Come, sit thee down upon this flow'ry bed,
>   While I thy amiable cheeks do coy,
> And stick musk-roses in thy sleek smooth head,
>   And kiss thy fair large ears, my gentle joy.
>
> (IV. i. 1–4)

Titania is "over-eares in love with him," like the star-struck waiting-women who became infatuated with John Earle, a leading actor of the 1620s, and sent for him to act in their privy chambers (Gurr 1992: 218). Actors and men behaving like actors (like

Lysander wooing Hermia) seduce women: "With feining voice verses of feigning love, / And stol'n the impression of her fantasy" (I. i. 31–2). Male mimesis and female spectatorship thus take seduction as their relatively benign paradigm.

Bottom as an actor, in fact, bears a rather surprising affinity with Richard III, probably Shakespeare's most notorious seducer, whose charm lies precisely in his capacity to play the ladies' man despite being physiologically ill-suited to the role. An accomplished actor – not an amateur like Bottom – he tests his capacities as both lover and villain by seducing the widow of the last man he murdered and by his direct addresses to the audience. Contemporary male commentators reported that women in the audience did indeed find Burbage's Richard III seductive. When Burbage played the role in 1602, one woman allegedly "greue soe farr in liking with him, that before shee went from the play shee appointed him to come that night unto hir by the name of Ri: the 3" (Rackin 1996: 42).

The animal attraction Richard III epitomizes and of which Bottom is a caricature was also pervasively associated with the corrupt nature of political authority, particularly in Bacon's essay "Of Deformity," which, though it reads like a description of Richard III, was probably provoked more directly by Elizabeth's hunchbacked, splayfooted, and physiognomically disfigured secretary, Robert Cecil.[12] Quasibestial Cecil nonetheless appears to have appealed not only to his female sovereign but also to Mary Herbert, Countess of Pembroke. John Aubrey's *Brief Lives* offers a scandalous report of their liaison:

> She was very salacious, and she had a Contrivance in the Spring of the yeare, when the Stallions were to leape the Mares, they were to be brought before such a part of the house, where she had a *vidette* (a hole to peepe out at) to looke on them and please herselfe with their Sport; and then she would act the like sport herselfe with *her* stallions. One of … [Mary Herbert's] great Gallants was Crooke-back't Cecill, Earl of Salisbury.
>
> (Aubrey 1949: 138; see also Boehrer 1994)[13]

Aubrey thus fantasizes the countess of Pembroke as a female spectator, a voyeur, who resembles Titania in her perverse predilection for equine masculinity, although she is unlike Titania in that she is completely in control of both spectacle and sexual encounter. Equally, Cecil is like the metamorphosed Bottom in his deformity but unlike the asinine Athenian in that despite being, according to Aubrey, anatomically subhuman, he remains politically potent.

Ironically, Titania's infatuation with Bottom is akin to Oberon and Titania's possibly pederastic desire for the Indian boy, the "changeling," who is the figure for erotic and mimetic substitution in the play. The boy is the prototype of the actor desired by both men and women and, presumably, desirable in both male and female roles.[14] Adult infatuation with juvenile masculinity was a distinctive feature of the transvestite stage. Elizabeth and Cecil were much taken with Peter Carew, a fourteen-year old who played Emilia in Richard Edwards's *Palamon and Arcyte* (which, like *A Midsummer Night's Dream*, is indebted to Chaucer for its material) in a performance at Corpus Christi, Oxford, in August 1566:

> being in her privy chamber, there was brought into her presence a very pretty boy named Peter Carew (son as I think of Dr. Carew, late Dean of Christ Church) who making an Oration to her in Latin, with two Greek Verses at the end, pleased her so much that she forthwith sent for Secretary Cecyll to hear it; who being come, she commanded the boy to pronounce it again, saying before he began, "I pray God, my fine boy, thou mayst say it so well as thou didst to me just before." Which being done according to her wish, she with Cecyll and divers eminent persons then present were much taken as well with the Speech as with the Orator.
>
> (Elliott 1988: 225)

Such a word-perfect boy makes a plausible female character because, like the changeling, he signals the aesthetically coherent, symmetrical order of mimesis. In contrast, Bottom, beast of burden, member of the nether world of the laboring masses, is the implausible instrument with which to impress the all-too-absorbent and retentive substance of female perception.[15]

Bottom makes a comically grotesque tragic lover whose encounter with Titania demonstrates disorderly erotic and outrageously asymmetrical mimetic relationships. The deformities of desire, however, are more than merely analogous to those of theatrical representation: they inhere in its very structure. Written in 1616, John Cocke's attack on the common player crucially situates the potential for distortion in both the mimetic process and in spectatorial perception: "If hee marries, hee mistakes the Woman for the Boy in Womans attire, ... But so long as he lives unmarried, he mistakes the Boy, or a Whore for the Woman" (Cocke quoted in Chambers 1923: 256–7). Dramatic representation is for Cocke configured as a series of inappropriate substitutions, like those Hermia, Helena, Lysander, and Demetrius play out in the erotic register, and those the mechanicals play out in a specifically theatrical one: "one must come in with a bush of thorns and a lantern and say he comes to disfigure or to present, the person of Moonshine" (III. i. 55–7).

Bizarre substitutions and improvisations were, however, also to be found in quite exalted theatrical circumstances. In an entertainment at the Scottish court in 1594, a lion was supposed to play exotic beast of burden and pull a chariot before the courtly spectators. In the end an African, apparently regarded as its human equivalent, understudied for the lion on the grounds that he was less likely to cause alarm among spectators.[16] The prospect of timorous spectators apparently brought the pressure of dramatic exigency to bear across the entire social spectrum:

Bottom: Let me play the lion too. I will roar that I will do any man's heart good to hear me. I will roar that I will make the Duke say "Let him roar again; let him roar again."

Quince: An you should do it too terribly you would fright the Duchess and the ladies that they would shriek, and that were enough to hang us all.

(I. ii. 63–9)

"Terrible" – that is histrionic – acting is what imperils women's sanity, or, alternatively, what allows an actor, even one as bad as Bottom, to become, indeed, "a lion among ladies" (III. i. 28).

Notably, Bottom's style of performance is just the sort that Hamlet cautions against not because it will alarm women (which is in fact overtly one of the objectives of theatre for him) but because it appeals to undiscerning plebeian spectators, "the groundlings, who for the most part are capable of nothing but inexplicable dumbshows and noise" (III. ii. 11–12). Hamlet's elitist theatre, perhaps modeled on the university dramatics, would not make "the unskillful laugh" but would play to the privileged, "the judicious," who "o'erweigh a whole theatre of others" (III. ii. 25–8). Bottom's asses ears, like those inflicted on Midas for preferring the music of Pan to that of Apollo, literalize exactly the impaired aesthetic sensibility that Hamlet has in mind. Bottom is thus alienated though not excluded from theatrical culture and, as such, can only "disfigure" that which he does not have the power to represent.

A Midsummer Night's Dream proposes the preposterous fantasy of plebeian mimesis. While they present no threat to the social order, the mechanicals are in a position structurally analogous to that of the apprentices who rioted at the Cockpit on Shrove Tuesday 1617, the "outcasts, raging against expensive pleasures denied to them" (Cook 1981: 253). Writing in 1654, Edward Sherburne recalls that plebeians

> besett the house round, broke in, wounded divers of the players, broke open their trunckes, & what apparrell, bookes, or other things they found, they burnt & cutt in peeces; & not content herewith, gott on the top of the house, & untiled it, & had not the Justices of Peace & Shrerife levied an aide, & hindred their purpose, they would have laid that house likewise even with the ground. In this skyrmishe one prentise was slaine, being shott throughe the head with a pistoll, & many other of their fellowes were sore hurt, & such of them as are taken his Majestie hath commaunded shal be executed for example sake.
>
> (Sherburbe quoted in Cook 1981: 252)

The stakes of representation or of the exclusion from representation, both cultural and political, are remarkably high. The play demonstrates the tension between the social classes during the mechanicals' rehearsals when Bottom fears that a hearty performance might be understood as a threat against the women of Theseus's court: "[I]f you should fright the ladies out of their wits they would have no more discretion but to hang us," (I. ii. 66–9) and that, the mechanicals concur: "would hang us, every mother's son" (I. ii. 62–70).

The threat of hanging in the political context of 1595, the year in which Shakespeare's play was written, was anything but an idle one. There were at least thirteen disturbances that year and, as Annabel Patterson points out, twelve of them took place at midsummer, between 6 and 29 June.[17] In theatres lower-class disruption ranged from that of apprentices who would "break in at playes … for three a groat, and crack Nuts with the Scholars in peny rooms again, and fight for Apples" to that of mobs who set out "to rase and pull downe" the theatre itself (Fletcher 1905–12: 194).[18] Importantly, many acts of violence in the audience were instances of class antagonism. For example, two butchers, Ralph Brewyn and John Lynsey, were arraigned in 1611 "for abusinge certen gentlemen at the playhouse called The Fortune," and in 1614 a yeoman, Richard Bradley, "assaulted Nicholas Bestney junior gentleman, and with a knife gave him two grievous wounds" (Cook 1981: 259).

Common criminality included stealing, stabbing, and fighting (Gurr 1992: 223). In 1638 a silkweaver, a belligerent Bottom figure named Thomas Pinnocke, was arraigned "for menacing and threatening to pull down the Redbull playhouse and strikinge divers people with a great cudgell as he went along the streets" (quoted in Cook ibid.).

In this cultural context *A Midsummer Night's Dream* offers a fascinating meditation on the question of access to cultural and, by extension, to political representation. Theseus, the voice of law and "cool reason," devoid of the mechanicals' simple faith in the awesome power of mimesis, rejoices in that incapacity of others to represent themselves, which he sees as a sign of appropriate deference, equating representation with political power. He recalls the nervous behavior of officials who have to speak before him:

> Where I have come, great clerks have purposèd
> To greet me with premeditated welcomes,
> Where I have seen them shiver and look pale,
> Make periods in the midst of sentences,
> Throttle their practised accent in their fears,
> And in conclusion dumbly have broke off.
>
> (V. i. 93–8)

Stage fright (the antithesis of Bottom's hearty, if flawed, performance) reassures Theseus about his power. In contrast, Hippolyta asserts: "I love not to see wretchedness o'ercharged, / And duty in his service perishing" (V. i. 85–6); in other words, she professes precisely those sensibilities which the mechanicals have disproportionately attributed to the female spectator. Elizabeth herself also professed such sentiments on a progress through Warwick (only eight miles from Stratford) in 1574 as a trembling local official made his welcoming speech. Elizabeth allowed the official to kiss her hand and said, "Come hither, little Recorder. It was told me that you would be afraid to look upon me or to speak boldly; but you were not so afraid of me as I was of you; and I now thank you for putting me in mind of my duty." In Stephen Greenblatt's interpretation, this episode is, "in effect, a theatrical performance of humility by someone with immense confidence in her own histrionic power" (1997: 47). This reading would align Elizabeth, then, not with Hippolyta but with Theseus, who prefers inarticulate subjects, appreciating "silence" and "modesty", over "the rattling tongue/ Of saucy and audacious eloquence" (V. i. 100–3).[19] Hippolyta, despite her initial sympathy with the mechanicals' predicament, becomes a badly behaved aristocratic spectator in due course but only after being instructed by her betrothed to value dumb-struck speechlessness: "Love, therefore … tongue-tied simplicity" (V. i. 104). Theseus teaches her to rejoice in what is essentially the failure of representation as an affirmation of his authority. Political and cultural representation here are not, as we might expect, irreducibly discontinuous but directly connected.

In their scorn for popular practises of representation, aristocratic spectators, both male and female, begin to look not altogether unlike riotous plebeians. Again, Elizabeth I is a case in point. The queen attended a number of student theatricals during her visit to Oxford in August of 1566 (the same visit on which she rewarded Peter Carew with a visit to her privy chamber). During the performance of *Palamon and Arcyte*, she interrupted actors and made comments to the audience. When one student actor, John Dalaper, forgot his lines and cried, "by ye masse & Got*es* blutt I am owte," Elizabeth and Cecil further humiliated him by yelling, "Goo thy way, God*es* pity what a knave it tis," and "thowe arte clir owte, thowe mayste be lowde to playe ye knave in any grownde in england" (Elliot 1988: 224). Elizabeth seems to have found the performance terribly amusing, because she is reported to have "laughed full harteleye afterwarde at su*m* of ye players" (ibid.: 226). What is disconcerting, not to say callous, about Elizabeth's reaction is that on this occasion, the first English dramatization of Chaucer's *Canterbury Tales*, there had been fatalities among the spectators at the start of the performance. In preparation for the royal visit, the hall staircase had been releaded, and when it collapsed at the beginning of the performance, three spectators were killed under its weight. Two of the dead were plebeians: a brewer named Pennie, and John Gilbert, a cook (ibid.: 220). Although the queen dispatched her surgeon to help (alas, he could recommend only speedy burial), the show went on.

The heterogeneous social backgrounds of audiences at the public theatre were, naturally, even more pronounced than any commingling that resulted from either royal watching or vernacular university dramatics. Thomas Dekker writes in *The Gull's Horne-booke*:

> the place [playhouse] is so free in entertainment, allowing a stoole as well to the Farmers sonne as to your Templer: that your Stinkard has the selfe-same libertie to be there in his Tobacco-Fumes, which your sweet Courtier hath: and that your Car-man and Tinker claime as strong a voice in their suffrage, and sit to

giue iudgment on the plaies life and death, as well as the prowdest *Momus* among the tribe of *Critick*.

(Dekker quoted in Cook 1981: 216)

The lower orders, who would not have been permitted to give their voice in parliamentary elections, were enfranchized in theatre to mimic the exercise of specifically political representation – suffrage – to which, in this society, only men of property were entitled. Significantly, in Dekker's description, women do not seem to have a voice in the theatre at all. If this is so, Elizabeth's vocality at Oxford may have been, in part, an exercise of royal prerogative. Whatever the case, the behavior of both aristocratic and plebeian theatregoers belies the shared community of theatrical experience celebrated in *A Midsummer Night's Dream*.

Groundlings are clearly the detritus of early modern society, but the actors, often, like the playwrights themselves, sons of glovemakers or erstwhile bricklayers, are little better. As an actor, even more than as a weaver, Bottom lacks both class status and skill, and yet it is through him more than any other character that the magic of theatre takes effect. It is, in a sense, Bottom's "hideous" acting that brings about his metamorphosis (he is, as we have noted, "translated" during rehearsals), a transformation that it is always the purpose of the actor to effect. The professional actor on the public stage represents a new social category in early modern England and one that confutes conventional demarcations between intellectual and artisanal labor. Bottom may be Shakespeare's apology for actors:

> I have had a most rare vision. I have had a dream past the wit of man to say what dream it was. Man is but an ass if he go about to expound this dream. Methought I was – there is no man can tell what. Methought I was, and methought I had – but man is but a patched fool if he will offer to say what methought I had. The eye of man hath not heard, the ear of man hath not seen, man's hand is not able to taste, his tongue to conceive, nor his heart to report what my dream was.

(IV. i. 201–10)

Bottom's speech, a parody of one of St. Paul's letters to the Corinthians, resonates quite remarkably with Montaigne's "An Apologie for *Raymond Sebond*," an essay essentially concerned with the problem of human perception (see Screech 1993: xxxiv), which demonstrates both a deep reverence for animals and a startling egalitarianism. In particular, the essay questions a hierarchy even more fundamental than that of gender or that of menial and mental labor, yet one to which Bottom's transformation implicitly refers, namely, the human dominion over nature:

> How knoweth he by the vertue of his understanding the inward and secret motions of the beasts? By what comparison from them to us doth he conclude the brutishnesse he ascribeth unto them? When I am playing with my Cat, who knowes whether she have more sport in dallying with me, than I have in gaming with her?
>
> (Montaigne 1897: 209)

Montaigne is appalled not only by "mans impudency touching beasts" (Montaigne 1897: 209) but by the idea that linguistic facility gives dominance. "[O]ur dumbe men," he observes, "dispute, argue and tell histories by signes. … And as for other matters; what sufficiency is there is us, that we must not acknowledge from the industry and labours of beasts? … We perceive by the greater part of their workes what excellency beasts have over us, and how weake our art and short our cunning is, if we goe about to imitate them" (ibid.: 211–14).

Nature has not bestowed upon humanity "the naturall sufficiency of brute beasts: So that their brutish stupidity doth in all commodities exceed whatsoever our divine intelligence can effect" (ibid.: 215):

> We are neither above nor under the rest. … And if we will take hold of any advantage tending to that purpose, that it is in our power to seize upon them, to employ them to our service, and to use them at our pleasure; it is but the same oddes we have one upon another.
>
> (Montaigne 1897: 222–5)

The Spanish theologian Raymond Sebond, widely regarded as a heretic, believed that God gave humanity two books, one metaphorical and one real: the "Book of All Creatures" (or the Book of Nature) and the Scriptures. After the Fall, the "Book of All Creatures" became illegible to humanity but nevertheless remains common to everyone, in a way that breaks down the distinction between lettered and unlettered persons (Screech 1993: xxv). At first glance this egalitarianism seems to refer purely to class and not at all to gender. But this is not, in fact, the case. Sebond's audience was primarily female: "divers ammuse themselves to read it, and especially Ladies, to whom we owe most service" (Montaigne ibid.: 186).

Montaigne in this sense takes it upon himself to represent Sebond's female readership. Female receptiveness is, then, the catalyst for Montaigne's project.

Crucially, Bottom's scrambled biblical quotation also refers us to the basic physiological requirements of sensory perception and thus to the fundamental conditions of spectatorship itself. A much later text, John Bulwer's *Philocophus: or, The Deafe and Dumbe Mans Friend* (1648), advertises itself as being about how "a man borne Deafe and Dumbe, may be taught to *Heare* the sound of *words* with his *Eie*" (Bulwer 1648: t.p.). A prefatory poem by Thomas Diconson offers the following exhortation:

> Rejoice you Deafe and Dumbe, your Armes extend
> T'embrace th'inventive goodnesse of a Friend!
> Who heere intends, for your reliefe, to Found
> An Academie, on Natvres highest ground:
> Wherein He doth strange mysteries unlocke,
> How all the Sences have one common Stocke.
> Shewes how indulgent Nature for each sence
> Wanting, allowes a double recompence.
> How she translates a sence, transplants an Eare
> Into the Eye, and makes the Optiques heare
> Inoculates an Eare with sight; whereby
> It shall performe the office of an Eie …
>
> (Bulwer 1648: A7–A8)

For John Bulwer there is a marked proximity between defective perception and the positive aspects of metamorphosis:

> the most remarkable properties of M. *Crispe*, who is wel known to be deaf, and among the rest he said, that a while ago he walking with him in the company of others, one asked him how his Brother did? My Brother (replied he presently) is very well, I *heard* from him but the other day: … He that had an Ear in his Eye, might well say, He heard from his Brother. And that the defect of the *Ear* in deaf men, may be supplied by the office of the *Eye*, or the defect of the *Eye* in blinde men by the office of the *Ear*, so that the *Ear* also may *see*; will not appear so paradoxical, if we consider the consent of *visibles* and *audibles*.
>
> (Bulwer 1648: D11ʳ)

Bulwer sees here an almost magical set of compensations and substitutions, precisely what is involved in the mechanics of theatrical representation: a lantern and a thorn bush can signify moonshine; Snug the joiner can impersonate a lion; and an inept tragedian can somehow transport us to the bower of the Queen of Fairies. In Bottom's dream the gendered and class divisions within the theatre and the eroticized substitutions inherent in dramatic representation parallel the division of the sensory faculties themselves. The outright deformity of the senses becomes in *A Midsummer Night's Dream*, as it does in Bulwer, the privileged site of apprehension and access to the divine.

Bottom's dream connotes not only the idea of the actor as agent of metamorphosis but also his reaction as a spectator to the "vision" of Titania's bower and, in so doing, refigures the relationship between spectator and spectacle.[20] The play's meditation on both the practical and quasi-divine aspects of mimesis, i.e., its capacity for metamorphosis, is instigated by a combination of bad plebeian acting and impaired female spectatorship. Not possessing a learned ear, Bottom is possessed of monstrously deformed capacity for perception. His misquotation from First Corinthians 2: 9–10 echoes the aesthetic disruption of Midas, who, as we have seen, was the archetypal barren spectator. Even prior to his transformation, Bottom declares: "I see a voice" (V. i. 191). In this declaration, he resembles certain uneducated women who attended Cambridge theatricals "only for what they could see" and, contemporaries complained, distracted those listening attentively to the Latin verse by cracking nuts (see Gurr 1987: 93–4).

However, it is not only Bottom's auditory perceptions that are profoundly impaired: he cannot see even his own transformation (though some productions have him catch his transformed image reflected in water). Yet in his "translation" Bottom is related to the satyr, originally the personification of satire, and as such, his distorted perceptions have a surprising critical and moral value. As John Marston asserts in *Pygmalion* in his defense of that genre: "Who would imagine that such squint-eyed sight / Could strike the world's deformities so right" (quoted in Kernan 1959: 136). That is, Bottom, becomes a figure for simultaneously impaired and intensified perception, of which the exemplary type is not the barren spectator but woman.

Spectatrix

The female spectator, like the anonymous and probably fictional gentlewoman in Cambridge with which I began, bears only a problematic relation to that handful of flesh-and-blood women whose attendance at the playhouses between 1567 and 1642 is part of the historical record: Elizabeth Williams, Mrs Tufton, Queen Anne, Queen Elizabeth, Queen Henrietta Maria, Lady Newport, Mrs Overall, Lady Jane and Nan Mildmay, Mrs James, Marion Frith, Ann Clifford, Mary Caldwell, and Margaret Cavendish, Duchess of Newcastle, along with an assortment of unnamed lower-class women; applewives, fishwives, etc. Paradoxically, the latter, though they are unnamed, like references to plebeian spectators in general, seem to imply a rather more embodied presence than that of the almost spectral, privileged female spectators (Gurr 1987: 60, 61, 64, 55–9). The list offers a vivid demonstration of the limits of empiricism in that, contrary to all expectation about securing female presence in the audience if not on the stage, we have, in fact, absolutely no concrete evidence for the now axiomatic assertion among critics that women were "more than half" Shakespeare's audience. While it is notoriously difficult to accredit any aspect of the social composition of such audiences and especially the ratio of privileged to plebeian spectators (though there is, as Ann Jennalie Cook has argued, more evidence for the former than the latter), the already troublesome demographics of spectatorship are exacerbated in relation to women. Andrew Gurr observes:

> Women playgoers provide the hardest evidence of the social composition of Shakespearean playgoers. They were, as a whole, the least literate section of society. Their reasons for playgoing were most open to question and most subject to attack. … [L]ittle of any assertion beyond the bare fact that women were present can be trusted. Hardly any statement on such an emotive question as the morals of women playgoers tells as much about audiences as it does about the man making the statement.
>
> (Gurr 1987: 57–8; see also 60)[21]

Sometimes even the "bare fact" of women's presence in the audience is not required in order to have them validate a performance. For example, in a prefatory poem to his comedy *Vertumnus* (1607) Matthew Gwinne writes of Queen Anne: "… *vtinam spectasset, læta: sed illam / Melpomene pridie lassarat, læserat Aiax.* …" ("[I]f only she had watched the play in happiness. But the day before Melpomene had tired her, and Ajax had harmed her") (Gwinne 1607: sig. B3ᵛ–B4ʳ). Although wearied and, signally, troubled by the previous day's theatrics, as a royal female spectator, Anne remains a powerful reminder of association between spectatorial power and women in the author's recollection of his play's performance.[22]

The importance accorded to the female spectator, even, or perhaps especially, when understood as a cultural phenomenon rather than an empirical category, does not bear out Stephen Orgel's assertion that: "[T]he success of any play was significantly dependent on the receptiveness of women" (Orgel 1996: 10–11).[23] As I have been arguing, receptiveness is a heavily freighted ideological construct. For example, while women might have been particularly "receptive" to Shakespeare, who, as François Laroque describes it, "transcribed onto the stage a tremendous range of sensation, which combined the spectacular and the fantastic with the deeply moving" (Laroque 1993: 119), it is also the case that this process involved more than merely doing something before others, striving to please an audience, but doing "something to" them. This is what Frank Whigham describes as "seizures of the will," "the act of grasping, of taking, of violating, of seizing control," which, in the Renaissance projections about spectatorship were particularly directed toward women (Whigham 1996: 1).

That violent female reaction (madness, confession, and amorous rapture) was the measure of performance in a theatre founded on the symbolic violence of excluding women from the stage neither invariably places women in a position of power nor guarantees women's pleasure.[24] In this early modern cultural context, current critical claims about women's putatively untroubled and enthusiastic attendance at the playhouse are decidedly problematic. Such assertions presuppose that, as a function of their position as consumers in the theatre, whatever went on, women must have "asked for it." My point is neither to discount the probability of women's pleasure in theatre, nor to insist on a rigid empiricism but rather to note that there is a tendency among critics to hypothesize not only women's presence in the theatre but also their reactions there, in a way that uncannily and uncritically perpetuates those early modern fantasies of female spectatorship that it has been my purpose to unravel.

Hysterics

The Cambridge gentlewoman with whom I began this chapter betrayed hysterical symptoms, which, long before Freud, were associated with sexual disorder rather than mimetic effectiveness. The Greek words for "womb," *hyster*, and, "actor", *histriones*, provide an etymological pun that lies at the heart of the gendered division of labor in theatre (though not the class division, to which I will shortly return) which I have been elaborating in this chapter: men acting – the meaner sort – and women – the better sort – acting up.

Freud shaped modern sensibilities about women "acting up" under the scientific rubric of hysteria. He began the famous 1932 lecture "On Femininity" with the following address:

> Ladies and Gentlemen ... Throughout history people have knocked their heads against the riddle of the nature of femininity –. ... Nor will *you* have escaped worrying over this problem – those of you who are men; to those of you who are women this will not apply – you are yourselves the problem.
>
> (Freud 1965: 100)

Reading this passage, one imagines gasps of consternation among the women in Freud's audience. But this is where the direct address to the female audience is most misleading, not to say entirely phatasmatic. Freud, having undergone an operation for mouth cancer, never actually delivered the lecture (see Felman 1993: 42). Like another of Freud's most notorious remarks, "What does a woman want?"[25] the lecture depends on an address to women but not on their reply. Though from Apuleius on, men have answered Freud's question to Marie Bonaparte about female desire with ribald certainty, Freud does not expect his female correspondent to solve the presumed riddle of femininity despite whatever claim she might have, on experiential grounds, for being able to do so. Freud erases female subjectivity even, or perhaps especially, when addressing women.

A certain skepticism is equally appropriate in relation to the energetic interpellations of women (notably, not just the ladies) in Shakespeare's audience:

> O men, for the love you bear to women – as I perceive by your simp'ring, none of you hates them – that between you and the women the play may please. If I were a woman I would kiss as many of you as had beards that please me, complexions that liked me, and breaths that I defied not. ...
>
> (*As You Like It*, V. Epi. 14–19)

>   ... I fear
> All the expected good w'are like to hear
> For this play at this time, is only in
> The merciful construction of good women,

> For such a one we show'd 'em: if they smile,
> And say 'twill do, I know within a while
> All the best men are ours; for 'tis ill hap
> If they hold, when their ladies bid 'em clap.
>   (*Henry VIII*, V. Epi.7–14)

Yet, the direct address to a female audience to whose desires the
play ostensibly caters, and to whom it cedes control of the play's
reception while they articulate the shaping fantasy of early modern
theatre, namely, that of female spectatorship, are, signally, an after-
thought. We can discern in the direct address to women what Juliet
Fleming has discovered in books ostensibly addressed to a female
readership, namely: "The covert movement through or beyond
women to a male audience that stands behind them ... which thus
enacts in the register of the literary that process of exchanging
women as symbolic property between men" (Fleming 1993: 164).
Crucially, the issue here and in the epilogues is not the idea of frightening women, which, as we have seen, is so central to the project of
male mimesis, but rather one of giving pleasure as opposed to giving offense – not to women but to men.

Like women in the audience of *Henry VIII*, the ladies of the French
court who visit Navarre in *Love's Labour's Lost*, have the power to
withhold their approval:

> Our wooing doth not end like an old play;
> Jack hath not Jill: These ladies' courtesy
> Might well have made our sport a comedy.
>   (V. ii. 864–6)

However, the notion of appealing to women while excluding them
from the work of representation has been revealed both as the central and the preposterous premise of the play, as the young noblemen
strive to entertain the ladies despite having banned ladies from the
court of Navarre.

The idea of women as relatively pliant and receptive female spectators implied by the epilogues sharply distinguishes them from the
plebeian audience. When the latter became restless, "It was not
then the most mimicall nor fighting man ... could pacifie; Prologues
nor Epilogues would prevaile" (Cook 1981: 227; Gurr 1992: 225).[26]
Such audiences were not passive, and they were an integral element
in the production of the play. For all that, there remained crucial
dimensions of representation from which women and

plebeians were barred, and no amount of deconstruction, no reevaluation of the status of consumption will alter this fact. In fact, power, though it may be negotiable, is not reversible, and the productions of the audience are not equivalent to the production on the stage.

Notes

Introduction

1 In his edition of *The Winter's Tale*, Stephen Orgel (1996: 155) argues for an actor in a bear suit rather than a real bear. However, his claim that there is no evidence for real bears in stage performance is contradicted by John Urson's troupe of dancing bears in Jonson's *Masque of Augurs* (1622). Further, circuses everywhere belie the curious claim that "no bear has ever been tame enough to be a reliable performer" (155–6). The possibility of a real bear remains.

2 In the fifteenth century existing images of whites were painted over with the figure of the black magus, and in the nineteenth century depictions of Ham which had hitherto been white suddenly began to be rendered as black (Braude 1997: 103–42, 120).

3 "All things considered," NPR, May 1997. Relating the question of visibility to stage transvestitism, Tracey Sedinger remarks: "Most critics ... assume that the crossdresser is, in a sense, visible. ... I argue that the crossdresser is not a visible object but rather a structure enacting the failure of a dominant epistemology in which knowledge is equated with visibility" (1997: 63–79, 64).

4 Harvey Firestein in *The Celluloid Closet* (1996) Dir. Rob Epstein and Jeffrey Friedman. Distributed by Sony Picture Classics.

5 Stephen Orgel writes, "It is certainly true that the professional theatre companies of Shakespeare's time included no women" (1996: 4).

6 Rose Brewer argues: "What is most important conceptually and analytically in this [black feminist] work is the articulation of multiple

oppressions. The polyvocality of multiple social locations is historically missing from analyses of oppression and exploitation in traditional
feminism, Black studies, and mainstream academic disciplines" (1993:
13).

7 David Bevington summarizes the argument about the play's performance as follows: "Presumably, Shakespeare's play was staged in 1606
or 1607, although we have no direct evidence of this. The only au-
thoritative text of *Anthony and Cleopatra*, that printed in the First Folio,
is of authorial origin rather than the playhouse. The Lord Chamber-
lain's records for 1669 note that the play was 'formerly acted at
Blackfriars,' without indication as to how often it was performed or
whether it was acted publicly at the Globe" (1990: 44).

   Michael Neill remarks, "The history of the various attempts made
to overcome the difficulties presented by the sheer scale of the play
and by the bafflingly contradictory character of its protagonists,
especially Cleopatra, make this limited history an especially telling
one" (1994).

8 The book to which I owe my title, Tania Modleski's *Feminism Without
Women: Culture and Criticism in a "Postfeminist" Age* (1991), argues: "the
once exhilarating proposition that there is no 'essential' female nature has been elaborated to the point where it is now often used to
scare 'women' away from making any generalizations about political
claims on behalf of a group called 'women' " (15). Modleski argues
that anti-essentialist thinking is in danger of dissolving the subject of
feminism – woman – altogether. She claims that women in anti-
foundationalist postmodern theory have become an almost
unrepresentable constituency in a maneuver that dangerously parallels the fetishistic disavowal of woman's difference, the dread of the
feminine, that is the motor of castration anxiety (22).

   In the context of early modern theatre, gender identities remained
sufficiently inflexible to prohibit women from the stage, and the danger
of the anti-essentialist argument is that it fetishistically disavows
difference altogether.

9 Sandra Richards also observes, "In pandering to the jaded tastes of
audiences, however, most of the Restoration plays in which actresses
had to appear became increasingly smutty and immoral" (1993: 15).

10 "The position of the Master of the Revels, jealously protecting court
privilege as much as he sought to suppress 'dangerous matter' made
him as much a friend of the actors as their overlord" (Dutton 1991:
248).

11 Margo Heinemann notes: "It is generally agreed that the particularly
radical surviving plays of this season and especially *A Game at Chess*
could be staged at all only because of exceptionally sharp division at
the top" (1993: 237).

12 Sovereignty is however, as David Kastan has demonstrated, unlike

other forms of social identity in that kingship performed onstage and kingship performed in life are alarmingly similar, both relying on the power of spectacle for their efficacy (1986: 459–75). That there are no real kings onstage is a representational dilemma that, Jean Howard argues, leads in the history plays to showing theatrical practise as either an external threat *to* monarchy or constitutive *of* monarchy (1994: 130).

13 For a detailed account of Continental eunuchs, see Elam 1996: 1–36.

14 In a parallel vein, Lorna Hutson argues that women function in humanist exchanges "as signs of credit between men in the traditional anthropological sense of alliance formation" (1994: 7).

1 "And all is semblative a woman's part"

1 On the political necessity of asserting women's physiological specificity, see Emily Martin 1987. On resistance postmodernism, see Ebert 1991: 113–35.

2 For a trenchant critique of Foucault's "body politics," see Fraser 1989: 62–3. See also Judith Butler 1990: 128–41.

3 For an excellent account of this phenomenon, see Morton 1990: 57–75.

4 There are other important and related statements with which I do not have space to engage here. There has been a lot of rethinking around biological essentialism, especially as it has been articulated in response to Irigaray's "womanspeak" and Cixous's *écriture feminine*. Also, there has been considerable debate as to whether the body exists outside discourse. Elizabeth Grosz argues, for example, that "the body can be seen as the primary object of social production and inscription" (1987: 1–16). See also Wolff, who argues "the critique of essentialism does *not* amount to proof that there *is* no body" (1990: 135). Both Wolff and Elizabeth Dempster try to locate new, liberatory understandings of the body in dance, but the result is a feminist rendition of the utopian excesses of the theorized bodies of Barthes and Foucault (1988: 35–54). See also Denise Riley 1988: 96–114. She remarks that "the very location of 'the sexual' in the body is itself historically mutable" (104).

5 For important treatments of these issues, see Wayne 1991, Paster 1993, Sawday 1995; and Hillman and Mazzio 1997.

6 See Fisher and Halley 1989.

7 Like Jardine, Stephen Orgel contends that homosexuality was the dominant form of eroticism in Renaissance culture (1989: 7–29). See also Woodbridge 1984: 154, 327.

8 See McLuskie 1989: 100–57 and 1987: 120–30; Ryan 1989: 88–9; Case 1988: 26–7; and Woodbridge 1984: 327.

9 Phyllis Rackin draws attention to the homophobic satire of Jonson's

Epicoene, thus demonstrating the important point that not all instances of transvestism were homoerotic (1987: 29–41, 31). Jean Howard points out that the social transgressions entailed in women's attendance at the theatre may well have been more directly related to the goings on in the auditorium than to the content of the plays: see "Scripts and/versus Playhouses: Ideological Production and the Renaissance Public Stage" in Wayne 1991.

10 In a different vein Juliet Dusinberre observes: "Restoration drama boasts neither female heroes nor male heroines. But the woman actor offers no challenge to the dramatists to understand femininity beyond surface appearance" (1985: 27).

11 See Ryan 1989, chapter 9, for an account of the limitations of deconstruction in Shakespeare studies.

12 See also Binns 1974: 95–120; Clark 1985: 157–83; Levine 1986: 121–43.

13 On Malvolio's class status, see Malcolmson 1991: 29–57.

14 *Certain Sermons or Homilies Appointed to be Read In Churches in the Time of Queen Elizabeth I, 1547–1571*(1908) London: SPCK: 334–5.

15 There is perhaps a "coded" reference to transvestism in the mention of the play's Italian parallel. If, as Margaret Maurer suggests, *Twelfth Night* is a "trick" play, Manningham might not have wanted to give the game away. Maurer, "Coming of Age in Illyria: Doubling the Twins in *Twelfth Night*," (unpublished). Nonetheless, the emphasis is all on the "device" against Malvolio, which reinforces the sense that this is the trick of the play .

16 Criticism since the Renaissance has also been preoccupied with Malvolio. See Craik and Lothian (eds) 1981: lxxix–xcviii. All quotations of *Twelfth Night* will follow this edition.

17 Malcolmson, in "What You Will" argues that social estate in *Twelfth Night* is "a matter of desire or will rather than birth or title" in order to praise willing service, as that of Viola to Orsino, and to condemn self-interest, represented by Malvolio (1991: 51).

18 Malvolio's connection with bawdy is consolidated by the fact that, despite his Puritan leanings, he is not above making a lewd jest himself, as when he describes Orsino's messenger to his mistress:

> Not yet old enough for a man, nor young enough
> for a boy; as a squash is before 'tis a peascod, or a
> codling when 'tis almost an apple. 'Tis with him
> in standing water, between boy and man. He is
> very well-favoured, and he speaks very shrewishly.
> One would think his mother's milk were scarce
> out of him.
>
> (I. v. 158–64)

"Peascod" and "codling" refer to Cesario's genitals. It would seem too, that Malvolio participates in the solitary pleasures of masturbation – playing with his jewel; a pretty common double entendre (II. V. 60–1) – despite editors' efforts to sanitize his lines.

19 Partridge argues that in this "nursery spell-out" of *cunt* and *piss* that "Shakespeare has not, after all, omitted the *n*; it occurs in 'and no T's,' [*sic*] as several discerning scholars have noted." "N, innuendoed or concealed or – especially in *and* (pronounced 'n') – representing *in*; connected with the ways in which words or sounds are – for instance, with suggestive pauses – delivered on stage. ... Mr. Aylmer Rose, in a long and valuable letter dated 2 October 1955, writes thus, concerning *Twelfth Night*, II. v. 87–9: 'Her very C's, her U's, and [pronounced "n," i.e. N] her T's; and thus makes she her great P's' [where, he implies, there is a significant pause before P's]. If my suggestion about the innuendoed N is correct, it draws attention to the necessity of considering the sound of words and the way in which they are delivered on stage" (1968: 151–2).

20 Valerie Traub offers an important critique of the heterosexist bias of the assumption "that love between women was readily available as a source of both humor and humiliation for members of Shakespeare's audience" (1991: 83). And indeed, while misapprehension of any sort may be a source of ridicule, this does not exclude the production of homoerotic play here.

21 I have borrowed this term from Sue-Ellen Case's "Toward A Butch-Femme Aesthetic" in Hart (1989): 282–99, especially 297.

22 See Rose 1988: 78; Scragg 1991: 1–16. A contemporary pun with a similar effect is "snatch," which means both theft (as in purse snatching), and a woman's crotch. Jane Gallop's *Thinking Through the Body* uses "snatches of conversation" as a subtitle in one of its chapters in order to suggest both female crotch and partial apprehension.

23 This is a possibility not entertained in Gail Kern Paster's reading of this episode. Paster claims that Malvolio's transgression is marked by the fact that he appears to have contravened the norms of urinary segregation (1993: 213). I am indebted to Fran Dolan for the reference to Quaife.

24 Further, the emphasis on the linguistic dimension of the sexualization and denigration entailed in the process of enforcing social hierarchy, links both Olivia and Viola, whose names, as Jonathan Goldberg has pointed out, are anagrammatic mirrors of one another and link both with Malvolio, to whose names his adds a negative prefix (1986: 216).

25 For a fascinating analysis of the image of Lucrece in Shakespeare's narrative poem, see Vickers 1985: 209–22.

26 "Everything pertaining to the female genitalia is comprehended in the term 'of nature' [*phuseos*], and the obscene term cunt [*cunnus*,]" wrote Caspar Bauhin (1560–1624), professor of anatomy and botany at Basel (Laqueur 1989: 107).

27 As Leonard Tennenhouse puts it, Orsino "aestheticizes love by dislodging it from its political body" (1986: 63).

28 In my view, materialism has not become impossible, but it is perhaps not quite so self-evident as it was, say in 1982 (see Barrett 1988) or even in 1985. See Newton and Rosenfelt (1985).

29 Rackin argues, "The Puritans closed the theaters, and a multitude of causes, which we are only beginning to understand, closed off many of the opportunities and possibilities that had been open to women at the beginning of the modern age" (1987: 38).

30 In relation to Arnaud du Tilh's impersonation of Martin Guerre, Greenblatt points out that "What is entirely unacceptable – indeed punishable by death in the everyday world – is both instructive and delightful in spaces specially marked off for the exercise of impersonation. For in these spaces, and only in these spaces, there is a widely shared social agreement on imposture" (1986: 219–20).

31 This remains true of Dollimore's chapter on cross-dressing in early modern England in *Sexual Dissidence* (1991).

32 Dollimore argues: "But what kind of resistance, if any, does a materialist criticism discover in Renaissance tragedy? I argued in *Radical Tragedy* that we find in this theatre not so much a vision of political freedom as a knowledge of political domination. But we simply cannot slide between the two, or assume that the second easily produces the first. This knowledge *was* challenging: it subverted, interrogated, and undermined the ruling ideologies and helped precipitate them into crisis. But history tells us time and again that from such crisis there may emerge not freedom but brutal repression. And such repression emerges not because the subversive was always contained, subversion being a ruse of power to consolidate itself, but because the challenge really *was* unsettling" (Dollimore 1990: 471–93, 482).

33 Phyllis Rackin, who in a fascinating comment argues for the positive nature of transvestism nonetheless points out that it is the stuff of male fantasy rather than female historical experience: "Thus, in Jonson's play [*Epicoene*], which subscribes to the neoclassical ideal of art as an imitation of life, gender also imitates life – both in a limited, literal sense, since the sex of Epicoene is finally revealed as male (the sex of the actor who played the part), and in a broader sense, since women in the play are subjected to the same calumny, stereotyping, and social restrictions that real women suffered in Jonson's world. For Lyly and for Shakespeare, the relation between art and life is complementary as well as reflective. ... Thus, in these plays the true gender of the transvestite figure turns out to be feminine, the opposite of the real sex of the boy who played her part. Similarly, the dynamics of the plots make femininity a desideratum rather than the liability it was in actual life" (1987: 33).

2 The castrator's song

1 John Marston, *Antonio and Mellida*, ed. W. Reavley Gair (1991).
2 On "Kinsayder," see Wharton 1994: 5; and Hardin 1982: 134–5. In the second edition of *Scourge* (1599), Marston's note to his asterisk reads: "Mark the witty allusion to my name." Notably, *Mar* used in exactly this sense was a common prefix to satirical names, for example, Marprelate.
    Joseph Hall's interests as evidenced by his authorship of *Mundus alter et idem* (trans. 1610), a satirical meditation on English social folly, set in a "Double-sex Isle, otherwise called Skrat or Hermaphrodite Iland," placed him well to decode Marston's pseudonym. In this text the hermaphrodites claim superiority over eunuchs because they are formed by nature, unlike the eunuchs, who are the product of castration. *The Discovery of A New World*, Englished by John Healy (London: 1609), 72.
3 Marston was perhaps more knowledgeable about European theatre than his contemporaries since he had an Italian wife, Maria Guarsi (Chambers 1923: vol. 3, 427; vol. 2, 263). Marjorie Garber wittily points out that the castrato as a "solution" to the Pauline injunction against women's speech occurred because "castration was apparently thought of as less morally problematic than the presence of women" (1992: 254).
4 Peter Stallybrass remarks that "recent criticism has been particularly concerned with the 'part' that the boy actor has which is not in his part. (I would want to suggest, incidentally, that that part has been peculiarly distorted [and enlarged] by being thought of as a 'phallus,' as if a boy's small parts weren't peculiarly – and interestingly – at variance with the symbolic weight of THE phallus.) Criticism has thus been concerned with the 'addition' which the boy actor brings to a female role" (1992: 64–83, 68).
5 While there was little to ground sexual difference in the Renaissance, there remained an absolute difference between the social status of men and women, and, as Stallybrass argues – Galenic medicine notwithstanding – difference was "organized through a fixation on the supposedly 'essential' features of gender" (1992: 73). Jones and Stallybrass observe that the "potential collapse of everyone into a single male sex had … been partially authorized both by classical myth and by the Church" and is "an example of the absorption of the Other into the Same" (1991: 80–111, 85).
6 R. Barbour has recently argued that boy actors were "prime agents of indeterminacy" and that they "enabled mutual enjoyments among persons perhaps otherwise divided by gender-based hostilities" (1995: 1006–22, 1007).
7 Laura Levine argues that it is only masculinity on the stage that has to be enacted in order to exist: "it is as if femaleness were the default

position, the thing one were always in danger of slipping into" (1994: 8). The antitheatricalists did not discount the power of theatrical illusion, but rather feared that wearing women's clothing could "literally 'adulterate' male gender" (4).

8 The play's misogyny is, indeed, softened only in those moments when we are made most aware of the fact that Kate's submission is performed by a young man.

9 As Lesley Ferris has argued, in early modern England males "substituted their own bodies to 'create' the female other, an aesthetic substitution which was considered superior to the real unaesthetic woman herself" (1995: 252).

10 Beier and Finlay suggest that the topography of freeman barber-surgeons in London indicates that their services were regularly required and that members of the profession were increasingly located near places of vice and resort (1986: 87, 95).
    For a comprehensive account of syphilis during the period, see Fabricius 1994 and Quétel 1990: chapters 3 and 4.

11 See Beck 1974, esp. 113–14.

12 Surgeon John Hall's *Historicall Expostulation Against The Beastlye Abusers, Both of Chyrurgerie and Physyke, in oure Tyme: With A Goodlye Doctrine and Instruction Necessarye to be Marked and Folowed, of All True Chirurgiens* (1844 [1565]) argues that "pernicious division hath been brought to confusion. … For as the physiciens thynke their learnying sufficient, without practyse or experience, so the chirurgien, for the moste parte, havying experience and practise, thinketh it unnedeful to have any learnying at all." While this seems initially a moderate position, the argument for learning here is largely aimed at keeping "ignorant, ye and foolyshe women" from "worke in so noble and worthy an arte" (The Percy Society 1844: xiv). On the separation of medicine and surgery, see also G. Parker 1920: 15.

13 *The Whole Worke of That Famous Chirurgion Maister John Vigo*, compiled by Thomas Gale (1586:16).

14 Castration is of course a standard fablio punishment for adultery, though there is no evidence that this corresponds to actual practise. Removal of the penis, however, would probably have been a form of execution rather than a penalty that left the victim alive minus his virile member, since medieval surgeons thought wounds had to be induced to produce "laudable pus" before they healed. Those who escaped medical assistance had better hopes for survival (Beck 1974: 12). There were of course infamous cases of castration in the medieval era, most notably that of Abelard, who was allegedly emasculated in his sleep by a practitioner deft in the religious rite of circumcision.

15 Scultetus, *Chyrurgeons Store-House* (1644: n. p.).
    Culpepper writes: "This part [the clitoris] sometimes is as big as a mans Yard, and such women were thought to be turned into men. The

causes: It is from too much nourishment of the part, from the looseness of it by often handling. The cure: It is not safe to cut it off presently; but first use Driers and Discussers, with things that a little astringe; then gentle casticks without causing pain, as burnt allum, Aegpyticum. Take Aegpyticum, oyl of Mastick, Roses, wax, each half an ounce. If these will not do, then cut it off, or tie it with a ligature of silk or Horse-hari, till it mortifie. Aetius teacheth the way of Amputation he calls it Nympha or Clitoris, between both the wings: but take heed you cause not pain or inflammation. After cutting, wash wuth wine with Mirtles, Bayes, Roses, Pomogranate-flowers boiled in it, and cypress nuts, and lay on an astringent Powder" (Culpeper 1653: IV, 3). I am indebted to Rachana Sachdev for references to Culpeper and Sharp. See her forthcoming essay "Sycorax in Algiers: Cultural Politics and Gynecology in Early Modern England" in (ed.) Dympna Callaghan *The Feminist Companion To Shakespeare* (Oxford: Blackwell, forthcoming). On the practise of clitoridectomy in France, see Katharine Park (1997: 170–93, esp. 183).

16 A prolapsed, gangrened uterus would have been surgically removed, but according to Audrey Eccles, it was unlikely that total hysterectomy was ever performed (1982: 81).

17 Women did, of course, come under the knife but more often in caesarian deliveries, for instance, than for clitoral excision. My argument is not, I would emphasize, incompatible with the view that intense misogyny has informed the history of medicine. See Blumenfeld-Kosinski (1990: 91–119). In his encyclopedic account of the subject, Harvey Graham records no early instances of the gynecological horrors perpetuated on women in the nineteenth century. Women's wombs may have been believed to wander to the detriment of their reason, but there seems to have been no attempt to pluck them out by way of a cure or, for that matter, to engage in the pseudo-scientific butchery of women's other genital and reproductive organs (1951). See also Traub (1995: 81–113).

18 The only other major theory of anatomical distinction in the Renaissance is Aristotle's "botched male" theory of nature's production of females. See Laqueur (1990: 99–100). To some degree, of course, patriarchy is always a one-sex model because it takes man as its paradigmatic norm.

19 *Sow* was probably the generic name for a pig, since *sowgelding* apparently refers to the practise of boar-gelding.

20 Roger Baker observes of the boy troupes: "The history of these children is sometimes pathetic. … It is also the familiar story of abuse and exploitation which, in at least one case, makes modern show business seem a positively tranquil occupation" (1968: 68–9).

21 See Sommerville (1992); Marcus (1978: ch. 3); Ariès (1962: 100–33). On adolescent sexuality and working conditions, see Ben-Amos (1994: 200–207, 40–68).

22 Laurie Maguire (1998) argues that *censor* may mean "cittern," a musical instrument that was a standard item in barbers' shops. The Oxford *Complete Works Of Shakespeare* offers scissor instead of *censor*. See also Maguire (1995).

23 I cannot agree. See also Chambers 1923: vol. 1, 371, who also misreads this reference.

24 The *OED* defines *freemartin* as "a hermaphrodite or imperfect female of the ox kind."

25 Quoted by Linda Phyllis Austern in a splendid musicological account of vocal impersonation, "'No women are indeed': the boy actor as vocal seductress in late sixteenth- and early seventeenth-century drama" (1994: 83–102, 88). My book was in press when Bruce R. Smith's important study, *The Acoustic World of Early Modern England* (Chicago: Chicago University Press, 1999) came out, and I regret being unable to take account of it here.

26 Stallybrass remarks, "To be aware of the fetishistic staging of the boy actor, of the insistence that we see what is not there to see, is to conceptualize the erotics of Renaissance drama in totally unfamiliar ways" (1992: 72).

27 See also Austern 1993: 343–54; and Austern 1994: 83–102.

28 In vocal crisis, then, there is a replaying of the entry into language, into that "lack" of being which is the irreducible condition of subjectivity: "In acceding to language, the subject forfeits all existential reality, and forgoes any future possibility of wholeness" (Silverman 1992a: 4)

29 It is interesting to compare the gay cult of diva worship with the Renaissance dissatisfaction with male simulations of female voice. Terri Castle ponders this phenomenon: "[p]erhaps one of the reasons that the most vocal diva admirers of the past two hundred years have tended to be homosexual men is that it is the least embarrassing for them – of all the modern sexual subgroupings – to enthuse in public over the female singing voice: the libidinal element inspiring enthusiasm is there, by happy circumstance, most artfully disguised and displaced" (1993: 202).

30 *Eunuchism Display'd* "written by a person of Honour" (London: E. Curll, 1718) reports on the title page the circumstances of its writing: "Occasion'd by a young Lady's falling in Love with Nicolini, who sang in the Opera at the hay-Market, and whom she had like to have married."

31 The celluloid chimera of woman in the classic Hollywood narrative serves as a fantasized means of circumventing castration:

> [I]n psychoanalytic terms, the female figure poses a deeper problem. She also connotes something that the look continually circles around but disavows: her lack of a penis, implying a threat of castration and hence sexual unpleasure. Ultimately, the meaning

of woman is sexual difference, the visually ascertainable absence of the penis, the material evidence on which is based the castration complex essential for the organization of entrance to the symbolic order and the law of the father. Thus the woman as icon, displayed for the gaze and enjoyment of men, the active controllers of the look, always threatens to evoke the anxiety it originally signified. The male unconscious has two avenues of escape from this castration anxiety: preoccupation with the re-enactment of the original trauma (investigating the woman, demystifying her mystery), counterbalanced by the devaluation, punishment or saving of the guilty object (an avenue typified by the concerns of the *film noir*); or else complete disavowal of castration by the substitution of a fetish object or turning the represented figure itself into a fetish so that it becomes reassuring rather than dangerous (hence overvaluation, the cult of the female star).

(Silverman 1994: 21)

3 "Othello was a white man"

1 As Hall notes, "Representations of Blacks, as well as actual Blacks, were an integral part of Scottish court entertainment during James VI's reign" (Hall 1991: 4).
2 Preston contended that Othello, the character, the *Moor* of Venice, was white.
3 There are famous "exceptions" to this rule, namely foreign performers and Moll Frith's musical performance. See Mann 1991: 246.
4 Valerie Wayne articulates the crucial recognition that whiteness was "the most visible complexion of European Renaissance society" (1991: 11). See also Adelman (1997) and Vitkus (1997).
5 "Savages and men of Ind" are referred to, for example, in *The Tempest*, II. ii. 57. In his analysis of early modern understandings of Africa, Eldred Jones points out: "the peoples of Africa … were strange, picturesque inhabitants of a strange, picturesque land. Their color was a striking feature which was frequently mentioned. Regardless of what the more informed writers may have said about the different colors of Africans, only their blackness seems to have registered firmly" (Jones 1965: 39).
6 Occasionally, where characters disguised as Moors need to uncover themselves quickly, masks rather than blackface were used to represent black skin, as in Robert Greene's *Orlando Furioso* (1592). See Jones 1965: 121.
7 I have used the Arden editions of Shakespeare throughout this chapter.
8 Similarly, Parry observes that Othello's references to his own "begrimed" face take on greater resonance when "what you have in

your mind as you write (or view) the play are the words spoken by an actor who can wash his grimy blackness off an hour or so after the words are spoken" (Parry 1990: 101).

 9 My thinking here is directed by Copjec's chapter "The Sartorial Superego" (Copjec 1994).

10 For a fascinating account of the notion of race and cosmetics in an unproduced eighteenth-century play, *The New Cosmetic or The Triumph of Beauty, A Comedy* (1790) by Samuel Jackson Pratt, writing under the pseudonym Courtney Melmoth; see Gwilliam 1994.

11 Barthelemy observes: "The desire of so many women (nineteen in three masques) to be freed of the sign of their otherness, the sign of their type, can neither be overlooked nor underestimated" (1987: 41). See also Jack D'Amico 1991: 53.

12 *Oxford English Dictionary*, s.v. "blackness."

13 Thomas Southerne's rendition of Aphra Behn's novella *Oroonoko*, for instance, substitutes a white woman for the black beauty Imoinda. Margaret Ferguson incisively observes, "This change may perhaps be explained as Southerne's bow to a strikingly gendered and also colored convention of the Restoration stage which I'm still trying to understand, namely that male English actors could appear in blackface but actresses evidently could not" (Ferguson 1994: 219–20).

14 "Painting apparently was not only practised by women, for male courtiers at the end of the sixteenth century occasionally coloured their faces" (Webb 1912: 208). See Drew-Bear 1994: 27–31.

15 For a discussion of the blazon tradition in *Lucrece*, see Vickers 1985.

16 Annette Drew-Bear argues that "In fact, extensive evidence exists that boy and adult players used makeup in Renaissance drama" (1994: 14).

17 My thinking here is indebted to Kaja Silverman's discussion of the formation of the subject in the mirror stage, which I think has considerable relevance to formations of racial identity, though it has never been addressed in that context (1992b: 90).

18 There is, of course, a Renaissance stereotype of the Italian woman as the dark lady. On the significance of Cyprus in the Renaissance see Neill 1984.

19 Other characters onstage probably also wore sumptuous dress, but the palate of colors used in these costumes was rather more muted than that used in the depiction of Moors. Andrew Gurr observes: "It was an age of glorious variety, in which, as always in the world of fashion, new names had constantly to be chosen as new shades of color were invented. Pepper, tobacco, sea-water, and puke (a dark brown) were a few of the many Elizabethan inventions" (1992: 181–2). None of these is a bright color.

   F. M. Kelly argues for the predominance of black clothes in social dress: "The importance of black in the collective colour-scheme of Elizabethan costume is apt to be underestimated ... it is probably safe to say that black would be the dominant note in any average Elizabethan crowd. … Brocades, cloth of gold and of silver were only worn by the greatest on occasions of state" (Kelly 1938: 44–5).

20 John Salway observes, "What the theatre reviewers of 1833 were, in effect, denying to Ira Aldridge was his capacity to represent a Black character in a white theatre" (1991: 121).

21 In Britain, *The Black and White Minstrel Show* was a highly popular television show until the 1970s. All of its minstrels were white men in blackface. Ironically, it was one of the first television shows to appear "in color."

22 In medieval drama, for instance, blackface is not so much an impersonation as a symbolic depiction.

23 I do not have space to attend to Cleopatra here. I will observe only that she is constructed to occupy a place of pure exhibition.

24 Similarly, when women use cosmetics, or when women act, not only is the use of make-up denigrated but they are still being themselves – naturally vain, deceitful, and so on.

25 Jordan (1968) observes that Africans had become virtually synonymous with slavery by the mid sixteenth century.

26 See Jordan 1968 on the development of racialist ideology, especially chapters 1 and 2. Phillipa Berry has pointed out that there were very positive connotations to blackness in the thinking of Renaissance humanists such as Ficino, Bruno, and della Miradolla. On the complex history of the marvel, see Stephen Greenblatt's brilliant *Marvelous Possessions* (1991).

27 See Parker 1994 for a compelling discussion of the parallels between the unfolding and discovery of "foreign parts" and female genitals.

28 "Shakespeare shows that the union of a white Venetian maiden and a black Moorish general is from at least one perspective emphatically unnatural. The union is of course a central fact of the play, and to some commentators, the spectacle of the pale-skinned woman caught in Othello's black arms has indeed seemed monstrous. Yet that spectacle is a major source of Othello's emotional power. From Shakespeare's day to the present the sight has titillated and terrified predominantly white audiences" (Vaughan 1994: 51). See also Vaughan and Vaughan 1997: 19–44; and Rosenberg 1961: 16–205.

4 Irish memories in *The Tempest*

1 Ireland was initially conquered by Strongbow in the eleventh century, vigorously colonized under James I, and absolutely crushed by Cromwell.

2 Sir John Davies, Edmund Spenser, Barnaby Rich, John Bale, and John Milton all had political offices that connected them to Ireland and matters Irish, and wrote about Ireland. As the editors of the collec-

tion *Representing Ireland* point out, "In the sixteenth and seventeenth centuries, aesthetic and political representation cannot easily be severed" (Bradshaw, Hadfield and Maley 1993: 1).

3 On the book's popularity, see Maxwell 1923. What Stephen Greenblatt observes in relation to the New World is also true of the English relation to Ireland: "There is almost no authentic reciprocity in the exchange of representations between Europeans and the peoples of the New World, no equality of giving and receiving" (Greenblatt 1991: 121).

4 On the fantasy of speechless Indians, see Greenblatt 1990: 38.

5 There are writings from some of the peoples conquered by Spain, such as the Aztecs, which remain illegible to Europeans.

On Spanish ideas of indigenous literacy, see Miguel Leon-Portilla 1962. While it was true that initial contact with groups in the Caribbean led Europeans to believe that Indians had no language, by the 1520s, Spaniards knew they would have to manage a very complex, highly literate civilization. See also Baker 1997a: 88.

6 "It is as well to be clear that there is nothing in *The Tempest* fundamental to its structure of ideas which could not have existed had America remained undiscovered," writes Frank Kermode in an introduction, which paradoxically established the incontrovertible centrality of the play's colonial theme (Kermode 1986: xxv). See also Skura 1989: 42–69; and Orgel 1987: 209. All subsequent citations of the play will be from the Oxford edition.

7 On Maori cultural forms which have been visually pervasive but discursively absent, see Thomas 1995: 90–121.

Michael Neill remarks, "Given the amount of political, military, and intellectual energy it absorbed, and the monies it consumed, Ireland can be seen (along with, significantly, the New World) one of the greatest and unexplained lacunae in the drama of the period" (Neill 1994b: 1, 1–132, 11). See also Shaw 1987: 26–39.

8 Hall also notes the connection between *The Tempest* and Africa, arguing that Caliban occupies multiple sites of difference (1995: 151). Fuchs argues for the play's "polysemous" context of both Ireland and the Mediterranean (1997: 1, 45–62). See also D. Baker, where he makes the exciting case that: "The 'connecting link' between Ireland and *The Tempest* is that both *are* connecting links, Ireland as a mediating zone between two sorts of domain [kingdom and colony], and *The Tempest* as a drama that is 'set' within its fluctuating, overinscribed borders" (Baker 1997b: 72). On questions of geography and colonialism in the play, see also Knapp 1992: 220; and Willis 1989: 279–80.

9 On twentieth-century notions of memory, see Taylor 1996.

10 See also Fergus Kelly 1995.

11 *Calendar of State Papers Ireland* (henceforward referred to as *CSPI*). On the oral tradition of bardic poetry, see Murphy 1948: 44.

12 E.C.S., *The Governmentt of Ireland under Sir John Perrot, 1584–8* (London 1626), item 7 (no pagination) of "Sir John Perrots opinion for the suppressing of rebellion, and the well governing of Ireland, written by him upon the Queenes comandment, in the time of the Earle of Desmonds and the lord of Baltinglasses rebellion 1582." Quoted in Marc Caball's unpublished paper "Aspects of sixteenth-century Elite Gaelic mentalities: a casestudy."

13 For a different perspective on change in the play, see Simonds 1997–8: 538–70.

14 "Ordinances Proclaimed at Limerick by Sir John Perrot, Lord President of Munster" (1571) in Maxwell 1923; *CSPI 1611–14*: xxiv; Henley 1928:1056.

15 Robin Headlam Wells' "Prospero and the Myth of the Musician King" strives to restore the play's music to the general field of neo-platonism.

16 Jonson's dedication to *Volpone*, quoted in Philip Edwards 1979: 137.

17 For opposing views, see Dunne 1980: 7–30; Simms 1987: 58–75. Again, for the view that the poetry is not political, see O Riordan 1990. For a brilliant critique of O Riordan, see Caball 1993: 87–96.

18 On the connections between Ireland and Wales, see Highley 1997: chapter 3.

19 See also MacLysaght 1950: 353–6; and Henley 1928: 187.

20 Stephen Orgel has observed that the play's "realities throughout are largely the products of Prospero's imagination, or of the imaginative recreation of his memory. 'Facts' have a tendency to appear and disappear ... in a way that defeats any attempt to find in the play a firm history or a consistent world" (1987: 25).

21 Paul Brown writes: "Caliban's eloquence is after all 'your language', the language of the coloniser. Obviously the play itself, heavily invested in colonialist discourse, can only represent this moment of excess through that very discourse: and so the discourse itself may be said to produce this site of resistance. Yet what precisely is at stake here?

"The answer I believe is scandalously simple. Caliban's dream is not the antithesis but the apotheosis of colonialist discourse. If this discourse seeks to efface its own power, then here at last is an eloquent spokesman who is powerless" (1985: 66).

Alison Findlay argues that Caliban's language is pre-lingual, feminine music (1994: 140).

22 "The hybrid – either the degenerate Englishman or the incompletely assimilated Irishman – could become, for colonial power, a figure of threatening ambiguity, and his language the site of unsettling contradictions" (D. Baker 1992: 37–61, 40).

23 On Caliban's language, see also Cronin 1997: 202–5.

24 Hall argues that Miranda is herself an emblem of purity and integrity (1995: 42).

Janet Adelman illuminates the nature of femininity in Shakespeare's plays: "*Macbeth* is a recuperative consolidation of male power, a consolidation in the face of the threat unleashed in *Hamlet* and especially in *King Lear* and never fully contained in those plays. In *Macbeth*, maternal power is given its most virulent sway and then abolished; at the end of the play we are in a purely male realm. We will not be in so absolute a male realm again until we are in Prospero's island kingdom, similarly based firmly on the exiling of the witch Sycorax" (Adelman 1996: 105–34,122–3).

25 "Asgalan" is contemporary Askalane, my mother's birthplace, a few miles outside Westport.

26 It would be anachronistic, however, to read Keating's fear of annihilation in the annals of English historians as a fear of cultural annihilation in general. Far from being a "monument to a doomed civilization" (Collins 1990: 42), Keating's history evinces a commitment to Counter-Reformation ideology.

27 Instructions from the King to Sir Arthur Lord Chichester, 5th June 1614, *CSPI 1611–14*: 482–3.

28 Richard Halpern remarks, "[D]espite their own fantasies it was the colonizers themselves who, in their relations with the colonized, held a virtual monopoly on rape and sexual violence. Readers who find themselves casuistically tallying Caliban's sexual assault against the prior wrongs done to him … are caught in a false historical premise, one which builds specious symmetries for conservative ends" (1994: 283).

29 Consequently, the English regarded tanistry and gavelkind as follows: "It is a custom among all the Irish, that presently after the death of any of their chief lords and captains, they do presently assemble themselves to a place, generally appointed and known unto them, to choose another in his stead; where they do nominate and elect, for the most part, not the eldest son, nor any of the children of their lord deceased, but the next to him of blood, that is the eldest and worthiest" (Spenser quoted in Maxwell 1923: 32–3).

30 Kevin Collins explains, "So we find that while in English we say, 'I have a book,' the corresponding Irish construction *Tá leabhar agam* means literally 'The book is at me' " (1990: 24).

31 Richard Halpern writes that the first significant deviation from Montaigne in Gonzalo's speech is the word "plantation," which, he argues, "signifies an exclusively European colony" (1994: 268).

32 Spanish Captain, Francisco Cueller *Account of the Irish* (1589) quoted in Maxwell 1923: 318.

33 An unknown traveler's account of Ireland, 1579, in Maxwell 1923: 320.

34 See also, "Certain Considerations touching the Plantation," by Sir Arthur Chichester, 27th Jan 1609, in *CSPI 1609–10*: 357.

35 Prospero certainly reserves for Caliban a distinctly familial loathing, which, as Stephen Orgel notes, "moves him to a rage that is otherwise reserved only for Antonio" (1987: 23).

36 The question of O'Neill's upbringing has been the subject of some dispute. Most historians believe he spent a considerable portion of his childhood with the Sidneys, but Hiram Morgan believes he never left Ireland and was fostered by the New English family of Giles Hovenden in Laois (1993).

37 Orgel comments elsewhere: "Except for this moment, Prospero's wife is absent from his memory, she is wholly absent from her daughter's memory: Miranda can recall several women who attended her in childhood, but no mother" (1986: 51).

38 Orgel points out that in dynastic terms, calling Caliban a bastard negates his claim to the island via his mother's line, a claim that was plausible in the context of European monarchy.

39 Dolan writes: "Accounts of domestic crime destabilize distinctions between powerful and powerless, victimizer and victim, oppressor and oppressed" (1994: 171).

40 Peter Hulme has argued, for example, that discursively "Caliban is the monster all the characters make him out to be" (1992: 108), and that Caliban is a "compromise formation" because he bears on the surface of his body the secret of his genesis, which is nothing less than the heterogeneous history of repressed otherness. As such, Caliban can exist only within discourse, which is why he baffles directors and the play's other characters. For Hulme, Caliban is "fundamentally and essentially beyond the bounds of representation" (ibid.).

  In Marina Warner's novel *Indigo* (1992) Caliban is deformed as a result of having been hamstrung by European invaders.

41 David Baker writes, "England's sense of herself as an imperial domain may have been produced at some earlier point by taking the conquered Irish (for instance) as Other, but eventually power excludes all traces of that Other, leaving power to address itself in its own self-confirming terms" (1992: 42).

5 What is an audience?

1 A comparison with the contemporary horror film is instructive here. Carol J. Clover in *Men, Women and Chainsaws: Gender in the Modern Horror Film* (1992) observes, "Still, what formal surveys and informal accounts there are bear out with remarkable consistency Stephen King's presumption that adolescent males hold pride of place. At theatre screenings, in any case, the constituencies typically break down, on order of size, as follows: young men, frequently in groups but also solo; male-female couples of various ages (though mostly young); solo 'rogue males' (older men of ominous appearance and/or reactions);

and adolescent girls in groups. The proportions vary somewhat from subgenre to subgenre and from movie to movie ... but the preponderance of young males appears constant. ... Young males are also .. . the slasher film's implied audience, the object of its address" (6, 23). See also Richmond-Garza (1997: 223–46).

2 To avert the possibility of female terror, Bottom suggests direct address to the women in the audience. As Laura Levine incisively argues, "By avoiding any semblance of verisimilitude, this strategy seeks to avoid the dangers of representation in the first place" (1996: 217). The mechanicals tread the giddy brink between radical skepticism and absolute faith when it comes to representation. They demystify every element of its operations in the firm belief that the ladies cannot help but succumb to the awesome powers of mimesis.

3 It seems implausible that metropolitan plebeians (we have no information about the provinces) who paid admission to such an unusual social space as a theatre could persist in the belief that events and players on the platform were perfectly real; see Maguire 1996: 68, 329.

4 "[S]pectators were repeatedly and consistently described in contemporary accounts as moved to emotions and responses (compassion, remorse, pity, tears) that were understood as feminine. This conception ... is remarkably consistent: it appears in arguments for and against the theater, in the prologues and epilogues to plays, in accounts of actual experience as well as in prescriptive directions" (Rackin 1996: 34–5).

5 Of course, the impact of plays on men as well as women was also of interest, especially to the antitheatricalists. John Northbrooke's 1577 antitheatrical treatise, *A Treatise wherein Dicing, Dauncing, Vaine playes, or Enterluds, with other idle pastimes, & c., commonly used on the Sabbath day, are reproved by the Authorities of the word of God and the auntieint writers*, addresses itself particularly to women in a way that presupposed a distinction between male and female spectatorship: "If you will learne howe to be false and deceyve your husbandes, or husbandes their wyves howe to playe the harlottes, to obtayne one's love, howe to ravishe, howe to beguyle, howe to betraye, to flatter, lye, sweare, forsweare, how to allure to whoredome, howe to murther, howe to poyson, howe to disobey and rebell against princes, to consume treasures prodigally, to moove to lustes, to ransacke and spoyle cities and townes, to bee ydle, to blaspheme, to sing filthie songs of love, to speake filthily, to be prowde, howe to mocke, scoffe, and deryde any nation ... shall not you learne, then, at such enterludes howe to practise them?" (Northbrook quoted in Gurr 1987: 205).

6 On the importance of Shakespeare's cues for performers, see Dessen 1995.

7 Levine points out that Theseus's address to Hippolyta: – "I wooed

thee with my sword, / And won thy love doing thee injuries. / But I will wed thee in another key – / With pomp, with triumph, and with revelling" (I. i. 16–19) – signals theatre as a means of transforming sexual violence, though she argues that the play shows theatre unable, in the end, to accomplish that transformation (1996: 222).

8 For a brilliant analysis of the mechanicals' capacities for misrepresentation, see Parker (1996: 83–115).

9 Harold Brooks identifies Moffett's play as a source for Shakespeare's comedy in his 1979 Arden edition of *Dream* (1979: lxiv).

10 Though I cannot prove that Shakespeare knew of it, despite the play's Athenian setting, the specifically genital implications of Bottom's transformation resemble a tradition in Attic vase painting in which satyrs are, not half-human-half-goat but half-human-half-ass. The Attic hybrids have animal ears, while their lower bodies often resemble that of a donkey, complete with a tail and hooves. Sometimes, however, the lower part of the anatomy is left intact save for enormous genitalia. Nor is this disproportion exclusively dependent upon the satyr's ithyphallicism, for the creature may be depicted with an astoundingly long but flaccid member (Lissarague 1990: 54, 53–81).

Jonathan Bate observes, "Shakespeare's often-observed self-conscious theatricality, what has become known as his 'metadrama', simultaneously reminds us that we are in the theatre and helps us to forget where we are. In that forgetting, we come as near as is humanly possible to a witnessing of metamorphosis. With Bottom himself, we in the audience may say, 'I have had a most rare vision'" (1993: 144).

11 This is an interesting deformation of the conventional image of marriage (much favored by Protestant theologians in the period) in which the wife clings like a vine to her husband, the elm on whom she is dependent to the point of parasitism. On conventional vine imagery, see Holland 1994: 216. See also Paster 1993: 138.

12 "Sickly as a baby, a delicate but clever child, he grew up with a definite curvature of the spine which led to the development of a noticeable hump. In adulthood his mere silent presence could disconcert otherwise bold and blustering men; his eyes especially seemed to probe beyond a superficial truth. Yet this was a society that saw many more gross physical imperfections in people through birth traumas and congenital defects, or the calamities of war, than would be seen in England today. … He had also, like his mother, a shallow declivity on the side of his forehead" (quoted in Haynes 1989: 11–12). He never grew beyond five foot, and had a splay-footed gait. He was known by Elizabeth as "Elf" and "Pigmy," but he was also called among other things, "Bossive Robin," "Microgibbous," and "Roberto il Diavolo" (ibid.: 12). James referred to him as his "spaniel."

Bruce Smith, pondering what made Richard III so appealing to women, writes:

> Was it Richard III's brusque way with Lady Anne that made him so appealing …? In asking questions about women and staged violence, we need to distinguish … three possibilities: women as objects, women as subjects, and women as subjects/objects. Perhaps women read themselves as the perpetrators of violence. In that case, they might have taken a particular pleasure in witnessing the punishment of sexual transactions that excluded them.
>
> (Smith 1995: 437)

13 For a critique of Aubrey, see Lamb 1990.

14 "According to traditional fairy lore, which Shakespeare would have found in Spenser and in Scot's *Discoverie of Witchcraft*, fairies were in the habit of exchanging their own (often monstrous) babies for particularly beautiful human infants; this practise could leave parents in doubt about the identity of their own children, especially when these acted wickedly or rebelliously. The use of the term '*changeling*' between Titania and Oberon is unusual in that it applies to the human boy rather than the fairy infant – indeed, the play never directly asserts that any child was substituted for the Indian prince. And the accounts of the 'changeling' process vary between traditional fairy abduction ('A lovely boy, stol'n from an Indian king,' says Puck [2. 1. 22]) and Titania's story, which suggests that she is raising the boy in homage to her dear (but unfortunately mortal) friend, the Indian queen" (Barkan 1986: 259). See also Hendricks 1996.

15 Bottom is like the man who operated the machinery of the printing press. This worker, known as a "horse," was the brute force behind the purely physical aspects of printing operation (with all the sexual connotations of that operation), who bore down to imprint the page (de Grazia 1996: 63–94, esp. 83).

16 At a dinner at the Scottish court on 30 August 1594, a chariot was drawn by an African: "This chariot, which should have been drawn in by a lion, (but because his presence might have brought some fear to the nearest, or that the sight if the lights and torches might have commoved his tameness) it was thought meet that the lion should supply that room" (*A true Account of the most Triumphant and Royal Accomplishment of the Baptism of … Prince Henry Frederick in Somer's Tracts*, 2d ed. (1809), ii. 179). See also Holland 1945: 150; and Hall 1995: 23.

17 Patterson argues that after *King Lear*, "Shakespeare was forced to admit that the popular voice had grievances he could no longer express comedically" (Patterson 1989: 56, 69).

18 Privy Council to Lieutenants of Middlesex, 12th February 1618. For an analysis of the play in terms of friction between men at opposite ends of the class spectrum, see Leinwand 1986: 11–30; and on Shakespeare's relation to the midsummer riots and the question of popular insurrection more generally, see Wilson 1993: 22–44.

19 For the opposing view, that Theseus is a generous spectator, see Craig 1983: 91–3.

20 This speech links Bottom with "satire," spelled *satyr* in Elizabethan England (Kernan 1959: 55–7) and derives from a classical tradition in which satire was spoken by rough and savage satyrs (ibid.: 54). Kernan points out that the first use in English of the word satyr to denote a form of writing occurs in Alexander Barclay's *The Shyp of Folys of the Worlde* (1509): "This present Boke myght have ben callyd nat inconveneyntly the Satyr (that is to say) the reprehencion of foulysshnes" (quoted in ibid.: 54).

21 Michael Hattaway argues that "it has been common among theatre historians to argue that the public playhouses were frequented for the most part by members of the 'lower orders' or 'the working class.' The basic demographic information is exceedingly scanty and there are grave dangers of distortion if we allow modern demographic categories to settle on the period" (Hattaway 1982: 47). There were apparently more women than men in early modern London, but again these statistics may not correlate with women's attendance at the theatre.

22 Jean Howard reminds us that women in the theatre became "subjects who looked" (Howard 1994: 79).

23 In fact, despite all critical conjecture to the contrary, we do not have historical evidence that women were controlling the content of the drama. Richard Levin goes so far as to posit a causal relationship between women in the audience and the content of the plays themselves, a hypothesis that has come under fire in relation to Restoration theatre. "[W]hile women were not represented at the production end of this industry, they certainly were at the consumption end, and so probably had some effect upon its products" (1997: 174). See also Gurr 1987: 57. Jean Howard more cautiously asserts, "[W]e know that women were in the public theatre in significant numbers and that the women who attended the theatre were neither simply courtesans nor aristocratic ladies; many seem to have been citizens' wives, part of that emergent group, 'the middling sort' " (1994: 76).

24 Judith Mayne observes of studies of female spectatorship in the cinema a critique that is pertinent to studies of the female audience of early modern theatre: "the tendency for the researcher to construct an image of the 'spectator' or the 'real viewer' every bit as monolithic as the 'subject' of dominant ideology. Now, however, the monolithic quality works in another direction, constituting a viewer who is always resisting, always struggling, always seemingly just on the verge of becoming the embodiment of the researcher's own political ideal" (1993: 61).

25 Letter to Marie Bonaparte quoted in Jones 1955: 421.

26 Disruptive aristocratic spectators are quite unlike Nell the grocer's wife in *Knight of the Burning Pestle*. "Her spectatorship is active, interventional and effective, even though many of her suggestions are nominally transmitted through her husband," Osborne has argued (Osborne 1991: 505).

Bibliography

A. S. (1697) *The Husbandman, Farmer and Grasier's Compleat Instructor*, London: Printed for Henry Nelme.

Adelman, Janet (1996) "'Born of Woman': Fantasies of Maternal Power in *Macbeth*," in Garner and Sprengnether (eds).

—— (1997) "Iago's Alter Ego: Race as Projection in Othello," *Shakespeare Quarterly* 48: 125–44.

Aers, Lesley, and Wheale, Nigel (eds) (1991) *Shakespeare in the Changing Curriculum*, London and New York: Routledge.

Agnew, Jean-Christophe (1986) *World's Apart: The Market and the Theatre in Anglo-American Thought, 1550–1750*, Cambridge and New York: Cambridge University Press.

Allen, Theodore W. (1994) *The Invention of The White Race*, Volume I: *Oppression and Social Control*, New York: Verso.

Anderson, Judith H. (1996) *Words That Matter: Linguistic Perception in Renaissance English*, Stanford: Stanford University Press.

Andrews, Kenneth R., Canny, Nicholas P., Hair, P. E. H., and Quinn, David B. (eds) (1978) *The Westward Enterprise: English Activities in Ireland, the Atlantic, and America 1480–1650*, Liverpool: Liverpool University Press.

Appleby, John C. (1991) "Women and Piracy in Ireland: From Gráinne O'Malley to Anne Bonny," in MacCurtain and O'Dowd (eds) (1991).

Appleby, Joyce Oldham (1978) *Economic Thought and Ideology in Seventeenth-Century England*, Princeton: Princeton University Press.

188   Bibliography

Apuleius, Lucius (1893 [1566]) *The Golden Ass of Apuleius*, trans. William Adlington, intro. Charles Whibley, London: David Nutt.

Ariès, Philippe (1962) *Centuries of Childhood*, London: Jonathan Cape.

Armstrong, Nancy, and Tennenhouse, Leonard (eds) (1989) *The Violence of Representation: Literature and the History of Violence*, London and New York: Routledge.

Armstrong, Philip (1996) "Watching *Hamlet* Watching: Lacan, Shakespeare and the Mirror Stage," in Hawkes (ed.) (1996).

Armstrong, R. A. (1825) *Gaelic Dictionary*, London: James Duncan.

Astington, John (1994) "Malvolio and the Eunuchs: Texts and Revels in *Twelfth Night*," *Shakespeare Survey* 46: 23–49.

Aubrey, John (1949) *Aubrey's Brief Lives*, ed. Oliver Lawson Dick, London: Secker and Warburg.

Austern, Linda Phyllis (1992) *Music in English Children's Drama of the Later Renaissance*, New York: Gordon and Breach.

—— (1993) "'Alluring the Auditorie to Effeminacie': Music and the Idea of the Feminine in Early Modern England," *Music and Letters* 74: 343–54.

—— (1994) "'No Women Are Indeed': The Boy Actor as Vocal Seductress in English Renaissance Drama," in Dunn and Jones (eds) (1994).

Baker, David J. (1992) "'Wildehirisseman': Colonialist Representation in Shakespeare's *Henry V*," *ELR* 22, 1: 37–61.

—— (1997a) *Between Nations: Shakespeare, Spenser, Marvell, and the Question of Britain*, Stanford: Stanford University Press.

—— (1997b) "Where is Ireland in *The Tempest*?" in Burnett and Wray (eds) (1997).

Baker, Roger (1968) *Drag: A History of Female Impersonation*, London: Triton Books.

Barbour, R. (1995) "'When I Acted Young Antinous': Boy Actors and the Erotics of Jonsonian Theatre," *PMLA* 110, 5: 1006–22.

Barish, Jonas (1981) *The Antitheatrical Prejudice*, Berkeley: University of California Press.

Barkan, Leonard (1986) *The Gods Made Flesh: Metamorphosis & the Pursuit of Paganism*, New Haven, CT: Yale University Press.

Barker, Deborah, and Kamps, Ivo (eds) (1995) *Shakespeare and Gender: A History*, London and New York: Verso.

Barker, Francis (1984) *The Tremulous Private Body: Essays on Subjection*, New York: Methuen.

Barrett, Michèle (1988) *Women's Oppression Today: The Marxist/Feminist Encounter*, London: Verso.

Barroll, Leeds (1997) "Defining Dramatic Documents," *Medieval and Renaissance Drama in England* 9: 112–26.

Barthelemy, Anthony Gerard (1987) *Black Face, Maligned Race: The Representation of Blacks in English Drama from Shakespeare to Southerne*, Baton Rouge: Louisiana State University Press.

Barton, Sir D. Plunket (1919) *Links Between Ireland and Shakespeare*, Dublin: Maunsel and Co.

Bashar, Nazife (1983) "Rape in England Between 1500 and 1700," in London Feminist History Group (ed.) *The Sexual Dynamics of History*, London: Pluto Press.

Bate, Jonathan (1993) *Shakespeare and Ovid*, Clarendon Press: Oxford.

Beck, R. Theodore (1974) *The Cutting Edge: Early History of the Surgeons of London*, London: Lund Humphries.

Beier, A. L., and Finlay, Roger (1986) *London, 1500–1700: The Making of the Metropolis*, New York: Longman.

Belsey, Catherine (1985) "Disrupting Sexual Difference: Meaning and Gender in the Comedies," in John Drakakis (ed.) *Alternative Shakespeares*, London: Methuen.

Ben-Amos, Ilana Krausman (1994) *Adolescence and Youth in Early Modern England*, New Haven: Yale University Press.

Bentley, Gerald Eades (1984) *The Profession of Player in Shakespeare's Time, 1590–1642*, Princeton: Princeton University Press.

—— (ed.) (1968) *The Seventeenth-Century Stage*, Chicago: University of Chicago Press.

Berger, Harry Jr. (1969) "Miraculous Harp: A Reading of Shakespeare's *Tempest*," *Shakespeare Survey* 5: 253–83.

—— (1989) *Imaginary Audition: Shakespeare on Stage and Page*, Berkeley: University of California Press.

Berry, Phillipa (1993) "Authorship Overshadowed: death, darkness, and the feminisation of authority in late Renaissance literature," in Biriotti and Miller (eds).

Bevington, David (ed.) (1990) *Antony and Cleopatra*, Cambridge: Cambridge University Press.

Billington, Sandra (1991) *Mock Kings in Medieval Society and Renaissance Drama*, Oxford: Clarendon Press.

Binns, J. W. (1974) "Women or Transvestites on the Elizabethan Stage? An Oxford Controversy," *Sixteenth-Century Journal* 5: 95–120.

—— (1990) *Intellectual Culture in Elizabethan and Jacobean England: The Latin Writings of the Age*, Leeds: Francis Cairns.

Binns, J. W., and Spevack, Marvin (eds) (1981) *Renaissance Latin Drama in England*, First Series, Hildesheim; New York: G. Olms.

Biriotti, Maurice, and Miller, Nicola (eds) (1993) *What is an Author?*, Manchester: Manchester University Press.

Bishop, W. J. (1960) *The Early History of Surgery*, London: Robert Hale.

Blumenfeld-Kosinski, Renate (1990) *Not of Woman Born: Representations of Caesarean Birth in Medieval and Renaissance Culture*, Ithaca: Cornell University Press.

Boehrer, Bruce Thomas (1994) "Bestial Buggery in *A Midsummer Night's Dream*," in Miller, O'Dair, and Weber (eds) (1994).

Bradshaw, Brendan (1978) "Native Reaction to the Westward Enterprise: A Case-Study in Gaelic Ideology," in Andrews, Canny, Hair, and Quinn (eds) (1978).

—— (1993) "Geoffrey Keating: Apologist of Irish Ireland," in Bradshaw, Hadfield, and Maley (eds) (1993).

Bradshaw, Brendan, Hadfield, Andrew, and Maley, Willy (eds) (1993) *Representing Ireland: Literature and the Origins of Conflict, 1534–1660*, Cambridge: Cambridge University Press.

Braude, Benjamin (1997) "The Sons of Noah and the Construction of Ethnic and Geographical Identities in the Medieval and Early Modern Periods," *The William and Mary Quarterly* 3d series, 54, 1: 103–42.

Breatnach, Pádraigh A. (1989) "Cú Chonnacht Ó Dálaigh's Poem before Leaving Aodh Ruadh," in Ó Corrain, Breatnach, and McCone (eds), 32–42.

Breitenberg, Mark (1996) *Anxious Masculinity in Early Modern England*, Cambridge: Cambridge University Press.

Brewer, Rose M. (1993) "Theorizing Race, Class, and Gender: The new scholarship of Black feminist intellectuals and Black women's labor," in James and Busia (eds) (1993).

Brinkley, Roberta Florence (1928) *Nathan Field, The Actor-Playwright*, New Haven: Yale University Press.

Bristol, Michael D. (1990) "Charivari and the Comedy of Abjection in Othello," *Renaissance Drama* 21: 3–21.

Brooks, Harold F. (ed.) (1979) *A Midsummer Night's Dream*, Arden Edition, London: Methuen.

Brown, Paul (1985) "'This thing of darkness I acknowledge mine': *The Tempest* and the Discourse of Colonialism," in Dollimore and Sinfield (eds) (1985).

Brugis, Thomas (1681) *Vade Mecum: or a Companion for a Chirurgion fitted for Sea, or land; Peace or War*, London.

Bulwer, John (1648) *Philocophus: or The Deafe and Dumbe Mans Friend*, London.

—— (1653) *Anthropometamorphosis: Man Transformed*, London.

Burnett, Mark Thornton, and Wray, Ramona (eds) (1997) *Shakespeare and Ireland: History, Politics, Culture*, Basingstoke: Macmillan.

Butler, Judith (1990) *Gender Trouble: Feminism and the Subversion of Identity*, London and New York: Routledge.

Caball, Marc (unpublished) "Aspects of sixteenth-century Elite Gaelic mentalities: a case study."

—— (1993) "The Gaelic Mind and the Collapse of the Gaelic World: An Appraisal," *Cambridge Medieval Celtic Studies* 25: 87–96.

Callaghan, Dympna (1989) *Woman and Gender in Renaissance Tragedy*, Atlantic Highlands: Humanities Press International.

—— (ed.) (forthcoming) *The Feminist Companion To Shakespeare*, Oxford: Basil Blackwell.

Campbell, Jill (1995) *Natural Masques: Gender and Identity in Fielding's Plays and Novels*, Stanford: Stanford University Press.

Canny, Nicholas (1982) "The Formation of the Irish Mind: Religion, Politics and Gaelic Irish Literature 1580–1750," *Past and Present* 95: 91–116.

Case, Sue-Ellen (1988) *Feminism and Theatre*, New York: Methuen.

—— (1989) "Toward A Butch-Femme Aesthetic," in Lynda Hart (ed.) *Making A Spectacle: Feminist Essays In Contemporary Women's Theatre*, Ann Arbor: University of Michigan Press.

—— (ed.) (1991) *Performance of Power*, Iowa City: University of Iowa Press.

Castle, Terri (1993) *The Apparitional Lesbian: Female Homosexuality and Modern Culture*, New York: Columbia University Press.

Cavell, Stanley (1969) *Must We Mean What We Say?*, Cambridge: Cambridge University Press.

Céitinn, Seathrún. See Keating, Geoffrey.

Chambers, Anne (1998) *Granuaile: The Life and Times of Grace O'Malley, c.1530–1603*, Dublin: Wolfhound Press.

Chambers, E. K. (1923) *The Elizabethan Stage*, 4 vols, Oxford: Clarendon Press.

Chapman, George (1970) *Mayday* in Alan Holaday (ed.) *The Plays of George Chapman: Comedies*, Urbana: University of Illinois Press.

Charney, Maurice (1979) "Female Roles and the Children's Companies: Lyly's Pandora in The Woman in the Moon," *Research Opportunities in Renaissance Drama*, 22: 37–43.

Chedgzoy, Kate (1995) *Shakespeare's Queer Children: Sexual Politics and Contemporary Culture*, Manchester: Manchester University Press.

Church of England (1908 [1623]) *Certaine Sermons or Homilies, Appointed to be read in Churches, in the Time of Queen Elizabeth I, 1547–1571*, London: Society for Promoting Christian Knowledge.

Clark, Alice (1982 [1919]) *Working Life of Women in the Seventeenth Century*, London: Routledge and Kegan Paul.

Clark, Sandra (1985) "'Hic Mulier, Haec Vir' and the Controversy over Masculine Women," *Studies in Philology* 82, 2: 157–83.

Clover, Carol J. (1992) *Men, Women, and Chainsaws: Gender in the Modern Horror Film*, Princeton: Princeton University Press.

Collins, Kevin (1990) *The Cultural Conquest of Ireland*, Dublin: The Mercier Press.

Conboy, K., Medina, N., and Stanbury, S. (eds) (1997) *Writing on the Body: Female Embodiment and Feminist Theory*, New York: Columbia University Press.

Cook, Ann Jennalie (1981) *The Privileged Playgoers of Shakespeare's London, 1576–1642*, Princeton: Princeton University Press.

Cook, Judith (1977) *Women in Shakespeare*, London: Macmillan

Copjec, Joan (1994) *Read My Desire: Lacan Against the Historicists*, Cambridge, MA: M.I.T. Press.

Cowhig, Ruth (1995) "Blacks in English Renaissance Drama and the Role of Shakespeare's *Othello*," in David Dabydeen (ed.) *The Black Presence In English Literature*, Manchester: Manchester University Press.

Craig, D. H. (1983) "The Idea of the Play in *A Midsummer Night's Dream* and *Bartholomew Fair*," in Donaldson (ed.) (1983).

Craik, T. W., and Lothian, J. M. (eds) (1981) *Twelfth Night*, New York: Methuen. [Arden Shakespeare]

Crooke, Helkiah (1631 [1615]) *Mikrokosmographia: A Description of the Body of Man*, London.

Cronin, Michael (1997) "Rug-headed kerns speaking tongues: Shakespeare Translation and the Irish Language," in Burnett and Wray (eds) (1997).

Culpeper, Nicholas (1653) *Directory for Midwives*, London.

D'Amico, Jack (1991) *The Moor in English Renaissance Drama*, Tampa: University of South Florida Press.

David, Richard (1951) *Love's Labour's Lost*, London: Methuen.

De Grazia, Margreta (1996) "Imprints: Shakespeare, Gutenburg and Descartes," in Hawkes (ed.) (1996).

Dekker, Rudolf, and Van de Pol, Lotte C. (1989) *The Tradition of Female Transvestitism In Early Modern Europe*, New York: St. Martin's Press.

Dekker, Thomas (1904) *The Gull's Hornebook*, ed. R. B. McKerrow, London: De La More.

De Lauretis, Teresa (1987) *Technologies of Gender: Essays on Theory, Film, and Fiction*, Bloomington: Indiana Univeristy Press.

Dempster, Elizabeth (1988) "Women Writing the Body: Let's Watch a Little How She Dances," in Susan Sheridan (ed.) *Grafts: Feminist Cultural Criticism*, London: Verso.

Dessen, Alan C. (1995) *Recovering Shakespeare's Theatrical Vocabulary*, Cambridge: Cambridge University Press.

Doanne, Mary Ann (1991) *Femmes Fatales: Feminism, Film Theory, Psychoanalysis*, London and New York: Routledge.

Dolan, Frances (1993) "Taking the Pencil Out of God's Hand: Art, Nature and the Face-Painting Debate in Early Modern England," *PMLA* 108, 2: 224–39.

—— (1994) *Dangerous Familiars: Representations of Domestic Crime in England 1550–1700*, Ithaca, NY: Cornell University Press.

Dollimore, Jonathan (1990) "Shakespeare, Cultural Materialism, Feminism and Marxist Humanism," *New Literary History*, 21, 3: 471–93.

—— (1991) *Sexual Dissidence: Augustine to Wilde, Freud to Foucault*, Oxford: Clarendon Press.

Dollimore, Jonathan, and Sinfield, Alan (eds) (1985) *Political Shakespeare: New Essays In Cultural Materialism*, Ithaca: Cornell University Press.

Donaldson, Ian (ed.) (1983) *Jonson and Shakespeare*, Atlantic Highlands: Humanities Press International.

Drake, St. Clair (1990) *Black Folk Here and There*, 2 vols, Los Angeles: University of California Press.

Drayton, Michael (1622) *Poly-Olbion*, ed. Richard Hooper, London: John Russell Smith, 1876.

Drew-Bear, Annette (1981) "Face-Painting in Renaissance Tragedy," *Renaissance Drama* 12 (new series): 71–93.

—— (1994) *Painted Faces on the Renaissance Stage: The Moral Significance of Face-Painting Conventions*, Lewisburg: Bucknell University Press.

Dubrow, Heather, and Strier, Richard (eds) (1988) *The Historical Renaissance: New Essays in Tudor and Stuart Literature and Culture*, Chicago: University of Chicago Press.

Dunn, Leslie, and Jones, Nancy (eds) (1994) *Embodied Voices: Female Vocality and Western Culture*, Cambridge: Cambridge University Press.

Dunne, Thomas (1980) "The Gaelic Response to Conquest and Colonization: The Evidence of the Poetry," *Studia Hibernica* 20: 7–30.

—— (ed.) (1987) *The Writer as Witness: Literature as Historical Evidence*, Cork: Cork University Press

Durham, Jimmie (1993) *A Certain Lack of Coherence: Writings on Art and Cultural Politics*, London: Kala Press.

Dusinberre, Juliet (1985) *Shakespeare and the Nature of Women*, London: Macmillan.

—— (1996) "Squeaking Cleopatras: Gender and Performance in *Anthony and Cleopatra*," in James C. Bulman (ed.) *Shakespeare, Theory, and Performance*, London and New York: Routledge.

Dutton, Richard (1991) *Mastering the Revels: The Regulation and Censorship of English Renaissance Drama*, London: Macmillan.

Eagleton, Terry (1986) *Against the Grain: Essays 1975–1985*, London: Verso.

—— (1990) *The Ideology of the Aesthetic*, Oxford: Blackwell.

Ebert, Teresa L. (1991) "Political Semiosis In/Of American Cultural Studies," *American Journal of Semiotics* 8, 1/2: 113–35.

Eccles, Audrey (1982) *Obstetrics and Gynaecology in Tudor and Stuart England*, Kent, OH: Kent State University Press.

Edwards, Philip (1979) *Threshold of a Nation: A Study in English and Irish Drama*, Cambridge: Cambridge University Press.

Elam, Keir (1996) "The Fertile Eunuch: *Twelfth Night*, Early Modern Intercourse, and the Fruits of Castration," *Shakespeare Quarterly* 47: 1–36.

Elias, Norbert (1978–82 [1939]) *The Civilizing Process*, trans. Edmund Jephcott, 2 vols, Oxford: Basil Blackwell.

Elliott, John R., Jr. (1988) "Queen Elizabeth at Oxford: New Light on the Royal Plays of 1566," *ELR* 18, 2: 218–29.

—— (1997) "Drama," in Nicholas Tyacke (ed.) *Seventeenth-Century Oxford*, Vol. 4 of *The History of the University of Oxford*, T. H. Aston, gen. ed., Oxford: Clarendon Press (1984–).

Epstein, Julia, and Straub, Kristina (eds) (1991) *Body Guards: The Cultural Politics of Gender Ambiguity*, London and New York: Routledge.

Erickson, Peter (1991) *Rewriting Shakespeare, Rewriting Ourselves*, Berkeley: University of California Press.

Fabricius, Johannes (1994) *Syphilis in Shakespeare's England*, London and Bristol, PA: Jessica Kingsley.

Falkiner, C. Litton (1904) *Illustrations of Irish History and Topography, Mainly of the Seventeenth Century*, London: Longman Green.

Feher, Michel, Naddaff, Ramona, and Tazi, Nadia (eds) *Fragments for a History of the Human Body*, 3 vols, New York: Zone Books.

Felman, Shoshana (1993) *What Does a Woman Want? Reading and Sexual Difference*, Baltimore: Johns Hopkins University Press.

Ferguson, Margaret (1994) "Women, 'Race,' and Writing in Early Modern England," in Hendricks and Parker (eds) (1994).

Ferguson, Margaret W., Quilligan, Maureen, and Vickers, Nancy J. (eds) (1986) *Rewriting the Renaissance: The Discourse of Sexual Difference in Early Modern Europe*, Chicago: University of Chicago Press.

Ferris, Lesley (ed.) (1993) *Crossing the Stage: Controversies on Cross-Dressing*, London and New York: Routledge.

—— (1995) "The Female Self and Performance: The Case of The First Actress," in Laughlin and Schuler (eds).

Findlay, Alison (1994) *Illegitimate Power: Bastards in Renaissance Drama*, Manchester: Manchester University Press.

Fisher, Sheila, and Halley, Janet E. (eds) (1989) *Seeking the Woman in Late Medieval and Renaissance Writings*, Knoxville: University of Tennessee Press.

Fleming, Juliet (1993) "The ladies' man and the age of Elizabeth," in Turner (ed.).

Fletcher, John (1905–12) *Wit Without Money*, in *The Works of Francis Beaumont and John Fletcher*, ed. Arnold Glover and A. R. Waller, 10 vols, Cambridge: Cambridge University Press, Vol. 2.

Forbes, Thomas Roger (1966) *The Midwife and the Witch*, New Haven: Yale University Press.

Foucault, Michel (1981) *The History of Sexuality, Volume One: An Introduction*, trans. Robert Hurley, Harmondsworth: Penguin.

Fraser, Nancy (1989) *Unruly Practices: Power, Discourse and Gender in Contemporary Social Theory*, Minneapolis: University of Minnesota Press.

Freud, Sigmund (1965) *New Introductory Lectures on Psychoanalysis*, trans. James Strachey, New York: W. W. Norton.

Fryer, Peter (1984) *Staying Power: The History of Black People in Britain*, London: Pluto Press.

Fuchs, Barbara (1997) "Conquering Islands: Contextualizing *The Tempest*," *Shakespeare Quarterly* 48: 1, 45–62.

Fuller, Thomas (1662) *The History of the Worthies of England*, London.

Fumerton, Patricia (1991) *Cultural Aesthetics: Renaissance Literature and the Practice of Social Ornament*, Chicago: University of Chicago Press.

Gale, Thomas. See Vigo, Giovanni da.

Gallop, Jane (1982) *The Daughter's Seduction: Feminism and Psychoanalysis*, Ithaca: Cornell University Press.

—— (1988) *Thinking Through the Body*, New York: Columbia University Press.

Garber, Marjorie (1988) "Descanting on Deformity: *Richard III* and the Shape of History," in Dubrow and Strier (eds).

—— (1992) *Vested Interests: Cross-Dressing and Cultural Anxiety*, London and New York: Routledge.

Garner, Shirley Nelson (1989) "Let Her Paint an Inch Thick," *Renaissance Drama* 20: 123–39.

Garner, Shirley Nelson, and Sprengnether, Madelon (eds) (1996) *Shakespearean Tragedy and Gender*, Bloomington: Indiana University Press.

Gent, Lucy, and Llewellyn, Nigel (eds) (1990) *Renaissance Bodies: The Human Figure in English Culture c. 1540–1660*, London: Reaktion Books.

Gibbons, Brian (ed.) (1980) *Romeo and Juliet*, New York: Methuen. [Arden Shakespeare]

Gillies, John (1994) *Shakespeare and the Geography of Difference*, Cambridge: Cambridge University Press.

Gilroy, Paul (1993) *The Black Atlantic: Modernity and Double Consciousness*, Cambridge, MA: Harvard University Press.

Gold, Barbara K., Miller, Paul Allen, and Platter, Charles (1997) *Sex and Gender in Medieval and Renaissance Texts*, NY: State University of New York Press.

Goldberg, Jonathan (1986) "Textual Properties," *Shakespeare Quarterly* 37: 213–17.

Gombrich, E. H. (1985 [1963]) *Meditations on a Hobby Horse And Other Essays On the Theory Of Art*, London: Phaidon Press.

Gottfried, Rudolf (ed.) (1949) *Prose Works*, Vol. 9 of *The Works of Edmund Spenser: A Variorum Edition*, ed. Edwin Greenlaw, Charles Grosvenor Osgood, and Frederick Morgan Padelford, 10 vols, Baltimore: Johns Hopkins University Press.

Graham, Harvey (1951) *Eternal Eve: The History of Gynaecology and Obstetrics*, Garden City, NY: Doubleday.

Granville-Barker, Harley (1927) *Prefaces to Shakespeare*, 5 vols, London: Sidgwick and Jackson, 1927–47.

—— (1952) *Prefaces to Shakespeare*, vol. 1, Princeton: Princeton University Press.

Great Britain. *The Public Record Office. Calendar of State Papers . . . Ireland*, ed. C. W. Russell and John P. Prendergast (1574–84), 3 (1608–10), and 4 (1611–14), London: Her Majesty's Stationery Office.

Greenblatt, Stephen (1986) "Psychoanalysis and Renaissance Culture," in Parker and Quint (eds) (1986).

—— (1988) *Shakespearean Negotiations: The Circulation of Social Energy In Renaissance England*, Berkeley: University of California Press.

—— (1990) *Learning to Curse: Essays in Early Modern Culture*, London and New York: Routledge.

—— (1991) *Marvelous Possessions: The Wonder of the New World*, Chicago: University of Chicago Press.

—— (1997) "General Introduction," in *The Norton Shakespeare*, ed. Stephen Greenblatt et al., New York: W. W. Norton.

Grosz, Elizabeth (1987) "Notes Towards a Corporeal Feminism," *Australian Feminist Studies* 5: 1–16.

Gurr, Andrew (1987) *Playgoing in Shakespeare's London*, Cambridge: Cambridge University Press.

—— (1992) *The Shakespearean Stage 1547–1642*, 3rd ed., Cambridge: Cambridge University Press.

Gwilliam, Tassie (1994) "Cosmetic Poetics: Coloring Faces in the Eighteenth Century," in Kelly and Von Mücke (eds).

Gwinne, Matthew (1607) *Vertumnus*, London.

Hall, John (1844) *An Historical expostulation: against the beastlye abusers, both of chyrurgerie and physyke, in oure tyme: with a goodlye doctrine and instruction, necessarye to be marked and followed, of all true chirurgiens*, ed. T. J. Pettigrew, London: Printed for the Percy Society by T. Richards.

Hall, Joseph (1609) *The Discouery of a New World, or, a Description of the South Indies, hetherto vnknowne. [A humorous translation of Bishop Hall's Mundus alter et idem by John Healy.]*, London.

Hall, Kim F. (1991) "Sexual Politics and Cultural Identity in The Masque of Blackness," in Sue Ellen Case (ed.) *The Performance of Power*, Iowa City: University of Iowa Press.

—— (1994) "'I rather would wish to be a Black-Moor': Beauty, Race and Rank in Lady Mary Wroth's Urania," in Hendricks and Parker (eds).

—— (1995) *Things of Darkness: Economies of Race and Gender in Early Modern England*, Ithaca: Cornell University Press.

Halliwell-Phillipps, J. O. (ed.) (1865) *The Remonstrance of Nathan Field, one of Shakespeare's Company of Actors, Addressed to a preacher in Southwark, who had been Arraigning Against the Players At the Globe Theatre in the Year 1616*, London.

Halperin, David M., Winkler, John J., and Zeitlin, Froma I. (eds) (1990) *Before Sexuality: The Construction of Erotic Experience in the Ancient Greek World*, Princeton: Princeton University Press.

Halpern, Richard (1991) *The Poetics of Primitive Accumulation: English Renaissance Culture and the Genealogy of Capital*, Ithaca, NY: Cornell University Press.

—— (1994) "'The Picture of Nobody': White Cannibalism in *The Tempest*," in D. Miller, S. O'Dair, and H. Weber (eds).

Hardin, R. F. (1982) "Marston's Kinsayder: The Dog's Voice," *Notes and Queries* 29, 2: 134–5.

Hattaway, Michael (1982) *Elizabethan Popular Theatre: Plays in Performance*, London and New York: Routledge.

Hawkes, Terence (ed.) (1996) *Alternative Shakespeares*: Volume 2, London and New York: Routledge.

Haynes, Alan (1989) *Robert Cecil, Earl of Salisbury, 1563–1612: Servant of Two Sovereigns*, London: Peter Owen.

Hazlitt, W. C. (1869) *The English Drama And Stage Under the Tudor and Stuart Princes, 1543–1664*, London.

Hedrick, Don (1995) "Framing O.J.: Tabloidation and 'Tragedy', or Analog Racism and Digital Racism," *Mediations* 19, 2: 4–14.

Heinemann, Margo (1993) "Drama and Opinion in the 1620s: Middleton and Massinger," in Mulryne and Shewring (eds).

Hendricks, Margo (1996) "'Obscured by Dreams': Race, Empire, and Shakespeare's *A Midsummer Night's Dream*," *Shakespeare Quarterly* 47, 1: 37–60.

Hendricks, Margo, and Parker, Patricia (eds) (1994) *Women, "Race," and Writing in the Early Modern Period*, London and New York: Routledge.

Henley, Pauline (1928) *Spenser in Ireland*, London: Longman.

Herford, C. H., and Simpson, Percy and Evelyn (eds) (1925–52) *Ben Jonson*, 11 vols, Oxford: Clarendon Press.

Highley, Christopher (1997) *Shakespeare, Spenser, and the Crisis in Ireland*, Cambridge: Cambridge University Press.

Hill, Errol (1984) *Shakespeare in Sable: A History of Black Shakespearean Actors*, Amherst: University of Massachusetts Press.

Hillman, David, and Mazzio, Carla (1997) *The Body In Parts: Fantasies of Corporeality in Early Modern England*, London and New York: Routledge.

Holland, Peter (ed.) (1994) *A Midsummer Night's Dream*, Oxford: Oxford University Press.

Horkheimer, Max, and Adorno, Theodor W. (1972) *Dialectic of Enlightenment*, trans. John Cumming, New York: Continuum.

Howard, Jean (1991) "Scripts and/versus Playhouses: Ideological Production and the Renaissance Public Stage," in Wayne (ed.) (1991).

—— (1994) *The Stage and Social Struggle In Early Modern England*, London and New York: Routledge.

Howard, Jean E., and O'Connor, Marion F. (eds) (1987) *Shakespeare Reproduced: The Text in History and Ideology*, London and New York: Routledge

Howe, Elizabeth (1992) *The First English Actresses: Women and Drama 1660–1700*, Cambridge: Cambridge University Press.

Hulme, Peter (1992) *Colonial Encounters: Europe and the Native Caribbean, 1492–1797*, London and New York: Routledge.

Hutson, Lorna (1994) *The Usurer's Daughter: Male Friendship and Fictions of Women in Sixteenth-Century England*, London and New York: Routledge.

Jagendorf, Zvi (1990) "*Coriolanus*: Body Politic and Private Parts," *Shakespeare Quarterly* 41, 4: 455–69.

James, Stanlie M., and Busia, Abena P. A. (eds) (1993) *Theorizing Black Feminisms*, London and New York: Routledge.

Jamieson, Michael (1968) "Shakespeare's Celibate Stage: The Problem of Accommodation to Boy Actors in *As You Like It, Anthony and Cleopatra*, and *The Winter's Tale*," in Bentley (ed.).

Jankowski, Theodora (1992) *Women In Power In Early Modern Drama*, Chicago: University Of Illinois Press.

Jardine, Lisa (1983) *Still Harping on Daughters: Women and Drama in the Age of Shakespeare*, Brighton: Harvester.

Jenkins, Harold (ed.) (1982) *Hamlet*, New York: Methuen. [Arden Shakespeare]

Johnson, Thomas. See Paré, Ambroise.

Jones, Ann Rosalind, and Stallybrass, Peter (1991) "Fetishizing Gender: Constructing the Hermaphrodite in Renaissance Europe," in Epstein and Straub (eds).

Jones, Eldred (1965) *Othello's Countrymen: The African in English Renaissance Drama*, Oxford: Oxford University Press.

Jones, Ernest (1953–7) *The Life and Work of Sigmund Freud*, 3 vols, New York: Basic Books.

Jones, Gayl (1998) *The Healing*, Boston: Beacon Press.

Jonson, Ben (1960) *Bartholomew Fair*, ed. E. A. Horsman, Cambridge, MA: Harvard University Press.

—— (1969) *Ben Jonson: The Complete Masques, 1572–1637*, ed. Stephen Orgel, New Haven: Yale University Press.

Jordan, Winthrop (1968) *White Over Black: American Attitudes Toward the Negro, 1550–1812*, Chapel Hill: University of North Carolina Press.

Kastan, David (1986) "Proud Majesty Made Subject: Shakespeare and the Spectacle of Rule," *Shakespeare Quarterly* 37: 459–75.

Keating, Geoffrey (*c.* 1634) *The History of Ireland (Foras Feasa ar Éirinn)*.

Kelly, F. M. (1938) *Shakespearean Costume for Stage and Screen*, London: Adam and Charles Black.

Kelly, Fergus (1995) *A Guide to Early Irish Law*, Dublin: Institute for Advanced Studies.

Kelly, Veronica, and Von Mücke, Dorothea (eds) (1994) *Body and Text in the Eighteenth Century*, Stanford: Stanford University Press.

Kermode, Frank (ed.) (1964) *The Tempest*, New York: Methuen. [Arden Shakespeare]

Kernan, Alvin (1959) *The Cankered Muse: Satire of the English Renaissance*, New Haven: Yale University Press.

King, T. V. (1971) *Shakespearean Staging 1599–1642*, Cambridge: Harvard University Press.

Knapp, Jeffrey (1992) *An Empire Nowhere: England, American, and Literature from Utopia to* The Tempest, Berkeley: University of California Press.

Knott, Eleanor, and Murphy, Gerard (1966) *Early Irish Literature*, London: Routledge and Kegan Paul.

Koestenbaum, Wayne (1993) *The Queen's Throat: Opera, Homosexuality, and the Mystery of Desire*, New York: Penguin.

Kott, Jan (1987) *The Bottom Translation: Marlowe and Shakespeare and the*

Carnival Tradition, trans. Daniela Miedzyrzecka and Lillian Vallee, Evanston: Northwestern University Press.

Lamb, Margaret (1980) Antony and Cleopatra *On the English Stage*, Rutherford, NJ: Fairleigh Dickinson University Press.

Lamb, Mary Ellen (1990) *Gender and Authorship in the Sidney Circle*, Madison: University of Wisconsin Press.

Laqueur, Thomas (1989) "Amor Veneris, vel Ducedo Appelatur," in Feher, Naddaff, and Tazi (eds).

—— (1990) *Making Sex: Body and Gender from the Greeks to Freud*, Cambridge: Harvard University Press.

Laroque, François (1993) *Shakespeare*, New York: Harry N. Abrams.

—— (1993) *Shakespeare's Festive World: Elizabethan Seasonal Entertainment and the Professional Stage*, trans. Janet Lloyd, Cambridge: Cambridge University Press.

Laughlin, Karen, and Schuler, Catherine (eds) (1995) *Theatre and Feminist Aesthetics*, Madison: Fairleigh Dickinson University Press.

Leinwand, Theodore P. (1986) "'I believe we must leave the killing out': Deference and Accommodation in *A Midsummer Night's Dream*," *Renaissance Papers*: 11–30

Lennon, Colm (1981) *Richard Stanihurst The Dubliner 1547–1618*, Dublin: Irish Academic Press.

Leon-Portilla, Miguel (1962) *The Broken Spears: The Aztec Account of the Conquest of Mexico*, London: Constable and Co.

Levine, Laura (1986) "Men in Women's Clothing: Anti-theatricality and Effeminization from 1579 to 1642," *Criticism* 28: 121–43.

—— (1994) *Men in Women's Clothing: Anti-theatricality and Effeminization, 1579–1642*, Cambridge: Cambridge University Press.

—— (1996) "Rape, repetition, and the politics of closure in *A Midsummer Night's Dream*," in Traub, Kaplan, and Callaghan (eds).

Levin, Richard (1989) "Women In the Audience", *Shakespeare Quarterly* 40: 165–74.

Little, Arthur L. (1993) "'An essence that's not seen': The Primal Scene of Racism in *Othello*," *Shakespeare Quarterly* 44, 3: 304–24.

Lissarague, François (1990) "The Sexual Life of Satyr," in Halperin, Winkler, and Zeitlin (eds).

Loomba, Ania (1996) "Shakespeare and Cultural Difference," in Hawkes (ed.) (1996).

Lott, Eric (1993) *Love and Theft: Blackface, Minstrelsy, and the American Working Class*, Oxford: Oxford University Press.

MacCurtain, Margaret, and O'Dowd, Mary (eds) (1991) *Women in Early Modern Ireland*, Dublin: Wolfhound Press.

MacLysaght, Edward (1950) *Irish Life in the Seventeenth Century*, 2d ed., Oxford: Basil Blackwell.

Maguire, Laurie E. (1995) "Cultural Control in *The Taming of the Shrew*", *Renaissance Drama* 26: 83–104.

—— (1996) *Shakespearean Suspect Texts: The "bad" quartos and their contexts*, Cambridge: Cambridge University Press.

—— (1998)"Petruccio and the Barber's Shop," *Studies in Bibliography* 51: 117–126.

Malcolmson, Christina (1991) "'What You Will': Social Mobility and Gender in *Twelfth Night*," in Wayne (ed.) (1991).

Mann, David (1991) *The Elizabethan Player: Contemporary Stage Representation*, London and New York: Routledge.

Marcus, Leah (1978) *Childhood and Cultural Despair*, Pittsburgh: University of Pittsburgh Press.

—— (1996) *Unediting the Renaissance: Shakespeare, Marlowe, Milton*, London and New York: Routledge.

Marston, John (1991) *Antonio and Mellida*, ed. W. Reavley Gair, Manchester: Manchester University Press.

Martin, Emily (1987) *The Woman In The Body: A Cultural Analysis of Reproduction*, Boston: Beacon Press.

Masten, Jeffrey (1997) "Is the Fundament a Grave?," in Hillman and Mazzio (eds) (1997).

Maurer, Margaret (unpublished essay) "Coming of Age in Illyria: Doubling the Twins in *Twelfth Night*."

Maxwell, Constantina (1923) *Irish History from Contemporary Sources 1509–1610*, London: George Allen and Unwin.

Mayne, Judith (1993) *Cinema and Spectatorship*, London and New York: Routledge.

McKendrick, Melveena (1989) *Theatre in Spain 1490–1700*, Cambridge: Cambridge University Press.

McLuskie, Kathleen (1987) "The Act, the Role, and the Actor: Boy Actresses on the Elizabethan Stage," *New Theatre Quarterly* 5: 120–30.

—— (1989) *Renaissance Dramatists*, Atlantic Highlands: Humanities Press International.

Miller, David Lee, O'Dair, Sharon, and Weber, Harold (eds) (1994) *The Production of English Renaissance Culture*, Ithaca: Cornell University Press.

Modleski, Tania (1991) *Feminism Without Women: Culture and Criticism in a "Postfeminist" Age*, London and New York: Routledge.

Moffett, Thomas (1599) *The Silkwormes, and their Flies*, London.

Montagne, Walter (1629 and 1659) *The Shepheard's Purse*, London.

Montaigne, Michel de (1897) *The Essayes of Michael Lord of Montaigne*, trans. John Florio, ed. Israel Gollancz, London: J. M. Dent.

—— (1993) *The Complete Essays of Michel de Montaigne*, ed. and trans. M. A. Screech, London and New York: Penguin Books.

Morgan, Hiram (1993) *Tyrone's Rebellion: The Outbreak of the Nine Years War in Tudor Ireland*, Woodbridge: Boydell Press.

Morris, Brian (ed.) (1981) *The Taming of the Shrew*, New York: Methuen. [Arden Shakespeare]

Morton, Donald (1990) "Texts of Limits, the Limits of Texts, and the Containment of Politics in Contemporary Critical Theory," *Diacritics* 20,1: 57–75.

Mullaney, Steven (1988) *The Place of the Stage: License, Play, and Power in Renaissance England*, Chicago: University of Chicago Press.

Mulryne, J. R., and Shewring, Margaret (eds) (1993) *Theatre and Government Under the Early Stuarts*, Cambridge: Cambridge University Press.

Murphy, Gerard (1948) *Glimpses of Gaelic Ireland*, Dublin.

Neely, Carol Thomas (1995) "Circumscriptions and Unhousedness: *Othello* in the Borderlands," in Barker and Kamps (eds) (1995).

Neill, Michael (1984) "Changing Places in *Othello*," *Shakespeare Survey* 37: 115–31.

—— (1989) "Unproper Beds: Race, Adultery, and the Hideous in *Othello*," *Shakespeare Quarterly* 40, 4: 383–412.

—— (ed.) (1994a) *Anthony and Cleopatra*, Oxford: Clarendon Press.

—— (1994b) "Broken English and Broken Irish: Nation, Language, and the Optic of Power in Shakespeare's Histories," *Shakespeare Quarterly* 45: 1–32.

Nelson, Alan H. (1990) "Women in the Audience of Cambridge Plays," *Shakespeare Quarterly* 41: 333–6.

Newman, Karen (1987) " 'And wash the Ethiop white': Femininity and the Monstrous in *Othello*," in Howard and O'Connor (eds).

Newton, Judith, and Rosenfelt, Deborah (eds) (1985) *Feminist Criticism and Social Change: Sex, Class, and Race in Literature and Culture*, New York: Methuen.

Novy, Marianne (1984) *Love's Argument: Gender Relations in Shakespeare*, Chapel Hill: University of North Carolina Press.

Ó Corrain, Donnchadh, Breatnach, Liam, and McCone, Kim (eds) (1989) *Sages, Saints and Storytellers: Celtic Studies in Honor of Professor James Carney*, Maynooth: An Sagart.

Orgel, Stephen (1986) "Prospero's Wife," in Ferguson, Quilligan, and Vickers (eds), 50–64.

—— (ed.) (1987) *The Tempest*, Oxford: Oxford University Press.

—— (1989) "Nobody's Perfect: Or Why Did the English Stage Take Boys For Women?" *The South Atlantic Quarterly* 88: 7–29.

—— (1996) *Impersonations: The Performance of Gender in Shakespeare's England*, Cambridge: Cambridge University Press.

—— (ed.) (1996) *The Winter's Tale*, Oxford: Oxford University Press.

O'Riordan, Michelle (1990) *The Gaelic Mind and the Collapse of the Gaelic World*, Cork: Cork University Press.

Orkin, Martin (1987) "*Othello* and the 'plain face' of Racism," *Shakespeare Quarterly* 38: 166–88.

Osborne, Laurie (1991) "Female Audiences and Female Authority in the *Knight of the Burning Pestle*," *Exemplaria* 3, 2: 491–517.

Palmer, William (1992) "Gender, Violence, and Rebellion in Early Tudor and Stuart Ireland," *The Sixteenth Century Journal* 23,4: 699–712.

Papp, Joseph (1988) "Foreword" in *A Midsummer Night's Dream*, ed. David Bevington, New York: Bantam.

Paquet, Sandra Pouchet (1992) "Foreword" in George Lamming, *The Pleasure of Exile*, Ann Arbor: University of Michigan Press.

Paré, Ambroise (1982 [1573]) *On Monsters and Marvels*, trans. Janis L. Pallister, Chicago: University of Chicago Press.

—— (1634; London 1649) *The Workes of That Famous Chirurgion Ambrose Parey translated out of Latine and compared with the French* by Th: Johnson, London.

Park, Katharine (1997) "The Rediscovery of the Clitoris: French Medicine and the Tribade, 1570–1620," in Hillman and Mazzio (eds) (1997).

Parker, G. (1920) *The Early History of Surgery in Great Britain*, London: A. C. Black.

Parker, Patricia (1994) "Fantasies of 'Race' and 'Gender': Africa, *Othello*, and Bringing to Light," in Hendricks and Parker (eds) (1994).

—— (1996) *Shakespeare from the Margins: Language, Culture, Context*, Chicago: University of Chicago Press.

Parker, Patricia, and Quint, David (eds) (1986) *Literary Theory / Renaissance Texts*, Baltimore: Johns Hopkins University Press.

Parry, J. H. (1990) "The Boyhood of Shakespeare's Heroines," *Shakespeare Survey*, 42: 99–109.

Partridge, Eric (1968) *Shakespeare's Bawdy: A Literary and Psychological Essay and A Comprehensive Glossary*, rev. and enl., London: Routledge and Kegan Paul.

Paster, Gail Kern (1993) *The Body Embarrassed: Drama and the Disciplines of Shame in Early Modern England*, Ithaca: Cornell University Press.

Patterson, Annabel (1989) *Shakespeare and the Popular Voice*, Oxford: Basil Blackwell.

Pearson, Jacqueline (1988) *The Prostituted Muse: Images of Women and Women Dramatists, 1642–1673*, New York: St. Martin's Press.

Pequigney, Joseph (1995) "The Two Antonios and Same-Sex Love in *Twelfth Night* and *The Merchant of Venice*," in Barker and Kamps (eds) (1995).

Phelan, Peggy (1993) *Unmarked: The Politics of Performance*, London and New York: Routledge.

Pocock, J.G.A. (1975) *The Machiavellian Moment: Florentine Political Thought and the Atlantic Republican Tradition*, Princeton: Princeton University Press.

Pye, Christopher (1990) *The Regal Phantasm: Shakespeare and the Politics of Spectacle*, London and New York: Routledge.

Quaife, G. R. (1979) *Wanton Wenches and Wayward Wives: Peasants and Illicit Sex in Early Seventeenth-Century England*, New Brunswick: Rutgers University Press.

Quétel, Claude (1990) *The History of Syphilis*, trans. Judith Braddock and Brian Pike, Baltimore: Johns Hopkins University Press.

Rackin, Phyllis (1987) "Androgyny, Mimesis, and the Marriage of the Boy Heroine on the English Renaissance Stage," *PMLA* 102, 1: 29–41.

—— (1996) "History into Tragedy: The Case of *Richard III*," in Garner and Sprengnether (eds) (1996).

Rainolds, John (1972 [1599]) *The Overthrow of Stage-Plays, by the way of controversy between D. Gager and J. Rainolds*, intro. J. W. Binns, New York: Johnson Reprint Corp.

Rastall, Richard (1996) *The Heaven Singing: Music in Early English Religious Drama*, Cambridge, UK, and Rochester, NY: D. S. Brewer.

Retamar, Roberto Fernandez (1989) *Caliban and Other Essays*, trans. Edward Baker, Minneapolis: University of Minnesota Press.

Richards, Sandra (1993) *The Rise of the English Actress*, Basingstoke: Macmillan.

Richmond-Garza, Elizabeth M. (1997) "'She Never Recovered Her Senses:' *Roxana* and Dramatic Representations of Women at Oxbridge in the Elizabethan Age", in Gold et al. (eds).

Ridley, M. R. (ed.) (1958) *Othello*, London: Methuen. [Arden Shakespeare]

Riley, Denise (1988) *"Am I That Name?" Feminism and the Category of "Women" in History*, Minneapolis: University of Minnesota Press.

Roberts, David (1989) *The Ladies: Female Patronage of Restoration Drama 1660–1700*, Oxford: Clarendon Press.

Robinson, Amy (1994) "It Takes One to Know One: Passing and Communities of Common Interest," *Critical Inquiry* 20: 4, 715–36.

Rogin, Michael (1987) *Ronald Reagan, the Movie and Other Episodes in Political Demonology*, Berkeley: University of California Press.

Rose, Mary Beth (1988) *The Expense of Spirit: Love and Sexuality in English Renaissance Drama*, Ithaca: Cornell University Press.

Rosenberg, Marvin (1961) *The Masks of* Othello: *The search for the Identity of Othello, Iago, and Desdemona by Three Centuries of Actors and Critics*, Berkeley: University of California Press.

Russo, Mary (1997) "Female Grotesques: Carnival and Theory," in Conboy, Medina, and Stanbury (eds) (1997).

Ryan, Kiernan (1989) *Shakespeare*, Atlantic Highlands: Humanities Press International, Inc.

Sachdev, Rachana (forthcoming) "Sycorax in Algiers: Cultural Politics and Gynecology in Early Modern England," in Callaghan (ed.) *The Feminist Companion To Shakespeare*, Oxford: Blackwell.

Salway, John (1991) "Veritable Negroes and Circumcised Dogs: Racial Disturbances in Shakespeare," in Aers and Wheale (eds) (1991).

Sawday, Jonathan (1995) *The Body Emblazoned: Dissection and the Human Body in Renaissance Culture*, London and New York: Routledge.

Scragg, Leah (1991) "Her C's, Her U's, Her T's," *Review of English Studies* 42: 1–16.

Scultetus, Johannes (1674) *The Chyrurgeons Store-House* …, London.

Screech, M. A. See Montaigne, Michel de.

Sedinger, Tracey (1997) "'If sight and shape be true': The Epistemology of Crossdressing on the London Stage," *Shakespeare Quarterly* 48: 63–79.

Shabazz, Betty (1997) "All things considered," National Public Radio.

Shapiro, Michael (1996) *Gender in Play in the Shakespearean Stage: Boy Heroines and Female Pages*, Ann Arbor: University of Michigan.

Sharp, Jane (1671) *The Midwives Book*, London.

Shaw, Kate (1987) "Landgartha and the Irish Dilemma," *Eire-Ireland* xiii: 26–39.

Shershow, Scott Cutler (1995) *Puppets and "Popular" Culture*, Ithaca: Cornell University Press.

Shyllon, Folarin (1977) *Black People in Britain 1555–1833*, Oxford: Oxford University Press.

Silverman, Kaja (1988) *The Acoustic Mirror: The Female Voice in Psychoanalysis and Cinema*, Bloomington: Indiana University Press.

—— (1992a) *Male Subjectivity at the Margins*, New York: Routledge.

—— (1992b) "The Lacanian Phallus," *Differences* 4,1: 84–115.

—— (1994) *Visual and Other Pleasures*, Bloomington: Indiana University Press.

Simonds, Peggy Muñoz (1997–8) "'My Charms Crack Not': The Alchemical Structure of *The Tempest*," *Comparative Drama* 31: 538–70.

Simms, Katharine (1987) "Bardic Poetry as a Historical Source," in Dunne (ed.).

Singh, Jyotsna (1994) "Othello's Identity, Postcolonial Theory, and Contemporary African Rewritings of *Othello*," in Hendricks and Parker (eds) (1994).

Skura, Meredith Anne (1989) "Discourse and the Individual: The Case of Colonialism in *The Tempest*," *Shakespeare Quarterly* 40: 42–69.

Smith, Bruce (1995) "Race, rap, rupture: R-rated futures on the global market," *Textual Practice* 9, 3: 421–44.

Smith-Rosenberg, Carroll (1989) "The Body Politic," in Weed (ed.) (1989).

Sommerville, John (1992) *The Discovery of Childhood in Puritan England*, Athens: University of Georgia Press.

Spenser, Edmund (1997) *A View of the Present State of Ireland*, ed. Andrew Hadfield and Willy Maley, Oxford: Blackwell.

Stallybrass, Peter (1986) "Patriarchal Territories: The Body Enclosed," in Ferguson, Quilligan, and Vickers (eds) (1986).

—— (1989) "'Drunk With the Cup of Liberty': Robinhood, the Carnivalesque, and the Rhetoric of Violence in Early Modern England," in Armstrong and Tennenhouse (eds) (1989).

—— (1992) "Transvestism and the 'body beneath': Speculating on the Boy Actor," in Zimmerman (ed.) (1992).

Stallybrass, Peter, and White, Allon (1986) *The Politics and Poetics of Transgression*, Ithaca: Cornell University Press.

Sterne, Laurence (1986 [1768]) *A Sentimental Journey*, Harmondsworth: Penguin.

Stubbes, Philip (1583) *The Anatomy of Abuses*, London.

Suleiman, Susan Rubin (ed.) (1985) *The Female Body in Western Culture: Contemporary Perspectives*, Cambridge: Harvard University Press.

Tayler, Edward (1991) *Donne's Idea of A Woman: Structure and Meaning in the Anniversaries*, New York: Columbia University Press.

Taylor, Gary (1996) *Cultural Selection: Why Some Achievements Survive the Test of Time – And Others Don't*, New York: Basic Books.

Tennenhouse, Leonard (1986) *Power On Display: the Politics of Shakespeare's Genres*, New York: Methuen.

—— (1989) "Violence Done To Women On the Renaissance Stage," in Armstrong and Tennenhouse (eds) (1989).

Thomas, Nicholas (1995) "Kiss the Baby Goodbye: Kowhaiwhai and Aesthetics in Aotearoa New Zealand," *Critical Inquiry* 22: 1, 90–121.

Thompson, Ann (1996) "Women/'women' and the stage," in Wilcox (ed.) (1996).

Thomson, Peter (1992) *Shakespeare's Professional Career*, Cambridge: Cambridge University Press.

Tillotson, Geoffrey (1933) "*Othello* and *The Alchemist* at Oxford in 1610," *The Times Literary Supplement*, 20 July, p. 494.

Tilton, Robert S. (1994) *Pocahontas: The Evolution of An American Narrative*, Cambridge: Cambridge University Press.

Tokson, Elliot (1982) *The Popular Image of the Black Man in Elizabethan Drama, 1550–1688*, Boston: G. K. Hall.

Tomlinson, Sophie Eliza (1995) "Theatrical Women: The Female Actor in English Theatre and Drama 1603–1670," unpublished dissertation, Darwin College, Cambridge University.

Traub, Valerie (1991) "Desire and the Difference it Makes," in Wayne (ed.) (1991).

—— (1995) "The Psychomorphology of the Clitoris," *Gay and Lesbian Quarterly* 2: 81–113.

Traub, Valerie, Kaplan, M. Lindsay, and Callaghan, Dympna (eds) (1996) *Feminist Readings of Early Modern Culture*, Cambridge: Cambridge University Press.

Turner, James Grantham (ed.) (1993) *Sexuality and Gender in Early Modern Europe: Institutions, texts, images*, Cambridge: Cambridge University Press.

Vaughan, Alden T., and Vaughan, Virginia Mason (1991) *Shakespeare's Caliban: A Cultural History*, Cambridge: Cambridge University Press.

—— (1997) "Before *Othello*: Elizabethan Representations of Sub-Saharan Africans," *The William and Mary Quarterly* 3d Series, 54, 1: 19–44.

Vaughan, Virginia Mason (1994) Othello: *A Contextual History*, Cambridge: Cambridge University Press.

Vickers, Nancy J. (1985) "This Heraldry in Lucrece's Face," in Suleiman (ed.).

Vigo, Giovanni da (1586) *The Whole Worke of That Famous Chirugion Maister Iohn Vigo … compiled and published by Thomas Gale, Maister in Chirurgerie*, London.

Vitkus, Daniel J. (1997) "Turning Turk in *Othello*: The Conversion and Damnation of the Moor," *Shakespeare Quarterly* 48: 145–76.

Vulpi, Frank (1996) "'Parmenides,' 'What-is-not,' and Some Seventeenth-Century English Metaphysical Poets," *Seventeenth Century News* 54: 47–8.

Wallerstein, Immanuel (1991) "The Ideological Tensions of Capitalism: Universalism Versus Racism and Sexism," in Wallerstein and Balibar (eds).

Wallerstein, Immanuel, and Balibar, Etienne (eds) (1991) *Race, Nation and Class: Ambiguous Identities*, London: Verso.

Walsh, Paul (ed.) (1957) *The Life of Aodh Ruadh O Domhnaill Transcribed from the Book of Lughaidh Ó Clérigh*, Dublin: Irish Text Society.

Walton, Kendall L. (1990) *Mimesis as Make-Believe: On the Foundations of the Representational Arts*, Cambridge: Harvard University Press.

Walvin, James (1971) *The Black Presence: A Documentary History of the Negro in England, 1555–1860*, London: Orbach and Chambers.

—— (1973) *Black and White: The Negro and English Society 1555–1945*, London: The Penguin Press.

Warner, Marina (1992) *Indigo*, New York: Simon and Schuster.

Wayne, Valerie (ed.) (1991) *The Matter of Difference: Materialist Feminist Criticism of Shakespeare*, Ithaca, NY: Cornell University Press.

Webb, Wilfred Mark (1912) *The Heritage of Dress: Being Notes on the History and Evolution of Clothes*, London: The Times Book Club.

Weed, Elizabeth (ed.) (1989) *Coming To Terms: Feminism, Theory, Politics*, London and New York: Routledge.

Wells, Robin Headlam (1994) *Elizabethan Mythologies: Studies in Poetry, Drama, and Music*, Cambridge: Cambridge University Press.

Wells, Stanley, et al. (eds) (1986) *William Shakespeare: The Complete Works*, Oxford: Clarendon Press.

Westlund, Joseph (1984) *Shakespeare's Reparative Comedies: A Psychoanalytic View of the Middle Plays*, Chicago: University of Chicago Press.

Wharton, F. (1994) *The Critical Rise and Fall of John Marston*, Columbia: Camden House.

Whigham, Frank (1996) *Seizures of the will in early modern English drama*, Cambridge: Cambridge University Press.

Whitelaw, Billie (1995) "Billie Whitelaw … Who He?" *Sunday Times*, 27 August, sec. 10, p. 13.

Wickham, Glynne (1959) *The Early English Stage, 1300–1660*, 4 vols, London: Routledge and Kegan Paul.

Wilcox, Helen (ed.) (1996) *Women and Literature in Britain 1500–1700*, Cambridge: Cambridge University Press.

Willis, Deborah (1989) "Shakespeare's *Tempest* and the Discourse of Colonialism," *Studies in English Literature* 29: 279–80.

Wilson, Richard (1993) *Will Power: Essays on Shakespearean Authority*, Detroit: Wayne State University.

Wiseman, Richard (1696) *Eight Chirurgical Treatises* …, 3rd ed., London.

Wolff, Janet (1990) "Reinstating Corporeality: Feminism and Body Politics," in Janet Wolff, *Feminine Sentences: Essays on Women and Culture*, Berkeley: University of California Press.

Woodall, John (1639 [1617]) *The Surgeon's Mate or Military and Domestique Surgery* …, London: Printed by Rob: Young for Nicholas Bourne.

Woodbridge, Linda (1984) *Women and the English Renaissance: Literature and the Nature of Womankind, 1540–1620*, Urbana: University of Illinois Press.

Woolf, Virginia (1929) *A Room of One's Own*, London: Hogarth Press.

Wright, Joseph (ed.) (1904) *English Dialect Dictionary*, Oxford: Henry Frowde.

Young, Sidney (1890) *The Annals of the Barber-Surgeons of London, Compiled from Their Records and Other Sources*, London: Blades, East, and Blades.

Zavarzadeh, Mas'ud (1991) *Seeing Films Politically*, Albany: State University of New York Press.

Zimmerman, Susan (ed.) (1992) *Erotic Politics: Desire on the Renaissance Stage*, London and New York: Routledge

Index

Wiseman, Richard 63
Wolff, Janet 29–30, 32
woman's body 10, 22, 34–5, 43;
    see also female genitals
women: absent from stage 2, 7,
    11, 14–15; as actors 16–17, 31,
    47, 82, 93; as audience 14–15,
    31, 141–6, 148, 151, 160; and
    bastardy legislation 5–6; and
    cosmetics 82–4; and masques

77, 81–2; in real life 11, 17; as
    spectacle 19, 41, 147; as
    workers 17
Woodall, John 54
Woolf, Virginia 11–12
Wright, Joseph 116

xenophobia 96

Zavarzadeh, Mas'ud 27–8